The Mathematics Curriculum

MATHEMATICS ACROSS
THE CURRICULUM

The Mathematics Curriculum: A Critical Review
was a project set up by the Schools Council at the University of Nottingham 1973–77

Members of the central project team were

Professor J. V. Armitage (Principal, College of St. Hild and
St. Bede, Durham), Director
Professor H. Halberstam (Department of Mathematics,
University of Nottingham), Co-Director (1975–77)
Mr. G. R. H. Boys (1973–76)
Mrs. J. A. Gadsden
Dr. R. B. Coates (1973–74)

The books in this series are

Geometry
From Graphs to Calculus
Mathematics across the Curriculum
Number
Algebra
Counting and Configurations
Mathematics in the World
Eleven to Thirteen

The Mathematics Curriculum

MATHEMATICS ACROSS THE CURRICULUM

Written for the Project by

JOHN LING

Published for the Schools Council by BLACKIE

ISBN 0 216 90342 4

First published 1977

Illustrator: Julie Gadsden

Published by Blackie and Son Limited, Bishopbriggs, Glasgow
and 450/452 Edgware Road, London W2 1EG

Printed in Great Britain by Thomson Litho Ltd., East Kilbride, Scotland

Preface

This book is one of a series produced by the Schools Council Project: *The Mathematics Curriculum—A Critical Review*. This Project was initiated by the Mathematics Committee of the Schools Council as a result of letters received from teachers asking for guidance on the vast amount of new mathematical literature which had been produced for schools during the 1960s. The Project was set up in 1973 and was based at the Shell Centre for Mathematical Education at Nottingham University.

It was felt that teachers, who faced a daunting array of mathematical literature and novel classroom material, would welcome a basis for constructive and critical discussion of the content of the school mathematics curriculum. Moreover, whilst the choice of syllabus, books, materials, methods and presentation belonged properly to the teacher, the range of choices was so vast as to make well-informed decisions consistent with professional integrity well nigh impossible; so that any advice implicit in these books, far from detracting from the teachers' role, would rather establish it.

The fundamental aim of the Project, therefore, is to help teachers to perform their own critical appraisal of existing mathematics syllabuses and teaching apparatus for secondary school pupils in the 11 to 16 age range, with the objective of making, for them, optimal choices. Such an aim, however fundamental it may be, is still inadequate. It was never the intention of those responsible for the Project that they should provide only a review of mathematical literature and apparatus, for an exercise of that kind would be obsolescent before the material could be published. Instead, the Project was conceived as a contribution both to initial and to post-experience in-service training, as well as providing helpful private reading.

Although the Project was not intended to be an exercise in curriculum development, it was almost inevitable and certainly desirable that a review of existing syllabuses should lead to a consideration of the possibility of a synthesis of "modern" and "traditional". I believe that such a synthesis is possible and, indeed, sorely needed. So, although we have not attempted to spell out an optimum syllabus, we have tried to identify the important ideas and skills which should be represented at school, and to show how so-called modern and traditional topics are related. We hope that one of the lessons which emerges from these books is that the two can be integrated in a unified presentation of mathematics and its applications. Perhaps the current numeracy debate will lead to syllabus revision. If so, it must be informed by the sound mathematical and pedagogical considerations to which end these books are devoted.

In order to focus as wide a range of experience as possible on the task, planning teams were established, each under the chairmanship of a potential author (an Editorial Fellow) and comprising representatives from Universities, Polytechnics, Colleges of Education, Schools, the Inspectorate and the Advisory Services. The material produced was referred to working groups of teachers across the country—from Cornwall and the Channel Islands to Northumberland. Moreover, the groups were invited to make original contributions as well as to comment on planning material. All the material thus made available was then referred once more to the original planning team, who now assume responsibility for advising the Editorial Fellow on the "final" write-up, which in some cases received further redaction by other writers. The result is now before the reader.

For the preparation of the present book the pattern of organization was modified. Each member of the planning team (with the exception of the Editorial Fellow) was himself chairman of a group convened to consider the relationship between mathematics and one particular subject or subject group, and to produce planning material. These groups contained both mathematicians and practitioners of other disciplines.

It is important in an enterprise of this kind that the final output should not misrepresent the concerns of teachers of other subjects. In many instances (particularly in physics and chemistry) there is no need to debate the inclusion of mathematical ideas and methods in a school course: the mathematics is an essential requirement, and the debate is about how best to meet the requirement. But in some other school subjects there is not so much of a consensus about the role of mathematics. Mathematicians will naturally welcome the greater use of mathematics in another discipline, but the justification for this use has to be found within that discipline itself. The mere fact that a topic lends itself to mathematical treatment may not be thought a sufficient reason for its inclusion, although the topic may win an honourable mention. Teachers of the subject concerned have their own conceptions of the contribution that their specialism makes to education, and have to ask whether the suggested topic is a sufficiently important part of a secondary school course in their subject to warrant inclusion. (Most of the references to "modern" mathematics in this book are to the *SMP* courses, as these are the texts with which the author was most familiar. However, readers will readily be able to supply their own equivalent references to other well-known courses.)

This book is concerned for the most part with those applications of mathematics which are at present of importance or of interest to some, if not all, teachers of each subject considered. We have no doubt that the work of finding further areas of common interest will continue elsewhere. If this book acts as a stimulus to such research, so much the better.

J. F. Ling

Acknowledgements

Contributions from a great many people have helped to shape and to improve this book, and their valuable work is gratefully acknowledged. In particular, I should like to mention the leaders of the subject-oriented groups:

Chemistry Mr. C. R. Barwell, formerly of Netherthorpe Grammar School, Staveley, Chesterfield

Biology Dr. B. Dudley, Department of Education, University of Keele

Technical Subjects Mr. G. H. Littler, Bishop Lonsdale College of Education, Derby

Geography/Economics Mr. K. E. Selkirk, School of Education, University of Nottingham

Physics Dr. D. M. Shipstone, School of Education, University of Nottingham

I should also like to thank Dr. R. P. Burn of Homerton College, Cambridge, for his help in writing the chapter on Art, and Professor J. F. Eggleston of the School of Education, University of Nottingham, for his most useful comments and suggestions for the Biology chapter.

The members of the subject groups were:

Mr. J. Bausor, Inspector of Science, I.L.E.A.

Dr. P. Brown, School of Education, University of Nottingham

Mr. P. Clarke, Ashfield Comprehensive School, Kirkby-in-Ashfield, Nottinghamshire

Mr. J. R. A. Cook, City of London School

Mr. P. Eastwood, Nottingham High School

Mr. D. S. Gibbons, Bishop Lonsdale College of Education, Derby

Miss M. Hartshorn, Henry Fanshawe School, Dronfield, Derbyshire

Mr. T. J. Heard, City of London School

Miss P. Hern, Alnwick College of Education, Northumberland

Mr. B. Hughes, North Riding College of Education, Scarborough

Dr. M. F. Ingham, Sedbergh School, Cumbria

Miss M. Jago, Malvern Girls' College, Worcestershire

Mr. S. E. Johnson, The Brunts Grammar School, Mansfield, Nottinghamshire

Sister Luke Keitch, Ursuline Convent, Wimbledon

Dr. C. R. Kitchin, Hatfield Polytechnic, Hertfordshire

Mr. P. Lowther, Borough Road College of Education, Isleworth, Middlesex

Mr. F. B. Mayock, Shoreditch College of Education, Egham, Surrey

Mr. R. W. Moore, Sedbergh School, Cumbria

Mr. R. D. Purseglove, Sutton Centre, Sutton-in-Ashfield, Nottinghamshire

Miss D. Scrowther, Alnwick College of Education, Northumberland

Mr. D. R. F. Walker, Loughborough College of Education

Dr. G. D. Yeoman, School of Education, University of Nottingham

Groups of teachers in North and South London, Cheshire and Salford assisted the Project by providing comments on and criticism of the planning material.

Lastly, both the publishers and I would like to acknowledge with gratitude permission to reproduce material from:

Nuffield Physics, *Nuffield Biology*, *Nuffield Combined Science*, *Nuffield Secondary Science* (Longman); Clarke *et al.*, *Biology by Inquiry*, (HEB); Brocklehurst and Ward, *A New Biology*

(Hodder & Stoughton); J. Rolfe *et al.*, *Oxford Geography Project* (OUP); B. P. Fitzgerald *et al.*, *Science in Geography* (OUP); J. Bourgoin, *Arabic Geometrical Pattern and Design* (Dover); and *Manipulative Skills in School Mathematics* (SMP);

examination questions set by the following Boards:
  Associated Examining Board, Oxford and Cambridge Schools Examination Board, Oxford Delegacy of Local Examinations, Joint Matriculation Board, East Anglian Examinations Board, East Midland Regional Examinations Board, and West Yorkshire and Lindsey Regional Examining Board;

and assistance received from:
  Halifax Building Society, and Silva Compasses (London) Ltd.

J. F. Ling

Contents

CHAPTER 1 **Introduction**   1
   1.1 The purpose of this book   1
   1.2 The relationship between mathematics
     and other subjects   1
   1.3 The teaching relationship   2
     Bibliography   4

CHAPTER 2 **A Mathematics Core Common to All Sciences** 5
   2.1 Arithmetic and numeracy   5
   2.2 Compound units   6
   2.3 Simple ratio and proportion   7
   2.4 Percentage   8
   2.5 Average   8
   2.6 Approximation, experimental error   8
   2.7 Standard index form   9
   2.8 Area and volume   9
   2.9 Graphs   9
   2.10 Venn diagrams, tree diagrams, matrices   10
   2.11 Flow diagrams   13
   2.12 Use of symbols   13

CHAPTER 3 **Mathematics in Physics**   14
   TOPIC SURVEY: TRADITIONAL COURSE   14
   3.1 Use of symbols   14
   3.2 Negative numbers   15
   3.3 Manipulation of numbers in standard
     index form   15
   3.4 Fractions and reciprocals   15
   3.5 Proportionality   15
   3.6 Graphs   18

   3.7 Use of calculating aids   20
   3.8 Use of tables   22
   3.9 Algebra   22
   3.10 Geometry and trigonometry   27
   3.11 Logarithmic scale   31

   TOPIC SURVEY: NUFFIELD COURSE   31

   PROBLEMS AND SOLUTIONS   35
   3.12 Problem-solving   35
   3.13 A selection of CSE and "O" Level
     questions   37

   FURTHER TOPICS   45
   3.14 Drawing exercises in geometrical optics   45
   3.15 Fermat's principle in geometrical optics
     and geography   46

CHAPTER 4 **Mathematics in Chemistry**   51
   4.1 Chemical terminology   51

   TOPIC SURVEY   52
   4.2 Use of symbols   52
   4.3 Decimal arithmetic, ratio and
     proportion   52
   4.4 Algebra   55
   4.5 Graphical work   56
   4.6 Difference notation   57
   4.7 Geometry and trigonometry   57
   4.8 Exponential functions   57
   4.9 Logarithms   57

FURTHER TOPICS   58
4.10 Crystals and crystal structure   58
4.11 Chemical equations and linear algebra   65

CHAPTER 5 **Mathematics in Biology**   68

TOPIC SURVEY   68
5.1 Sets, flow diagrams   68
5.2 Percentage, and similar calculations   70
5.3 Inverse proportion   72
5.4 Compound units: rates   72
5.5 Gradient   73
5.6 Enlargement, scale factor, ratio, volume,
     surface area   73
5.7 Graphs   75
5.8 Statistics   77
5.9 Probability   79
5.10 Field work   82

CHAPTER 6 **Mathematics in Geography**   83

TOPIC SURVEY   83
6.1 Scale   83
6.2 Coordinates   83
6.3 Bearings   84
6.4 Spherical geometry: great circles, lati-
     tude and longitude, etc   84
6.5 Map projections   84
6.6 Contour maps, gradient   85
6.7 Statistical tables, graphs and diagrams   85
6.8 Use of graphs in formulating a model   86
6.9 Indices, percentage   88
6.10 Functions of location, spatial distri-
     butions, isopleth maps, loci   89

6.11 Time-distance and cost-distance maps   93
6.12 Networks: graphical aspects   94
6.13 Matrices   97
6.14 Mathematical models: algebraic models   97
6.15 A geometrical model: central place
     theory   99
6.16 Optimization problems: linear
     programming   101
6.17 Arithmetic and geometric progressions   103
6.18 Random numbers: simulation   103
6.19 Statistical methods   104

CHAPTER 7 **Mathematics in Economics and Social Studies** 107

TOPIC SURVEY   107
7.1 Arithmetic and simple graphs   107
7.2 Percentage   108
7.3 Use of graphs in formulating a model   109
7.4 Note for mathematics teachers on
     elasticity of demand   111

CHAPTER 8 **Mathematics in Technical Subjects**   112

TOPIC SURVEY   113
8.1 Decimal arithmetic, mensuration, ratio   113
8.2 Scale   115
8.3 Properties of parallel lines: proportional
     division, enlargement   115
8.4 Geometrical constructions   116
8.5 Loci   118
8.6 Orthographic projection   121

CHAPTER 9 **Mathematics in Domestic Subjects**   124
9.1 House Purchase   125

9.2 Consumer Education   125

9.3 Cookery   125

9.4 Furnishing a room   126

9.5 Needlework   126

CHAPTER 10 **Mathematics in Games and Physical Education**   128

GAMES AND ATHLETICS   128

10.1 Geometrical construction and mensuration   128

10.2 Geometrical problems   128

10.3 Algebraic structure   130

10.4 Combinatorial problems   130

10.5 Scoring and ranking systems   131

ORIENTEERING AND EXPEDITION   132

MODERN EDUCATIONAL DANCE   134

CHAPTER 11 **Mathematics and Art**   137

APPENDIX 1 **Manipulative Skills up to the Age of 16**   142

APPENDIX 2 **Some Statistical Topics** 143

A2.1 Non-parametric statistical tests 143

A2.2 Kendall's coefficient of rank correlation 145

INDEX   147

Now, of my threescore years and ten,
Twenty will not come again,
And take from seventy springs a score,
It only leaves me fifty more.

(A. E. Housman: *A Shropshire Lad*)

1 Introduction

1.1 The Purpose of This Book

The main purpose of this book is to act as an aid and catalyst in co-operation between teachers of mathematics and teachers of other subjects which use mathematics. The ways in which it might prove useful may be summarized as follows.

(i) In the past fifteen years or so there have been many changes in school courses in other subjects as well as in mathematics. In some cases the mathematical content has altered, becoming more, less or different. Many mathematics teachers will not have had the time to follow these changes. In this book the most significant newer applications of mathematics in school are explained for their benefit.

(ii) Some recent reports and articles (see page 4) have dealt in general terms with the mathematical requirements of school chemistry, physics and biology. The survey in this book differs from these by going into greater detail, covering more subjects, and giving actual examples and problems (including questions from CSE and GCE examinations) to show *what* mathematics is used and *how* it is used. Where necessary, the use and presentation of the mathematics are examined critically. Also considered are the implications for each "user" subject and for mathematics itself of what is being done in the other subject.

(iii) The mathematics teacher will find in this book examples of applied mathematics (using the term in its broadest sense) which he can use to demonstrate to pupils the usefulness of the mathematics they are studying, in the knowledge that such examples are of *genuine* interest to, say, chemists or geographers. Whether the reference to such an application is timely or welcome from his colleague's point of view can be discovered

only by consultation. In conducting the surveys in this book, it has been a guiding principle that only applications of mathematics which have to date been considered by at least some teachers of other subjects to be of significance in their own teaching have been described in any detail. In any instance where a more speculative line of thought has been pursued, this has been clearly stated. No doubt there are many potential applications of mathematics whose importance will one day be recognized by curriculum developers, and mathematics teachers have a natural interest in seeing the range of applications extended. But as it is, the range is wider than many teachers of mathematics realize.

(iv) A knowledge of what will be needed by pupils studying other subjects will give the mathematics teacher reasons for including mathematical topics he might otherwise have omitted from his teaching, or for emphasizing skills he might otherwise have underrated. It might also tip the balance in favour of one particular approach or teaching method.

(v) For science teachers, major problems have been caused by changes in mathematics courses. Where differences of approach in mathematics impinge directly upon science, the reasons behind the differences are elucidated. However, it is appreciated that a book like this may help, but cannot necessarily solve the problems. The primary responsibility for communication between its members lies with the teaching team.

1.2 The Relationship between Mathematics and Other Subjects

The relationship between mathematics and another subject

which uses mathematics is usually described as being in three stages:

(i) First there is the formulation of a possible mathematical model. This may itself involve stages: choosing measures, using graphical or other methods to detect possible relationships between measures, etc.

(ii) Having formulated the model, we may then subject it to purely mathematical manipulation; for example we may solve an equation, or examine the conditions under which a solution exists.

(iii) The translation of the results into the language of the other subject will determine which further manipulations need to be carried out. The results may be compared with other experimental data to see if deductions from the model are confirmed in practice or whether some modification of the model is required. They may predict phenomena as yet undiscovered. Where the model in question is well established, manipulation of it may be used to solve practical problems, as for example in engineering or planning.

These three stages may be illustrated by an example from school physics.

(i) Measurement of the pressure and temperature of a fixed volume of gas produces values which appear to satisfy a linear law (exhibited by drawing a graph). By itself this suggests a mathematical model of the relationship between pressure P (in cm of mercury) and temperature θ (in degrees C) of the form $P = a\theta + b$. If however, the results from several different samples of gas are plotted along a single pair of axes, the graphs in figure 1.1 are obtained.

(ii) By using the mathematical transformation of "change of origin", the mathematical relationship between pressure and temperature can be written in the simple form $P \propto T$, where $T = \theta + 273$. This leads directly to the idea of "absolute temperature" (P being theoretically zero when the absolute temperature is zero).

(iii) Mathematical manipulation of the relation $P \propto T$ in its equivalent form $P_1/P_2 = T_1/T_2$ can be used to solve a practical problem such as finding the maximum temperature to which a gas-filled container can be heated when the maximum pressure it can safely withstand is known.

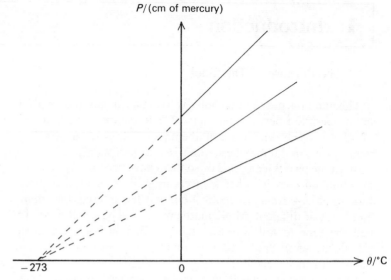

Figure 1.1   Relationship between temperature and pressure for different samples of gas.

Other aspects of this three-stage model can be illustrated from work done in school in the 11–16 age range. Recently introduced topics in school geography (described in chapter 6) illustrate well the very first stage in applying mathematics, which is to decide on what to use as a measure of some feature of interest; how, for example, to measure the degree of compactness of a country. However, as a model in terms of which to discuss the teaching of mathematics and science, it has serious shortcomings which are considered in the next section.

1.3   The Teaching Relationship

The three-stage model may accurately represent the relationship between mathematics and other subjects considered as entities in themselves. It *may* also accurately represent the way in which an applied mathematician goes about his job. However, from the point of view of the teacher, it fails to take account of the fact that at the school level pupils do not have to hand a body of abstract mathematics available for use in modelling. Rather, the pupils are in the process of acquiring mathematics, and here the concrete instance precedes the abstraction. The statement

> If I have three apples in a basket and then add another four, there will be seven apples in the basket.

is not an *application* of the pure mathematical statement $3+4 = 7$, except from a very sophisticated standpoint. It is rather one of the concrete starting points from which the abstraction of "pure" arithmetic proceeds. In teaching mathematics to children, teachers are constantly looking for a concrete entry from which to abstract and generalize, both because the mind demands it, and because in this way pupils see reasons for developing mathematical skills.

The most fruitful kind of topic for demonstrating the nature of the relationship between another subject and mathematics and thereby linking the teaching of the two, would be one which starts from a point in the other subject and leads to mathematics which is either new to pupils or takes them further in an idea they have already met. The mathematics would lead to results of interest in the other subject and would advance the pupils' understanding of it. The change-of-origin transformation as it occurs in the derivation of the pressure law considered in the previous section provides a small-scale example of a mathematical idea which arises naturally in a scientific application.

A major difficulty attends the search for such concrete starting points. This is that very often the use of mathematics in another subject is compounded with conceptual difficulties within that subject itself. The idea of density and pressure, for example, are difficult ones for children to grasp, quite apart from the arithmetic involved. As a contrast, the geographical idea of a transport network is a good concrete starting point for a study of planar graphs, as it presents no great conceptual problem; children are familiar with roads, railways, etc.

Science teachers sometimes complain that mathematics teachers, when teaching proportion, use artificial and uninteresting examples about ditch-digging, instead of scientific instances. However, the mathematics teacher's choice of example is guided by consideration of the relative ease with which the mathematical pattern will become apparent. (In the later years of the 11-16 year range, regard has also to be paid to the fact that the other subjects studied by pupils in a mathematics class may be different.) In a sense this mathematical idea—proportion—has to become pure before it can be applied elsewhere. Amongst teachers of science, there is universal recognition of the difficulty which many pupils experience in applying their mathematics; this is more properly seen as testimony to the difficulty inherent in the process rather than simply to inadequacy of mathematics teaching.

For teachers of all subjects, the most important link between subjects is the fact that it is the same pupils who are trying to learn all of them. In this sense all teaching is team teaching. The teachers, of whatever subject, who have been concerned with the various stages of producing this book were unanimous in affirming the inappropriateness, even the destructiveness, of narrow subject-orientation amongst teachers. It is essential that there should be discussion and co-operation between teachers of mathematics and of other disciplines in individual schools; the mode of co-operation (inter-disciplinary courses, regular inter-departmental meetings, etc.) is secondary to the fact of it. It would be untrue to say that curriculum development has often proceeded within each subject without *any* concern for inter-disciplinary relationships (the mathematical guidance given to teachers in, for instance, *Nuffield Combined Science* is very welcome), but often the traditional autonomy of individual departments in a school, where choice of course is concerned, has resulted in dislocations and communication problems which give every appearance of mutual indifference. Teachers of related subjects often do not know the mathematical capabilities of their pupils—which topics they have met and how far they understand them. It is the pupils who suffer the consequences.

Bibliography

N. G. G. Webb, "Developing a Good Relationship between Mathematics and Science", *School Science Review*, March 1973, pp. 441–9.

A. J. Malpas, "Mathematics and Science in the Secondary School", *Education in Science*, April 1973, pp. 27–32.

"Mathematics and School Chemistry" (Report by British Committee on Chemical Education), *Education in Science*, January 1974, pp. 14–21.

J. Bausor, "Mathematics and Science: Uneasy Truce or Open Hostilities?" *Mathematics Teaching*, September 1974.

"Mathematics for Biologists" (Report by a joint working party of the Royal Society and the Institute of Biology), *Education in Science*, November 1974, pp. 23–30.

"The Relationship between Mathematics and Physics at Pre-"O" Level Stage," *Education in Science*, September 1976, pp. 18–20. (This article summarizes a report by a joint working party of the Royal Society and the Institute of Physics, published by the latter.)

N. G. G. Webb, "Correlating the Teaching of Mathematics and Science," *International Journal of Mathematical Education in Science and Technology*, **6**, 1 (1975), pp. 105–10.

Modern Mathematics and its Implications for Physics Teaching, Scottish Centre for Mathematics, Science and Technical Education, August 1975.

Crossing Subject Boundaries (Schools Council Project "Mathematics for the Majority"), Chatto and Windus Educational, 1974.

Modern Mathematics in the Science Lesson, SMP 1977.

2 A Mathematics Core Common to All Sciences

In this section are considered those mathematical topics which occur in all the sciences. Those which are of an elementary but fundamental nature are likely to give rise to problems with pupils of moderate ability. Indeed for such pupils this range of mathematical ideas may constitute the limit to which they may advance in understanding quantitative science. For this reason, the exposition below concentrates on the problems likely to be experienced by mathematically average pupils, but even so, some of the comments and suggestions may have a more general usefulness.

2.1 Arithmetic and Numeracy

DECIMAL ARITHMETIC

An understanding of the decimal system of measurement and the ability to add, subtract, multiply and divide decimals are the most fundamental mathematical requirements of science. There are certain technical problems which may be considered first, but there are deeper problems of understanding as well.

Pupils who make mistakes in the "mechanical" or routine processes of arithmetic may be confused if the science teacher, in his attempt to help them towards a correct answer, uses a method different from that which the pupils have previously been taught. For example, one mathematics textbook advocates, as a first method, multiplication of decimals as follows: $3.8 \times 7.2 = 38 \times 0.1 \times 72 \times 0.1 = 2736 \times 0.01 = 27.36$.

This method may be superseded later, but a science teacher may find in one class pupils at various stages using different methods.

Children are often taught to "move the figures one place to the left" rather than to "move the decimal point one place to the right." Also there are two commonly used methods of subtraction: "decomposition" and "equal additions".

However, these are secondary to the main problem, that of understanding. Division in particular presents difficulties of understanding. Recognizing this, the authors of *Nuffield Combined Science**have this to say in connection with an activity at the beginning of the course which involves finding the thickness of a penny from the fact that 80 pennies have a total thickness of 13 cm (*NCSTG 3*, Mathematics Appendix):

The danger which the activity is trying to avoid is to write glibly

80 pennies are 13 cm thick,
1 penny is $\frac{13}{80}$ cm thick.

and then to carry out a long division sum.... Any method which uses the child's common sense and which he understands is to be preferred to trying to force all such problems into a fixed pattern.

Children can be shown how to approach the answer by the series of steps indicated in the following table:

Number of pennies	80	40	20	10	5	1
Thickness of pile in cm	13	6·5	3·25	1·6	0·8	0·16

If halving is felt to be easy, then if we had started with a pile of 64 pennies we could have found the thickness of one by halving each time. This also leads on to powers of 2 which might help when we later come to need powers of 10.

*The following abbreviations are used throughout chapters 2–5:
NPTG: *Nuffield Physics Teachers' Guides* (Longman);
NCSTG: *Nuffield Combined Science Teachers' Guides* (Longman);
NB: *Nuffield Biology* Pupils' Texts (where revised edition is meant this is stated) (Longman);
NBTG: *Nuffield Biology Teachers' Guides* (Longman);
NC: *Nuffield Chemistry* (Longman);
SCISP: Schools Council Integrated Science Project published under the title *Patterns* (Longman);
SMP: *School Mathematics Project* (CUP).

(One might ask: Why not start with 100 pennies? However the mechanical procedure of moving the decimal point (or the figures) may have been learnt but not really understood. The halving process aids understanding.)

Science teachers often report that their pupils have difficulty with simple arithmetic, and mathematics teachers are blamed for not providing the necessary drill. However, the recurrent difficulties can also be taken as an indication that "simple" arithmetic is not so "simple" to children as we think it should be. We, the teachers, have had constant practice at it for years, and the effect of that practice may have been to obscure any early misgivings we might have had about the meaning of what we were doing.

NUMERACY

Numeracy is the most fundamental objective of a secondary school mathematics course. Numeracy does not mean merely the ability to add, subtract, multiply and divide. It also means knowing when to do one of these things, and what conclusion to draw from the answer.

For example, a common procedure in experimental biology is to compare the effects of different treatments by calculating percentage changes rather than absolute changes. The wider definition of numeracy would include the ability to recognize the circumstances in which it is appropriate to draw conclusions from data in this way. If this understanding of numeracy is adopted, then teachers of science are as involved in the teaching of numeracy as mathematics teachers. As in the elementary example of the pile of pennies described above, every application of division can be used to help the pupil's understanding of the process, and to smooth the way towards its fluent use.

ELECTRONIC CALCULATORS

Electronic calculators are likely to become the most widely used calculating aid in scientific calculations, but their use by pupils at school raises problems which have already become a common topic of discussion amongst teachers concerned with numerical skills. The fear is that automatic recourse to button-pushing on the part of the pupil will result in erosion of the basic number sense which ought to be operational when a calculator is unnecessary or inappropriate, e.g. when making an order-of-magnitude calculation—perhaps to check the reasonableness of an answer obtained with the calculator.

The extent to which the use of calculators extends or destroys number appreciation cannot be determined as yet. However, even when a calculator is used, pupils have to understand which particular operations on the data are necessary to obtain the answer and also how to interpret that answer. It may be that the abolition of the drudgery involved in carrying out arithmetical processes will allow more time to be spent on achieving an understanding of the operations themselves and on the interpretation of results.

2.2   Compound Units

Measures such as density and pressure, which are obtained as quotients of other simple measures, give rise to great difficulties in understanding (see, for example, *NPTG 1*, pp. 134 ff, on density). Pupils may have difficulty in carrying out the arithmetic involved, but they are more likely to have difficulty in understanding the scientific concepts.

There is a warning here for mathematics teachers who, in a laudable attempt to make mathematics seen to be useful, set density calculations to young pupils as simple examples involving quotients and products. If such a problem has to be accompanied by the statement of a rule,

$$\text{density} = \text{mass/volume}$$

then one might as well give the problem "pure".

The "table" method used for division in *Nuffield Combined Science* (*TG3*, p. 107) is suggested for the teaching of density:

Number of cm cubes	40	20	10	1
Mass (grams)	120	60	30	3

The idea of *population density* as it appears in geography also has its difficulties. The population density of a country is generally non-uniform, and giving a value for it involves an imagined uniform re-distribution.

The use of index notation in SI compound units (such as $m\,s^{-1}$, $kg\,m^{-3}$ or kg/m^3, etc.) is best delayed in the early stages. Just as children may start reading with the initial teaching alphabet and progress to standard spelling, so they can use "metres per second" or "kilograms per cubic metre" if they understand them better.

2.3 Simple Ratio and Proportion

Extensive use is made of ratio and proportion in chemistry and physics, and the topics are considered at greater depth in chapter 3. A simple application of proportion occurs in the following example (*NB 4*, pp. 49–50).

The number of microscopic animals in a small given sample of water may be too great to be counted under the microscope. So the sample is diluted with pure water to a total volume of, say $50\,cm^3$, and then the number of animals in a sample of $0.25\,cm^3$ (measured with a pipette) is counted. Supposing that 5 animals are counted, estimate the number of animals in the original sample of water.

The "simplicity" in this example is that of the steps involved in the calculation, when set out as follows:

5 animals in $0.25\,cm^3$
implies
20 animals in $1\,cm^3$;
which implies
1000 animals in $50\,cm^3$.

Each step involves an "easy" (i.e. whole number) multiplying factor, if the move from $0.25\,cm^3$ to $50\,cm^3$ is made via $1\,cm^3$. (Since the use of $0.25\,cm^3$ as a sampling volume is common, this transition may become a matter of routine.) Often it is possible to design an experiment so as to avoid arithmetical difficulties.

The ability to work with simple ratio and proportion has a usefulness beyond its direct application in examples such as that described above. Simplifying the arithmetic so that whole-number factors are involved is the basis of much approximation and rough estimation. An example from chemistry (worked in full on p. 54) will illustrate this.

To find the heat of combustion per mole of carbon (for a definition of "mole", see p. 51), it is necessary to find the heat produced by the burning of $12\,g$ of carbon. Suppose that $0.411\,g$ of carbon gave, on burning, $3.12\,kcal$.

To obtain a rough answer, we can use the (approximate) relations:

$$0.411 \xrightarrow{\times 10} 4 \xrightarrow{\times 3} 12,$$

and obtain

$$3.12 \xrightarrow{\times 10} 31 \xrightarrow{\times 3} 93.$$

Ratio and proportion are difficult concepts for children to grasp, as numerous experiments and tests have shown. In a study of proportional reasoning in children ("Proportional Reasoning and Control of Variables in Seven Countries", in *Advancing Education Through Science-Oriented Programs* Report 1D/25, June 1975, Berkeley, California) R. Karplus gave a sample of pupils aged 13–15 a picture of "Mr Short" together with 9 standard paper-clips. The children were told that Mr Short has a friend, called Mr Tall, and that the heights of Mr Short and Mr Tall, when measured in buttons, are 4 and 6 buttons respectively. The children were asked to measure Mr Short's height using paper-clips (and to say how they did it). The answer was in fact 6 paper-clips. They were asked two questions: (1) How tall is Mr Tall when measured in paper-clips? (2) How wide is Mr

Tall's car in buttons if its width is 14 paper-clips? Of his sample of British children, only 16 per cent of the boys and 11 per cent of the girls understood and used ratio correctly. Very popular was an "additive" strategy yielding the answer 8 to the first question.

Proportionality and the reasons for its difficulty, are considered further below (p. 15). Further investigation is at present being carried out at Chelsea College, London by the project "Concepts in Secondary Mathematics and Science".

2.4   Percentage

Pupils need to be able to understand a statement such as: "between 60 and 95 per cent of the mass of a living organism is made up of water". They may also be required to obtain one quantity as a percentage of another. In some biology texts, pupils are given a recipe—sometimes with a specimen worked example—for how to obtain a percentage. Clearly the authors are very pessimistic about the pupils' level of mathematical attainment, but prefer to supply techniques than to explain the processes. One can see their point. Their interest is in drawing conclusions from the percentages obtained, and they feel that the point of the experiment may be obscured if teacher and pupils get bogged down in the business of explaining the rationale behind the arithmetic. However, rather than resort to a "method" carried out without understanding, it may be better to obtain an approximate result by a more easily understood approach such as a conversion graph, which has the advantage of exhibiting visually the percentage idea as a whole (figure 2.1).

Percentage is used in physics, for instance when stating the efficiency of a machine or transformer, and occasionally in chemistry when describing the composition of a substance.

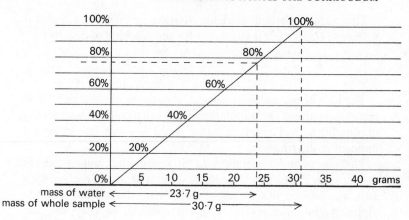

Figure 2.1   Percentage conversion graph.

2.5   Average

The calculation of the arithmetic mean of a number of single experimental results occurs frequently throughout elementary science. For median and mode, see chapter 5, p. 77.

2.6   Approximation, Experimental Error

The ability to obtain a "good" rough approximation, and to reject an answer on order-of-magnitude grounds, is an important part of numeracy. The ability develops with experience, and can be nurtured as much in science lessons as in mathematics lessons.

"Rounding off" to so many decimal places or significant figures is frequent in experimental work. One method of expressing experimental results which are subject to inherent experimental error is to give a range, e.g. $3{\cdot}20 \pm 0{\cdot}05$.

2.7 Standard Index Form

The need for an economical notation to handle the very large and very small numbers which occur throughout science, whose scope encompasses the sub-atomic and the astronomical, provides a linkage with mathematics.

In the *Nuffield Physics Teachers' Guide 1* (pp. 143 ff) there is a suggestion for a "halfway" stage in the progress towards standard index form. This is to write a large number such as 250 000 000 in two columns, figures and noughts. This scheme is developed to give a multiplication rule:

	Figures	Noughts
250 000 000	25	7
× 200 000 000	× 2	+ 8
	50	15

From this an advance is made via "followed by 7 noughts" to "multiplied by ten 7 times" and so to the notation "$\times 10^7$", so that 250 000 000 is written as 25×10^7.

> After some more practice with that form, pupils may then be ready to make one further change, the reduction of the first number before the power of 10 to one which has only one digit before the decimal point. If this last form ("standard form") seems to add a sense of difficulty, teachers should postpone that and stick to one of the earlier forms all the way through the present important arithmetic for atoms (*NPTG 1*, p. 145).

If a calculator with scientific notation is available, this may help with explanations. Particularly useful in this respect are those calculators in the CBM range which have EXP↑ and EXP↓ keys. These enable the exponent to be raised and lowered, with consequent shifting of the decimal point.

Manipulation of numbers in standard index form (as opposed to understanding the notation and being able to make simple comparisons) is a separate issue, and is dealt with in the separate science sections.

2.8 Area and Volume

The ideas of area and volume and their respective units of measurement figure a great deal in elementary science, but calculation using standard mensuration formulae (apart from "length × breadth" for a rectangle—and even this can be mis-applied by pupils to an irregular quadrilateral) need not be required. Drawing an area on graph paper and counting squares is a respectable way of finding real areas.

The treatment of volume in *Nuffield Combined Science* (*TG 3*, p. 241) is based upon counting cubes rather than the application of a formula. The authors comment:

> The step from measuring the volume of regular solids to that of any shape regular or irregular is important and one that should not be rushed. In the past it has been an aspect of measuring that has not been covered by mathematics departments at an early stage and this has led to difficulties later.

2.9 Graphs

The ability to read a graph—in the full sense, that of reading the story it has to tell—is worth putting alongside numeracy as a further important objective of any mathematics course (see *From Graphs to Calculus*, a book in the present series). Science text-books include a vast number of bar charts, graphs and pie charts, some examples of which are given later in the separate sections.

A commonly recurring mistake of nomenclature in science texts arises in the use of the term "histogram". The word is properly applied to a graph in which the *area* enclosed between two ordinates represents frequency or relative frequency. In a *histogram* showing the frequency distribution of height (in cm) in a population of men, the unit on the vertical scale is not frequency, but frequency per centimetre (this point is dealt with in greater detail in chapter 6, page 91). However the word *histogram* is often wrongly applied to any bar chart showing frequencies, and sometimes to a bar chart which has nothing to do with frequency. In the former case "frequency graph" or "frequency chart" would be a correct description.

In drawing a graph, the main preliminary points—labelling of axes, choice of scales, decision as to whether a discrete or continuous graph is appropriate—need to have been established as a mathematical sub-routine.

In mathematics lessons the drawing of Cartesian graphs of functions may be preceded by other forms of graphical representation, such as "arrow diagrams". The use, where appropriate, of graphs of this kind by science teachers would also help pupils to realize that there is a common language. The arrows in the table below bring out the functional relationship involved.

Voltage (volts)	Current (amperes)
4	→ 0·4
3	→ 0·3
2	→ 0·2
1	→ 0·1

The charts made from paper tape (which are used in Nuffield courses, see p. 32) may give rise to problems over the transition from what looks like a discontinuous bar-chart to a continuous graph (see *NCSTG 3*, p. 243).

There are instances where the interpretation of a graph arising in a scientific context leads to a mathematically interesting idea. One such case has been mentioned in the previous chapter.

Pie charts are often used in science to illustrate the percentage breakdown of some quantity. It is useful to have available a circular protractor with a percentage scale for drawing pie charts.

The concept of proportion is involved in the construction of pie charts, and teachers sometimes try to introduce them too early.

2.10   Venn Diagrams, Tree Diagrams, Matrices

These diagrammatic ways of exhibiting relationships between things, or sets of things, or between the definitions of words, are not specifically mathematical. Since their use has been most evident in newer approaches to mathematics teaching, many teachers think of them as mathematical ideas which may be "applied" to their subjects. However, the notion of a set, together with the relation of membership of a given set, is pre-mathematical. In fact the idea is taught to children by using examples drawn from common experience, such as the fact that foxes and mice live on land, goldfish in water, and newts both on land and in water.

Some examples illustrating the ubiquitous usefulness of diagrammatic and matrix presentation of relationships are given in figure 2.2.

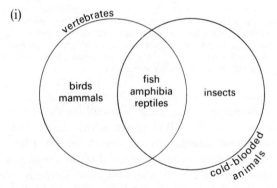

Fig. 2.2   Diagrammatic and matrix representations of relationships (part (iii) due to G. T. Woods; other similar examples can be found in Leisten, *Education in Chemistry*, Jan. 1969, pp. 19–20).

(ii)

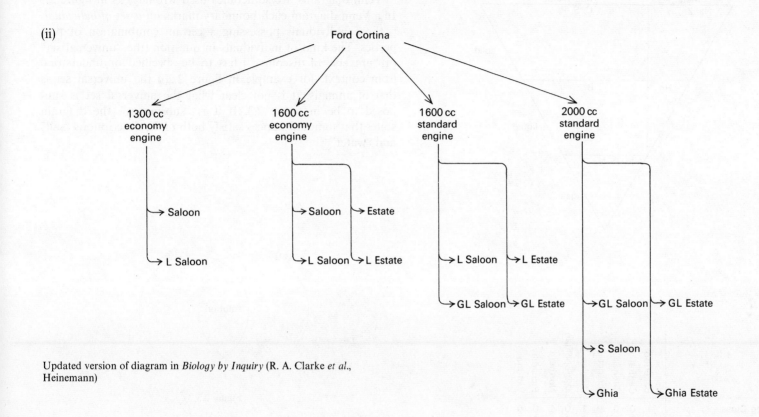

Updated version of diagram in *Biology by Inquiry* (R. A. Clarke *et al.*, Heinemann)

(iii)

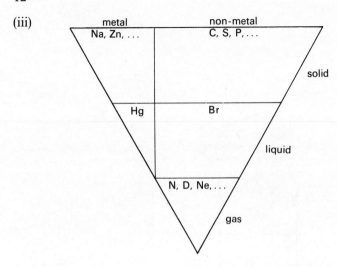

Venn diagrams are sometimes used wrongly, as in figure 2.3 In a Venn diagram each boundary marks off *a set of individuals* —those individuals possessing a certain combination of properties. The kind of individuals in question (the "universal set" or "universe of discourse") has to be specified or understood from context; for example in figure 2.2(i) the universal set is that of animals. It is not clear what the universal set is supposed to be in figure 2.3. If it is "substances", the diagram states that some substances satisfy both of the descriptions "salt" and "water".

(iv)

	Bakerloo	Central	Circle	District	Jubilee	Metropolitan	Northern	Piccadilly	Victoria
Charing Cross	1	0	0	0	1	0	1	0	0
Euston	0	0	0	0	0	0	1	0	1
Kings Cross, St. Pancras	0	0	1	0	0	1	1	1	1
Liverpool Street	0	1	1	0	0	1	0	0	0
Paddington	1	0	1	1	0	1	0	0	0
Victoria	0	0	1	1	0	0	0	0	1
Waterloo	1	0	0	0	0	0	1	0	0

In this matrix '1' denotes that the station is on the line and '0' that it is not.

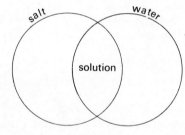

Figure 2.3.

2.11   Flow Diagrams

As with Venn diagrams, flow diagrams are not specifically mathematical. In chemistry and biology the complexities of the carbon and nitrogen cycles have always been presented in the form of flow diagrams. Of particular usefulness, in a variety of contexts, are flow diagrams giving a programme of instructions (see also pages 35 and 68).

An example from chemistry is shown in figure 2.4.

2.12   Use of Symbols

This topic is considered on page 14.

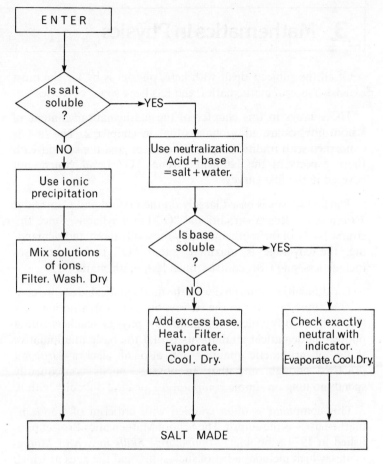

Figure 2.4   Program of instructions for preparing a salt.

3 Mathematics in Physics

Of all the subjects dealt with here, physics is by far the most extensive user of mathematics, and has been so for centuries.

The surveys in this chapter of the mathematical content of school physics are additional to that in chapter 2. The first is concerned with traditional physics courses, and the second with those aspects of the Nuffield Physics "O" Level course not covered in the first survey.

The first survey is based largely on the Oxford and Cambridge Examination Board's traditional "O" Level syllabus. Since this course is one of the mathematically most advanced and demanding, the coverage is maximal; other "O" Level syllabuses include less, and CSE courses much less, mathematics.

The difficulties connected with the mathematical ideas are considered topic by topic in the survey, but it is worth noting here that a frequently voiced complaint by physics teachers about pupils' mathematical attainments is that the basic manipulative skills—of arithmetic mainly, but also of algebra—are not practised enough, and that, in physics, pupils consequently spend too long on simple computation, or have difficulty with it.

This complaint is often coupled with criticism of "modern" mathematics as the culprit. The School Mathematics Project published in 1974 a booklet, *Manipulative Skills in School Mathematics*, which includes a list of such skills, and the ages at which pupils of various abilities should be proficient in them. This list may be found in Appendix 1, p. 142.

TOPIC SURVEY: TRADITIONAL COURSE

3.1 Use of Symbols

Scientists use letters to stand for *quantities*. A quantity is a product of a number and a unit. Mathematicians use letters to stand for pure numbers. Thus a scientist will write "Let mass of copper be m ... thus $m = 5g$," whereas a mathematician might prefer "Let mass of copper be m g ... thus $m = 5$". The reason for the scientists' preference are explained in an article by J. Bausor (*Mathematical Gazette*, June 1975). Both systems are consistent, but conflict arises if pupils are penalized in one context for what is regarded as acceptable in another, and confusion arises when pupils mix up the two systems. It would be simpler if one or other became an agreed system, but the important point as far as mathematics teachers are concerned is that pupils should be clear as to what the symbols they use stand for. Instead of writing "Let x be the number of apples and y the number of pears", a pupil will often write "let x = apples, y = pears". Later in the same piece of work "$3x + 4y$" will be misinterpreted as "3 apples and 4 pears".

One particular consequence of the scientific use of symbols is worth noting. If length = 3 cm, then length/cm = 3. It has been suggested that this notation should be used in tables of numerical values and for labelling the axes of graphs:

Length/cm	3	5	6
Tension/N	18	22	24

It is so used in the publications resulting from the Schools Council Integrated Science Project.

3.2 Negative Numbers

The measurement of temperature is an obvious, indeed everyday, example of the use of negative numbers. The difference $\theta_1 - \theta_2$ between two temperatures θ_1, θ_2 shows the common sense behind the appropriate sign-rule in such a case as $\theta_1 = 20°C$, $\theta_2 = -30°C$.

Other instances requiring the use of negative numbers include negative displacements, velocities and accelerations, and the sign conventions for the lens and mirror formulae in optics.

The notation for negative numbers favoured in many modern courses in mathematics (including *SMP*) differs from the traditional one. The distinction between "subtract 3" (the operation) and "minus 3" (the number now referred to as "negative 3") is shown by writing the latter as $^-3$.

3.3 Manipulation of Numbers in Standard Index Form

As well as multiplication and division of numbers in standard index form, the addition of very unequal numbers sometimes occurs. An instance would be $1 + 8 \times 10^{-6}$, arising from the linear expansion formula $l = l_0(1 + \alpha\theta)$.

3.4 Fractions and Reciprocals

The use of the formulae
$$\frac{1}{u} + \frac{1}{v} = \frac{1}{f} \quad \text{and} \quad \frac{1}{R} = \frac{1}{R_1} + \frac{1}{R_2}$$
involves the manipulation of reciprocals and fractions.

3.5 Proportionality

Proportionality is a mathematical concept of fundamental importance in physics. It is also a very difficult idea for pupils to grasp. Here are some instances of proportionality in physics:

Direct Proportionality

Hooke's law for a spring	extension $\propto$ load
Pressure law for a gas	pressure $\propto$ absolute temperature
Charles' law for a gas	volume $\propto$ absolute temperature
Ohm's law	voltage $\propto$ current
Electrolysis laws	mass $\propto$ time
	mass $\propto$ current
	leading to
	mass $\propto$ current $\times$ time
Friction	frictional force $\propto$ normal reaction
Snell's law of refraction	$\dfrac{\sin i}{\sin r} = $ constant.

Inverse Proportionality

Boyle's law	$P \propto \dfrac{1}{V}$
Variation of frequency (of note) with length of string (or pipe)	$f \propto \dfrac{1}{l}$

Other types of proportionality

Pendulum	time of swing $\propto \sqrt{(\text{length})}$
Stretched string	frequency $\propto \sqrt{(\text{tension})}$
Gravitation	force $\propto \dfrac{1}{(\text{distance})^2}$

WHY IS PROPORTIONALITY A DIFFICULT IDEA?

Whilst at junior school, normal children develop their ability to handle relationships. But the relationships with which they are able to deal mentally are those between objects which are either actually present, or between objects similar to those with which they have had direct experience and so can readily imagine. In Piagetian terms these children are at the stage of concrete operational thought. At about the age of eleven years, bright pupils begin to develop the ability to use these same relationships when dealing with abstractions. They are entering the stage of formal operational thought. Average pupils do not enter this stage until fourteen or fifteen years of age, and some pupils of below average ability may never do so.

A ratio is an abstraction in that it does not consist simply of a pair of lengths, masses or whatever, but of a conceived relationship between the members of the pair. Proportionality implies a relationship of equality between two ratios. It is a relation between relations, and so we should not expect pupils to be able to understand proportionality until they reach ages which, depending upon their abilities, approximate to those stated above.

PROPORTIONALITY IN MATHEMATICS AND SCIENCE

Experimental measurements made to detect or verify a proportionality relationship will at best yield only approximate proportionality, so pupils will need a previous understanding of exact, i.e. mathematical, proportionality. If concrete examples are used to help fix the idea, they must not be such as to present conceptual problems themselves. For an example of inverse proportion relatively free from these extra conceptual problems, mathematics teachers have often used the relation between speed and time taken for a given journey, or between length and breadth of a rectangle of given area. The "cause" of the inverse proportionality is evident in each case: the fixed distance or the fixed area. In Boyle's law the constancy of the product PV is not intuitively clear, neither is this product given a name. So the pupil has to be allowed time to abstract the idea of proportionality— as a mathematical pattern—before he can confidently apply it in science.

DIFFERENT METHODS OF OPERATING WITH DIRECT PROPORTIONALITY

The complexity of the relation

$$\frac{Y_1}{X_1} = \frac{Y_2}{X_2}$$

enables it to be structured in various ways. The usual nongraphical method of testing for direct proportionality is to compute Y/X for each pair. In this case the appropriate symbolic form for the relation is $Y/X = $ constant.

When a known proportionality is used in a calculation, several methods are possible:

(i) *The "multiplier" method*

Given X_1, Y_1, X_2, work out X_2/X_1 and multiply Y_1 by that. In *Nuffield Physics Teachers' Guide 1* (p. 51) the wording "Y goes as X" is recommended. SCISP suggests (*Patterns, Teachers' Guide 1*, p. 6) "when X doubles, Y doubles, and so on", but the main difficulties for pupils arise when fractional multipliers are needed.

In *Nuffield Secondary Science* (*Theme 4, Harnessing Energy*, pp. 114–5) teachers are recommended to avoid a formal statement of Ohm's law. The relationship between voltage V, resistance R, and current I is summarized as:

(a) With the same value of V, if R increases, I will decrease; the current can only be kept at the same value by increasing the voltage.

(b) To keep I at the same value:
If R is doubled, V is doubled.
If R is halved, V is halved.
If R is increased ten times, so is V.
If R is 0·1 of its original value, so is V.

(c) If V is unchanged and R increases, I will decrease.
If R is doubled, I is halved.
If R is 0·1 of its original value, I is increased ten times.

(ii) *Substitution method*

Substitute known values in

$$\frac{Y_1}{Y_2} = \frac{X_1}{X_2} \quad \text{or} \quad \frac{Y_1}{X_1} = \frac{Y_2}{X_2}$$

and then cross-multiply. This latter process is a particular *bête noire* of mathematics teachers, but there is no denying its usefulness as a routine. If introduced before the idea of proportionality is properly understood, it will do nothing to aid understanding of the *relation*, even though right answers to *individual* computations may be facilitated. But this does not mean that cross-multiplication should be absolutely anathematized.

As with all equation-solving, pupils should examine the answer they obtain critically. The ability to do this, like the ability to get an approximate answer without a routine like cross-multiplication, is an indication of whether proportionality is really understood or not.

(iii) *Finding the constant of proportionality*

The known pair X_1, Y_1, are used to find the value of k in the relation $Y = kX$. This is then used to find Y_2 from $Y_2 = kX_2$.

(*Nuffield Physics Teachers' Guide 1* (pp. 51 and 201) notes that this method "diverts attention from the structure of the relationship" and should be avoided as far as possible. Its preferred method is (i) above.)

If the values of X and Y are exhibited as proportional sets of pure numbers, e.g.

$$\begin{Bmatrix} 2, & 3, & 4, & 5 \\ 2\cdot6, & 3\cdot9, & 5\cdot2, & 6\cdot5 \end{Bmatrix}$$

the value of k is the *scale factor*. If, however, the values of X

and Y are physical quantities, k is a quotient of two quantities, i.e. a *rate*.

X (seconds)	2	3	4	5	$k = 1\cdot3$ litres/second.
Y (litres)	2·6	3·9	5·2	6·5	

(iv) *Slide-rule method*

A single setting of the A and B scales (or the C and D Scales) exhibits all the related pairs in a given proportionality relation, together with the scale factor (rate). It is thus related to method (iii) rather than to method (i).

OTHER TYPES OF PROPORTIONALITY

(*a*) $Y \propto X^2$

The methods for detecting or verifying $Y \propto X^2$ are based upon

$$\frac{Y}{X^2} = k \quad \text{or} \quad Y = kX^2.$$

In calculations, the four methods given above become:

(i) Work out $(X_2/X_1)^2$ and multiply Y_1 by this. This is based upon

$$\frac{Y_2}{Y_1} = \left(\frac{X_2}{X_1}\right)^2$$

(ii) Substitute in

$$\frac{Y_2}{Y_1} = \frac{X_2{}^2}{X_1{}^2}$$

and cross-multiply.

(iii) Obtain k in $Y = kX^2$, etc.

(iv) On a slide rule, use D and B (or C and A) scales.

(*b*) *Inverse proportionality*

Detection or verification is based on

$$\frac{Y}{1/X} = k \quad \text{or} \quad XY = k.$$

Methods of calculation are:
(i) Find X_2/X_1 and *divide* Y_1 by this.
(ii) Substitute in $X_1Y_1 = X_2Y_2$.
(iii) Obtain k in $Y = k(1/X)$.
(iv) On a slide rule, use C and CI scales.

As it is possible to employ different, but algebraically equivalent, ways of thinking about proportionality, it is evident that there is scope for confusion when pupils do not have a clear conception of the equivalence of these methods to *their* understanding of proportionality.

3.6   Graphs

Graphical work may be divided into two types.
(i) A graph may be used to "tell a story" about some phenomenon. An instance of this is given in figure 3.1. The pupil needs to be able to read the "story"—to interpret maxima, minima, gradients, discontinuities. One deduction from this particular graph is that the density is greatest at 4°C.

(ii) A graph may also be used as a tool, aiding the formulation of a mathematical model of the relation between measures.

STRAIGHT LINE THROUGH THE ORIGIN

The most commonly used is a straight-line graph through the origin, representing direct proportionality. The mathematical connection needs to be understood if the method is used; experimental results rarely provide an exact fit. There are particular modifications which arise naturally in physics out of the attempt to achieve the simplest possible statement of a physical law.

(i) *Hooke's Law*
If a graph of length against load is drawn, a change of origin as indicated in figure 3.2 leads to the simple proportionality

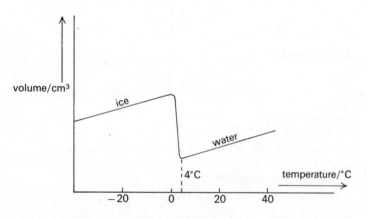

Figure 3.1   The change in volume of a fixed mass of ice and water with changing temperature.

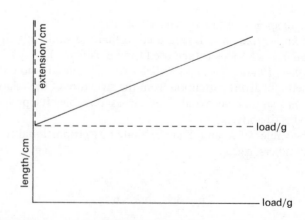

Figure 3.2   Hooke's Law.

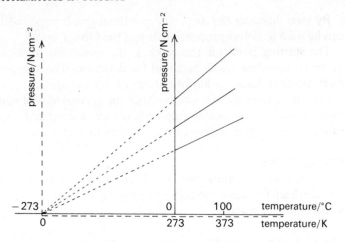

Figure 3.3   Pressure Law.

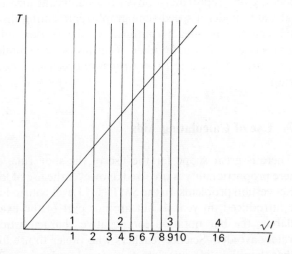

Figure 3.4   Special graph paper for detecting proportionality of the form $T \propto \sqrt{l}$.

law "extension $\propto$ load". Because the new variable *extension* has a name and an obvious physical significance, the change of origin is easy to understand. This is a simple case in which a concrete instance provides an introduction to a mathematical idea (change of origin), which would involve greater difficulty if presented to pupils in the context of abstract mathematics.

(ii) *Pressure Law*

This instance is discussed more fully in the introduction (p. 2). It is of interest mathematically as a change-of-origin transformation where the new origin is not on the *y*-axis (figure 3.3); but, far more than this, it is of interest as it emphasizes that choice of axes is in itself arbitrary, although guided in practice by considerations of simplicity.

(iii) *Variation of period of pendulum with length*

Another interesting development of the straight-line graph through the origin is the transformation of a scale, for example plotting $\sqrt{l}$ rather than l on the *x*-axis in order to detect a proportionality of the form $T \propto \sqrt{l}$. There is scope here for some joint work between physics and mathematics teachers. (The chapter on "Searching for Functions" in *SMP Book 4* should be of interest to physics teachers.) In particular, if both scales, l and $\sqrt{l}$, are shown as in figure 3.4, a transition may be made to the idea of special graph paper where the spacing of numbers on the *x*-axis leads directly to a straight-line graph through the origin whenever $y \propto \sqrt{x}$.

The transformation from a curve such as $T = 2\sqrt{l}$ (not easily recognized) to a straight line (easily recognized) can also be shown as in figure 3.5. The curve is made into a straight line by "bunching up" numbers on the *x*-axis. (In other cases it is done by "stretching".) The amount of squashing together increases as the curve gets flatter.

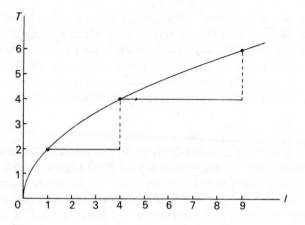

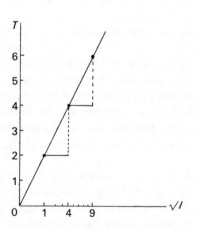

Figure 3.5   Transformation of the graph $T = 2\sqrt{l}$.

By interchanging the axes, one produces graph paper which can be used to detect proportionality of the form $Y \propto X^2$.

The starting point for this work is the usefulness in science of the straight-line graph as a tool for detection. The suggested mathematical ideas—transformation of scales, special graph paper—have their uses in science. Also, the general idea of scale-transformation and special graph rulings has widespread application—logarithmic scales, normal probability paper, etc.

LINEAR LAWS

Linear laws are formulated in different ways, and the relation between each form and the corresponding graph has to be understood (figures 3.6 and 7).

AREA UNDER A GRAPH

The most obvious case considered in physics in which the area under a graph represents a physically significant measure is that of the area under a speed-time graph representing distance. An approach to this idea is outlined in the section on Nuffield Physics (see p. 32, where other instances of areas under graphs are mentioned. See also *From Graphs to Calculus*, a book in this series).

3.7   Use of Calculating Aids

There is great scope for the use of the slide rule, especially where proportionality is involved. However the use of logarithms raises certain problems. In the *SMP* "O" Level course logarithms are introduced (in year 4) but are not part of the examination syllabus; the bar notation for negative characteristics is deliberately avoided. Science teachers who prefer to use logarithms rather than the slide rule (which is introduced in year 2 in *SMP* and then used throughout), often instruct pupils in the mechanical

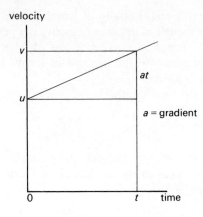

Figure 3.6   Graph of $v = u + at$.

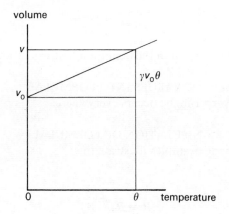

Figure 3.7   Graph of $v = v_0(1 + \gamma\theta)$.

processes involved, and mathematics teachers complain that there is no understanding on the part of the pupils.

Logarithms do have certain advantages over the slide rule for arithmetical calculations:

(i) They do not involve scale reading. Many pupils are liable to make mistakes in reading the logarithmic scales on a slide rule.

(ii) They incorporate a mechanical procedure for obtaining the order of magnitude.

The first stages of the teaching sequence in mathematics would be:

(i) Multiplication and division of numbers in standard index form.

(ii) Contrast between the comparatively easy addition and subtraction of indices with the laborious long multiplication and division, leading to the suggestion that it might be possible to write, for example, the 2·63 in $2·63 \times 10^5$ also as a power of 10.

(iii) Interpolation on the graph of $y = 10^x$ to find an approximate value of x for a given value of y.

Able pupils might appreciate that

$$(10^{0·3})^{10} = 10^{0·3} \times 10^{0·3} \times \ldots \times 10^{0·3}$$
$$= 10^3 = 1000$$

But

$$2^{10} = 1024 \approx 1000$$

hence

$$2 \approx 10^{0·3}$$

(iv) Using tables to convert e.g. $2·63 \times 10^5 \times 5·91 \times 10^{-3}$ into $10^{0·420} \times 10^5 \times 10^{0·772} \times 10^{-3}$

The slide rule has a great advantage over logarithms (and electronic calculators) where proportionality is concerned, in that it displays *all* the related pairs in a proportionality. This is also true to some extent of a table such as a ready reckoner! For a discussion of electronic calculators, see chapter 2, page 6.

3.8   Use of tables

The usual mathematical tables—squares, square roots, reciprocals, sines, cosines, tangents—are used in various places throughout the course. *SMP* and *Modern Mathematics for Schools* have opted for 3-figure tables, which are usually adequate for the level of accuracy of data, and which avoid the problems caused by difference columns.

3.9   Algebra

NOTATION

In addition to Roman and Greek letters to denote physical quantities, physics often makes use of primed and suffix notations. It is not unknown for a pupil to be unable to apply the algebra he knows because letters other than x and y are used!

SETTING UP OF FORMULAE

In order to set up a formula, we need a clear understanding of the physical measures, and the relations between them. However, analogous problems from the common stock of experience can be used by mathematics teachers to aid understanding of this process, which is of crucial importance in the formulation of a mathematical model. Simple formulae are often merely the symbolic statements of definitions, for example

$$\text{density} = \frac{\text{mass}}{\text{volume}}.$$

Some instances of setting up formulae are given below. The route to the formula in each case may be made easier for the pupils by considering numerical examples first.

(i) Suppose a rod, initially of length l cm is heated through $\theta°$C. The coefficient of linear expansivity is α per K (per $°$C).

For a 1$°$C temperature rise, a rod of length l cm increases its length by αl cm. So the increase in length for a $\theta°$C rise in temperature is $\alpha l\theta$ cm.

If l_θ cm is the final length,

$$l_\theta = l + \alpha l\theta$$
$$\therefore l_\theta = l(1 + \alpha\theta).$$

Another way of approaching this example is to translate a definition in words of the coefficient of linear expansivity into a formula

$$\alpha = \frac{l_\theta - l}{l\theta}$$

This translation requires considerable understanding.

(ii) The acceleration/time relationship $v = u + at$, written in the form

$$a = \frac{v - u}{t}$$

is an algebraic version of the definition of acceleration.

SUBSTITUTION OF VALUES INTO FORMULAE

This, not surprisingly, occurs everywhere.

ALGEBRAIC MANIPULATION OF FORMULAE

The following examples illustrate this:

(i) The derivation of

$$\frac{1}{R} = \frac{1}{R_1} + \frac{1}{R_2}$$

(for resistors in parallel) from $V = I_1 R_1$, $V = I_2 R_2$, $V = IR$ and $I = I_1 + I_2$.

(ii) The derivation of

$$s = ut + \tfrac{1}{2}at^2$$

and

$$v^2 = u^2 + 2as.$$

(iii) Obtaining v from

$$\frac{1}{u} + \frac{1}{v} = \frac{1}{f}$$

given, say, $u = 3 \cdot 5$, $f = 2 \cdot 5$. This is done by substituting in the given formula to obtain

$$\frac{1}{3 \cdot 5} + \frac{1}{v} = \frac{1}{2 \cdot 5}$$

rather than by re-arranging to make v the subject.

(iv) Re-arrangement of formulae, such as the transition from

$$T = 2\pi \sqrt{\frac{l}{g}} \quad \text{to} \quad g = \frac{4\pi^2 l}{T^2}$$

which is used in an experiment with a simple pendulum to calculate g.

SIMPLE LINEAR EQUATIONS

Examples of equations arising in problem-solving will be found on page 37. The most complicated type occurs in calculations in connection with the "method of mixtures" in calorimetry, but these are not often demanded. A problem involving moments (the balancing of a beam) can lead to a linear equation.

Difficulties are found in schools where the solution of a linear equation is taught in mathematics by a "flow diagram" method, and this has not been explained to science teachers. On the general question of modern approaches to equations, see below.

SIMULTANEOUS LINEAR EQUATIONS

Examples of these will be found in the problems section (p. 37).

EQUATIONS IN PHYSICS AND IN *SMP*

The ways in which equations arise and are treated in traditional physics courses and in the *SMP* mathematics course are somewhat different. This is true to some extent in the case of simple linear equations, but particularly true of simultaneous linear equations.

In the *SMP* treatment the primary notion is that of mapping or function. (In the *SMP* numbered books the terms *mapping* and *function* are not synonymous, the latter being a special case of the former. In the (later) lettered books the terms are synonymous. The latter usage is followed here.) A given mapping associates with each element (*object*) in a set (called the *domain* of the mapping) an element (*image*) in a set called the *codomain* (which may be the same set as the domain itself). For example, the function $y = x^2 + 2$ (as written in traditional notation) is described in the terminology given above as follows:

The domain, i.e. the set of values of x, could be the set of real numbers. The reason for saying "could be" rather than "is" is that, in a particular case, we might be interested in a restricted set of values for x such as non-negative numbers only. (This is the case with $y = \sqrt{x}$ for example, since no real value can be found for y when x is negative.) The domain for a mapping has to be specified. In this case let the domain be the set of all positive real numbers.

For each real-number object x, the formula specifies the image as the number $x^2 + 2$. Thus, if the object is 3, the image is 11. If the letter m is used to stand for the mapping, then we may write the relationship between 3 and 11 in the pictorial form

$$3 \xrightarrow{\; m \;} 11$$

This can be read as "m maps 3 onto 11".

The general formula, written in the same form, is

$$x \xrightarrow{\ m\ } x^2 + 2$$

An alternative form is $m: x \mapsto x^2 + 2$.

The image of x under the mapping m is written $m(x)$. So we can also write $m(x) = x^2 + 2$.

The total effect of the mapping m on all members of the domain may be exhibited in a graph. As an alternative to the usual Cartesian graph (figure 3.8), an arrow graph is often used (figure 3.9).

Another way of thinking of the function m is as a series of operations carried out on the input x to yield the output $x^2 + 2$. This may be pictured as a flow diagram:

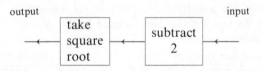

If in the arrow graph (figure 3.9) the domain and codomain are interchanged, and the direction of the arrows reversed, the resulting graph is that of the *inverse* function (figure 3.10).

The flow diagram for the inverse function is obtained by reversing the one above, and replacing each operation by the corresponding inverse ("undoing") operation, thus:

An *equation* arises when the following problem is posed: suppose that it is known that the image of a certain object under the function m is 17. What is the object?

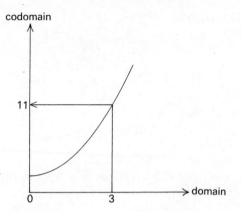

Figure 3.8 Cartesian graph.

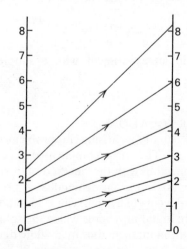

Figure 3.9 Arrow graph.

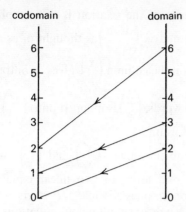

Figure 3.10   Arrow graph of inverse function.

Using the first flow diagram, the problem may be represented thus:

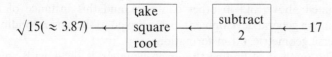

Using the second (inverse) flow diagram, the solution is obtained thus:

$\sqrt{15}(\approx 3.87)$ ← | take square root | ← | subtract 2 | ← 17

Such is the flow-diagram method for solving

$$x^2 + 2 = 17.$$

The calculation of particular images and objects, whilst important, is secondary to the development of a "global" view in which each type of function is seen as a whole entity. Mathematicians are more interested in the differences between the two parts of figure 3.11 than in the computation of individual points on either graph. These two examples are deliberately selected in order to demonstrate to physicists the advantages of the function-orientated approach.

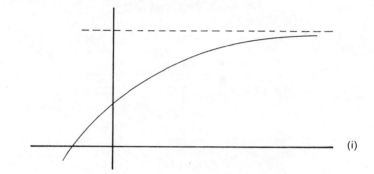

(i)

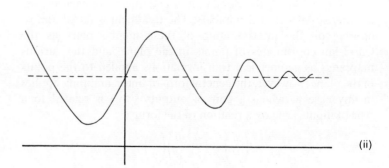

(ii)

Figure 3.11.

The flow-diagram method as described above is limited to equations which can be put in the form $f(x) = a$, and in which the unknown x is mentioned once only. Linear equations arising in physics are sometimes of the form $f(x) = g(x)$, as in the following simple example on moments (figure 3.12). The equation has to be solved in the traditional way:

$$50x = 20(10-x) + 10(20-x)$$

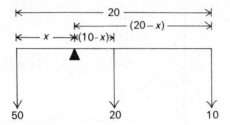

50   20   10

Figure 3.12.

In *SMP*, simultaneous linear equations arise when considering mappings in which the domain and codomain are each the set of *ordered pairs* of real numbers. The treatment is based almost entirely on the interpretation of these number-pairs as the Cartesian coordinates of points in the plane, and the various mappings as geometrical transformations applied to the points of the plane; however, the general form of linear mapping applies in any case in which a pair of outputs (x',y') is related to a pair of inputs (x,y) by a relation of the form

$$\begin{pmatrix} x' \\ y' \end{pmatrix} = \begin{pmatrix} a & b \\ c & d \end{pmatrix} \begin{pmatrix} x \\ y \end{pmatrix}$$

This relation is equivalent to two simultaneous linear relations:

$$x' = ax + by$$

$$y' = cx + dy$$

but the matrix form of the relation is that emphasized in the *SMP* course. The matrix $\begin{pmatrix} a & b \\ c & d \end{pmatrix}$ is thought of as an "operator" which, operating on the column $\begin{pmatrix} x \\ y \end{pmatrix}$, gives as output the column $\begin{pmatrix} x' \\ y' \end{pmatrix}$. Or, in other words, $\begin{pmatrix} x \\ y \end{pmatrix}$ is mapped onto $\begin{pmatrix} x' \\ y' \end{pmatrix}$ by a function given by the first formula.

The inverse problem—given $\begin{pmatrix} x' \\ y' \end{pmatrix}$ find $\begin{pmatrix} x \\ y \end{pmatrix}$—would lead, if written in the second form, to two linear equations. But the method of solution emphasized in *SMP* starts from the single matrix equation. A pair of simultaneous equations such as

$$2x + 3y = 2$$

$$4x + 7y = 5$$

are first re-cast in matrix form as

$$\begin{pmatrix} 2 & 3 \\ 4 & 7 \end{pmatrix} \begin{pmatrix} x \\ y \end{pmatrix} = \begin{pmatrix} 2 \\ 5 \end{pmatrix}.$$

The solution is obtained by finding the inverse matrix.

Pupils will already have met the idea of inverse function (as outlined above and in other contexts), and this instance of it fits into a general development, being linked to the corresponding inverse geometrical transformations.

The method of finding the inverse matrix is dealt with, and the equation is solved by writing

$$\begin{pmatrix} x \\ y \end{pmatrix} = \begin{pmatrix} 2 & 3 \\ 4 & 7 \end{pmatrix}^{-1} \begin{pmatrix} 2 \\ 5 \end{pmatrix}$$

The matrix notation and the ideas of transformation (mapping) and inverse are developed because of the great range of their applicability when extended to any situation where an ordered set (vector) of outputs is obtained from an ordered set (vector) of inputs by premultiplication by a matrix.

Applications of matrix algebra occur in science, in probability and statistics, but in all of these at a relatively high level of sophistication. The kind of simultaneous equations arising in physics problems can be illustrated by the following example.

When a certain cell is connected to a 5-ohm resistor, a current of 7 amperes flows in the circuit. When the resistance is increased to 8 ohms, the current falls to 3 amperes. Calculate the e.m.f. and the internal resistance of the cell.

If E volts is the e.m.f. of the cell and r ohms its internal resistance, then application of Ohm's law to the circuit in each case yields the simultaneous equations

$$7 = \frac{E}{5+r} \quad (1); \qquad 3 = \frac{E}{8+r} \quad (2).$$

This problem *can* be put into matrix form and solved as follows:

$$(1) \Rightarrow 7(5+r) = E \Rightarrow 35+7r = E \Rightarrow E-7r = 35$$

$$(2) \Rightarrow 3(8+r) = E \Rightarrow 24+3r = E \Rightarrow E-3r = 24.$$

Thus

$$\begin{pmatrix} 1 & -7 \\ 1 & -3 \end{pmatrix} \begin{pmatrix} E \\ r \end{pmatrix} = \begin{pmatrix} 35 \\ 24 \end{pmatrix}$$

(Incidentally, what "output" is represented by the vector $\begin{pmatrix} 35 \\ 24 \end{pmatrix}$?)

$$\Leftrightarrow \begin{pmatrix} E \\ r \end{pmatrix} = \begin{pmatrix} 1 & -7 \\ 1 & -3 \end{pmatrix}^{-1} \begin{pmatrix} 35 \\ 24 \end{pmatrix} \text{etc.}$$

The point of the matrix representation is lost. The entries in the matrix are of no clear significance, and the vector $\begin{pmatrix} E \\ r \end{pmatrix}$ is not in any clear relationship to $\begin{pmatrix} 35 \\ 24 \end{pmatrix}$. The problem has had to be forced into the matrix mould.

The traditional language of equations is more appropriate here. This language speaks of "unknowns", and of equations as statements connecting the unknowns. There is a rule of thumb that we need as many independent equations as there are unknowns, and there are techniques for "unscrambling" equations.

Although the standard "elimination" method is dealt with in *SMP* (and extended to simultaneous inequalities) it is not emphasized. Evidence for this comes from an examination of the revision exercises in *Book 5*—the final book of the course—and from the "O" Level papers themselves. Further details of different methods of solving simultaneous equations are given in *Algebra*, a book in this series.

3.10   Geometry and Trigonometry

GEOMETRICAL PROPERTIES OF PARALLEL LINES, ISOSCELES TRIANGLES, CIRCLES.

Most of the applications of these topics are to geometrical optics. They are well illustrated by the following explanation of the formula $f = \frac{1}{2}r$, where f is the focal length and r the radius of curvature of a concave spherical mirror of small aperture.

CR, being the radius of the circle (which is the section of the sphere by the plane of the paper), is normal to the circle at R (figure 3.13).

By the law of reflection, angle $x =$ angle y. But

$$\text{angle } x = \text{angle } z \text{ (alternate angles).}$$

Thus $y = z$, and hence $\triangle$FCR is isosceles. Hence

$$\text{FR} = \text{FC.}$$

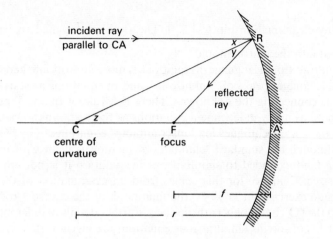

Figure 3.13   Reflection of light by a concave spherical mirror.

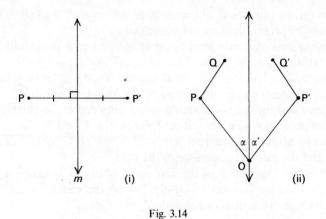

Fig. 3.14

If R is close to A, then FR is practically equal to FA. Thus

$$f = \tfrac{1}{2}r.$$

A NOTE ON REFLECTION

Reflection, as it appears in mathematics courses, is a transformation of the plane. If m is the axis of reflection, then the image of P is defined as P′, where PP′ is bisected perpendicularly by m (figure 3.14(i)). In other words m is the axis of symmetry of P and P′, and symmetry is invoked as the explanation of the following features of figure 3.14(ii):

$$P'Q' = PQ; \quad \alpha' = \alpha; \quad OP' = OP.$$

In geometrical optics the fundamental law of reflection is "angle of incidence = angle of reflection", and the fact that m bisects PP′ at right angles has to be established from a consideration of figure 3.15, where two rays emerging from P are

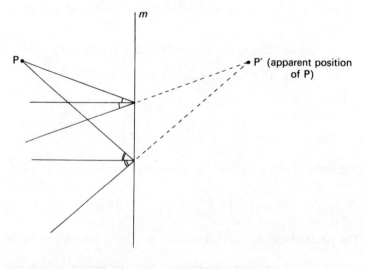

Fig. 3.15   Reflection in a plane mirror.

shown. The physics lies in answering the question: why does a plane mirror produce biaxial symmetry of object and image?

Geometrical optics produces some interesting geometrical construction work. The topic is pursued further in section 3.14.

SIMILAR TRIANGLES

Similar triangles in figure 3.16 are used to establish the formula

$$\text{magnification} = \frac{\text{height of image}}{\text{height of object}} = \frac{v}{u}.$$

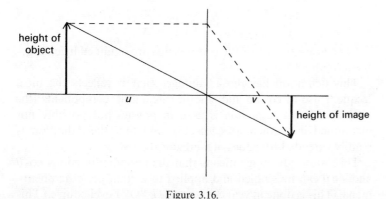

Figure 3.16.

In *SMP* pupils are introduced (year 2) to the geometrical transformation of *enlargement from a centre*, illustrated in figure 3.17. This idea can be related directly to the lens example.

VECTORS

The vector quantities used in physics are force, velocity and acceleration. These are represented by directed line-segments, and both triangle and parallelogram forms of the addition law are used. The second is preferred for forces, since it draws

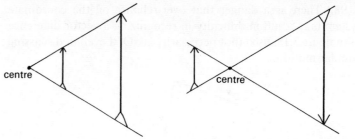

enlargement with positive scale factor   enlargement with negative scale factor

Figure 3.17.

attention to the point of application, which is significant in the case of a force, though not for a vector in general. (The term *resultant* is common in physics but *sum* is usually used in mathematics.)

The vectors studied in school mathematics—displacement vectors—do not represent something else, so their law of addition is relatively easy to understand. When coordinate geometry is used, a vector is specified by a number-pair whose two components are the changes in the two coordinates of every point undergoing the given displacement.

Thus, for example, $\begin{pmatrix} 3 \\ -2 \end{pmatrix}$ specifies a displacement or translation in which (2,4) moves to (5,2) and, in general, (p,q) moves to $(p+3, q-2)$.

The vector law of addition

$$\begin{pmatrix} a_1 \\ a_2 \end{pmatrix} + \begin{pmatrix} b_1 \\ b_2 \end{pmatrix} = \begin{pmatrix} a_1 + b_1 \\ a_2 + b_2 \end{pmatrix}$$

is easy, and an arithmetic of vectors as lists of numbers soon develops.

Vectors are introduced in this way in SCISP (*Patterns, Vol. 2,* p. 98.) There is a danger that over-reliance on the coordinate system may result in difficulty in recognizing a vector difference as in figure 3.18, used (not necessarily at "O" Level) in discussing circular motion.

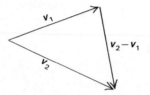

Figure 3.18.

PYTHAGORAS' THEOREM

The theorem is used in the calculation of the resultant of two perpendicular vectors.

TRIGONOMETRY

The sine function appears in Snell's law of refraction, and calculation of the critical angle for a substance involves the solution of

$$\sin \theta = \frac{1}{n}$$

where n is the refractive index. Sines and cosines may be used to calculate components of forces.

In the traditional treatment of trigonometry, sine, cosine and tangent are defined as quotients of the sides of a right-angled triangle:

$$\sin \theta = \frac{\text{opposite}}{\text{hypotenuse}}; \quad \cos \theta = \frac{\text{adjacent}}{\text{hypotenuse}}; \quad \tan \theta = \frac{\text{opposite}}{\text{adjacent}}.$$

In *SMP Book 2*, cosine and sine are defined as components of a unit vector (whereas in the CSE course (*Books E, F*) they are defined as the coordinates of a point P, where OP = 1 unit and angle XOP $= \theta$).

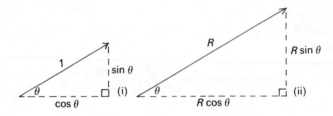

Figure 3.19.

For a non-unit vector the components are obtained by enlargement (figure 3.19).

This definition has the advantages that it reflects the most frequent use of cosine and sine in calculating components (the equivalent term *resolution* is used in physics but possibly not mentioned in mathematics lessons), and that the definition is readily extended to values of θ greater than 90°.

This latter advantage means that the periodic functions $\cos \theta$ and $\sin \theta$ can be studied and applied to certain periodic phenomena. (This is done in year 3 in the *SMP* "O" Level course.) This mathematical work is not used much at present in "O" Level physics, mainly because it is restricted to certain mathematics courses. At most the term *sine curve* may be used to describe a wave-form.

In the *SMP* treatment of trigonometry, $\tan \theta$ is defined as

$$\frac{\sin \theta}{\cos \theta}.$$

In applications to right-angled triangles, figure 3.20 shows the form of the relationship which is used.

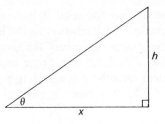

Figure 3.20 $h = x \tan \theta$.

MENSURATION

The formula for the circumference of a circle is used in obtaining a formula for the velocity ratio of a screw. Area calculations are involved when dealing with laminas and the trapezoidal area under a velocity-time graph. Calculations of the area of a circle, and the volumes of a cylinder and a sphere, arise in the determination of molecular size from the diameter of an oil-film obtained from a spherical oil drop. Other instances of mensuration will be found in section 3.13 (example 8, p. 40).

3.11   Logarithmic scale

This scale is used in the presentation of the range of sizes of physical objects, the time scale of the universe, and the electro-magnetic spectrum.

TOPIC SURVEY: NUFFIELD COURSE

Owing to lack of space it is impossible to give here a detailed account of the *Nuffield Physics* course. The five *Teachers' Guides* are informative for mathematics teachers unfamiliar with the course. However, one cannot give an account of the mathe-matical content of the course without giving some idea of its aims and the thinking behind it (*NPTG 4*, p. 65).

> Science today is not just a pile of measured results like a table of densities or some values of g; nor is it a set of formulae connecting measurements, like $s = \frac{1}{2}gt^2$. We try to build a connected frame of knowledge, in which models of nature—stretched by imaginative thinking based on experimental results—enable us to think and plan, to check the models themselves to some extent, to predict, to guide more investigations, and over all to discuss our own knowledge. It is the growing edge that most scientists enjoy, the doing and thinking to extend the frame of knowledge, rather than the wealth of facts and rules already accumulated. Unless young people understand some-thing of that attitude they will be out of tune with modern science.

The word *model* in this quotation is being used in a wider sense than simply that of mathematical model. But in so far as the course aims to make pupils participate in the scientific activity of modelling, then the appreciation of the part played by mathematics is integral.

Some comments from the *Nuffield Physics Teachers' Guides* on elementary topics in mathematics have already been noted. The account which follows, apart from the first entry, is concerned with the mathematical content of years 3, 4 and 5 of the course.

THE OIL-FILM EXPERIMENT (YEAR 1)

The oil-film experiment to estimate the size of an oil molecule appears near the end of the first year of the course. In spite of the fact that many simplifications and approximations are made (and these may themselves give rise to difficulty in under-standing), the concepts involved and the indirectness of approach (the thickness of the film is obtained from its volume and its area) are rather difficult for pupils at the first-year stage. This is a criticism voiced in many quarters.

SPEED-TIME CHARTS (YEAR 3)

An approach to speed-time charts and their interpretation is made by using a device called a *ticker timer* which produces

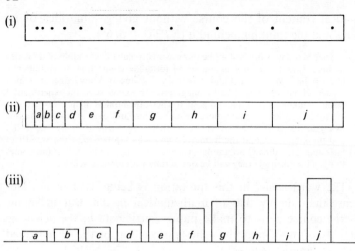

Figure 3.21   The construction of a speed-time chart.

Although it is clear that the total height of all the columns is the distance travelled, the transition to the idea that the *area* under a speed-time graph represents the distance travelled is recognized as being a difficult one. Some examples of graphs whose areas represent something are given to pupils. An example is shown in figure 3.22, but there is no reason why the idea

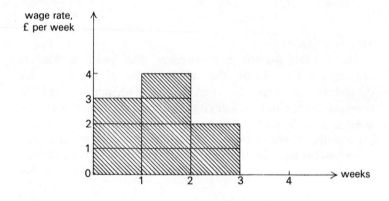

Figure 3.22.

a record on paper-tape of the motion of the object to which it is attached. An example is shown in figure 3.21 in a simplified form.

The ticks are produced at regular time-intervals (50 per second). If a suitable unit of time is chosen, the distances travelled in each of the time units can be marked off on the tape. The unit (ten ticks, called a *tentick*) is chosen on practical rather than mathematical grounds. This is done for the tape illustrated in figure 3.21(ii), using a unit of one tick. The length of each section, being a distance covered in unit time, gives the (average) speed for that part of the motion. The tape is then cut and the pieces placed side by side (figure 3.21(iii)). The resulting chart is a picture of the motion, showing speed against time. (An alternative approach is to calculate the set of speeds and then plot an ordinary graph.) Arithmetical difficulties can occur in the conversion from the tape units to centimetres per second.

should not have been introduced already in the mathematics course (at present it does not appear until year 5 in *SMP*). The fact that the area under a speed-time graph represents the distance travelled is used to establish the formula $s = ut + \frac{1}{2}at^2$. Similar methods for obtaining kinetic energy ($= \frac{1}{2}mv^2$) from a graph of momentum against velocity, and "work done" from a force against distance graph, are also indicated later in the course.

KINETIC THEORY (YEAR 4)

The derivation of the formula $PV = \frac{1}{3}Nmv^2$, where P is the pressure, and V the volume of a mass of gas consisting of N molecules, each of mass m and velocity v, is a central part of the work on kinetic theory. It is suggested to teachers that a numerical case is worked through first, before the algebraic version is given.

The algebra is worth giving in full (*NPTG 4*, p. 203):

> We arrive very carefully at the change of momentum $2mv$ at each impact.
>
> We call the length of the box a. We take the total distance vt that such a molecule will travel in a time t, and find how many return trips the molecule will make in time t; that is $vt/2a$ trips.
>
> We find the total change of momentum at one end face of the box in the time t; that is $(2mv)(vt/2a)$. Then we must multiply by the number of molecules available for this, which is $\frac{1}{3}N^*$; and we divide by the area of the end face, say bc. That gives us the pressure, $\frac{1}{3}Nmv^2/abc$.
>
> $$P = \tfrac{1}{3}Nmv^2/abc$$
>
> or
>
> $$PV = \tfrac{1}{3}Nmv^2$$
>
> since abc is the volume V.

Lest this be classified as a mathematical requirement of the course, the following comment on it should be noted (*NPTG 4*, p. 187):

> [It] is not a result to be memorized, nor should the full argument of "deriving" it from simple assumptions be learnt by heart as something that can be produced in an examination without the candidate knowing quite what he is doing. Somehow, we want every pupil to feel he knows what he and the teacher are doing when they arrive at that statement. That suggests for one thing that we should use different methods for classes of different ability; and for another thing that we should stimulate and encourage pupils to follow such a story through with the teacher without expecting it to be fully reproducible afterwards.
>
> "Ah, but a man's reach should exceed his grasp, or what's a heaven for?"

DIFFUSION (YEAR 4)

The argument here, which leads to an estimation of the size of an air molecule, is recognized as being difficult. The idea of random walk is involved, together with the average distance travelled from its starting point by a particle making N jumps,

---

* Seeing that the number of available molecules is $\frac{1}{3}N$ is a very difficult step.

---

each of length s, in random directions. A simulation is suggested to "verify" the rule

$$\text{average distance} = s\sqrt{N}$$

This is an interesting simulation; although used here for molecules, the set-up can be described comprehensibly in general terms (or picturesquely, as "drunkard's walk").

CIRCULAR MOTION (YEAR 5)

A central feature of the work in year 5 is the quantitative treatment of circular motion. If the geometrical approach is thought by the teacher to be too hard, then an experimental investigation is suggested (*NPTG 5*, p. 45).

> Where the (geometrical) derivation must be avoided, we have three choices: (1) give up most of the physics of satellites and planetary systems, and atomic particles; (2) treat those things, but take out all quantitative discussions, so that physics seems to lose its backbone; (3) justify $F = mv^2/R$ by experimental tests.... We wonder whether a slow pupil will not have as much difficulty in following the argument of the test as in following through a carefully taught derivation?

The methods of derivation suggested are (i) a method based upon the intersecting-chords theorem; and (ii) a method based upon vector change, and using similar triangles. In both cases a limit is involved, and teachers are advised not to labour the point.

The algebra involved in the theory of the fine-beam tube experiment to measure e/m is worth quoting in full (*NPTG 5*, p. 69):

$$eV = \tfrac{1}{2}mv^2 \qquad (1)$$

$$Bev = \frac{mv^2}{R} \qquad (2)$$

B in (2) is obtained from $F = BCL$ (current balance).

Calculate v first, rather than eliminate v. (This eases the algebra, and v is of interest anyway.)

From (1) and (2)

$$\frac{Bev}{eV} = \frac{mv^2/R}{\frac{1}{2}mv^2}$$

$$\therefore \frac{Bv}{V} = \frac{2}{R}$$

$$v = \frac{2V}{BR}$$

Substitute for v in (1) to obtain e/m.

ASTRONOMY (YEAR 5)

Astronomy is taught as the history of a theory.

The five regular polyhedra have a walking-on part (in an ancient Greek theory), but the main mathematical content occurs in the treatment of Kepler's laws of planetary motion. Here is the derivation, from Newton's laws of motion and gravitation, of Kepler's third law.

A planet of mass m moves with speed v in a circle of radius R around a Sun of mass M. G is the gravitational constant.

$$\frac{GMm}{d^2} = \frac{mv^2}{R} \tag{1}$$

$$d = R \tag{2}$$

$$v = \frac{2\pi R}{T} \tag{3}$$

$$\therefore \frac{GMm}{R^2} = \frac{m(2\pi R/T)^2}{R}$$

$$\therefore \frac{GMm}{R^2} = \frac{4\pi^2 mR^2}{T^2 R}$$

$$\therefore \frac{R^3}{T^2} = \frac{GM}{4\pi^2} = \text{constant.}$$

On Kepler's second law, the *Teachers' Guide* comments (*NPTG 5*, p. 191):

Newton gave a geometrical proof, using changes of momentum as vectors. This proof, in simplified form, should be offered to pupils in average and faster groups. Most of them would not be able to reproduce it, and may even remember the showing of it with something of a headache; yet it is a derivation they should see done, as part of their contact with a great piece of work.

The proof is too long to be given here. It involves vector change, and an application of the geometrical result that triangles on the same base and between the same parallels are equal in area.

LIGHT WAVES (YEAR 5)

Estimation of the wavelengths of light from measurements of Young's fringes involves understanding the geometry of figure 3.23.

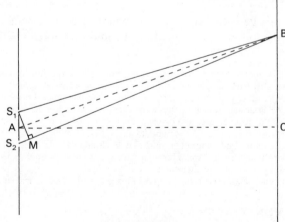

Figure 3.23.

$\triangle S_1 S_2 M$ is (very nearly) similar to $\triangle ABC$

$$\therefore \frac{S_2 M}{S_1 S_2} = \frac{BC}{AB}$$

THE RADIUS OF THE EARTH

Obtaining the angle of elevation of the sun by using a pole and shadow, followed by either a scale drawing or a trigonometric calculation, is a hackneyed procedure leading to a result which, because not connected with anything else, is of little interest. An interesting extension of this procedure is to calculate (or obtain from a simplified scale drawing) an approximate value for the radius of the earth from the angles of elevation recorded simultaneously at two places a long distance apart (say 300 miles or so) on the same line of longitude. The method is described in *NPTG* 5, pp. 134–6.

PROBLEMS AND SOLUTIONS

3.12   Problem-Solving

The section following this consists of a selection of representative examination questions involving mathematics, taken from recent CSE and "O" Level papers. The present section is concerned with some of the difficulties experienced by pupils in solving problems in physics.

(i) The translation from a physical to a mathematical statement of a problem (i.e. the entry into a mathematical model of a physical situation) is often the most difficult step of all, and this is true at all stages (see in section 3.13, examples 3, 5, 6, 9, 17). This difficulty is not confined to physics. In *SMP* pupils make use of elementary linear programming to solve problems which are stated non-symbolically. This work is valuable largely because of the practice it gives in the difficult business of translating into symbols. In traditional courses problems in words leading to an equation or pair of equations do the same job.

(ii) Many problems in "O" Level physics are "multi-stage" problems, requiring several steps for their solution, so that as well as a knowledge of the necessary physics and mathematics, an appropriate strategy is demanded. Whilst in many cases the strategies are fairly standard (e.g. section 3.13, example 3), there are many others in which the pupil must develop and follow a strategy of his own (examples 4, 5).

Science teachers may find that flow diagrams are helpful when explaining the approach to solving a problem, and pupils may find such diagrams useful when formulating their own strategies. The problem chosen here to illustrate the formulation of a strategy comes from an "O" Level physics paper (London, January 74, Question A1):

A balloon of volume $2000\,m^3$ is filled with hydrogen of density $0{\cdot}09\,kg/m^3$. If the mass of the fabric is $100\,kg$ and that of the pilot $75\,kg$, what will be the greatest mass of equipment that can be carried when operating in air of density $1{\cdot}25\,kg/m^3$?

The solution depends on two fundamental principles.

(i) When floating, the upthrust on the balloon is equal to the total weight of fabric, hydrogen, pilot and equipment.
(ii) Archimedes' Principle: the upthrust is equal to the weight of air displaced.

Unless the pupil knows that these physical laws are relevant to the problem, he can make no headway at all. (Often one of the principles underlying the problem is more or less given in the first part of the question.)

When these two principles have been recalled as being relevant, a flow diagram for solving the problem may be started by drawing two boxes.

(1)   (2)

From box (1) the diagram proceeds as below, the order of *thinking* being upwards.

From box (2) it can go as below.

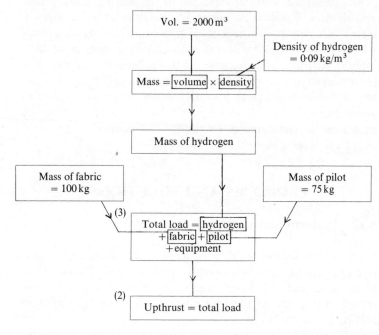

The use of flow diagrams, even fragmentary ones, may help pupils to structure their problem-solving. The account above starts *inside* the problem and works *outwards* towards the data. Often pupils will write down all the data and then calculate a few things from the data without knowing how they will be fitted together. The construction of a flow diagram helps in the fitting together.

The type of strategy illustrated above is reminiscent of the older style of geometrical problem in mathematics, in which a pupil had to say to himself, "In order to prove A, I must first prove B,...".

continued opposite

There is a tendency in some recent "O" Level mathematics papers for questions to be split up into parts, in such a way that the solution to each part helps the candidate to tackle the next. The job of deciding a strategy has been done for the candidate, and he has merely to follow the implied line of thought (itself not necessarily an easy task). Whereas such questions, set as exercises, may help pupils to see the need for a strategy (provided they reflect on the solutions when completed), it may be that simpler problems with fewer hints would be more valuable training for tackling the sort of question considered in this section.

In this solution the box labelled (3) is the focus, and in the final form (1), (2) and (3) can be drawn as shown below.

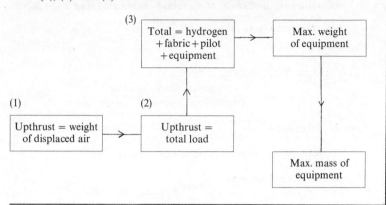

(3)

| Total = hydrogen + fabric + pilot + equipment | → | Max. weight of equipment |

(1) (2)

| Upthrust = weight of displaced air | → | Upthrust = total load |

| Max. mass of equipment |

3.13 A Selection of CSE and "O" Level Questions

This representative collection of examination questions has been included mainly in order that mathematics teachers may see (or be reminded of) the mathematical attainment expected of the candidates.

Examples 1 and 2 are taken from the papers of one of the CSE Boards which divides its course into a core plus options. The examples are drawn from the options, and will thus be attempted by pupils who have undertaken special studies in these areas. As such they are considerably more demanding than those questions appropriate to the core.

EXAMPLE 1 (EM, May 74, Question 2B 8)

Each of the cells in the circuit diagram has an e.m.f. of 2V and no internal resistance.

(a) (i)   Are the cells connected in series or parallel?
　　(ii) What is their total e.m.f.?
　　(iii) Calculate the total resistance in the circuit.

(iv)   What reading is shown by ammeter A_1?
(v)   What reading is shown by ammeter A_2?
(vi)   When the switch S is depressed, what effect, if any, does this have on the readings of the ammeters A_1 and A_2?
(vii) What is the reading shown by the voltmeter V?

(b) (i)   What is meant by a short circuit?
　　(ii) Why, when a short circuit occurs, is the electricity likely to cease flowing?
　　(iii) To which part of an appliance is the earth wire usually connected?
　　(iv) What is the purpose of the earth wire?

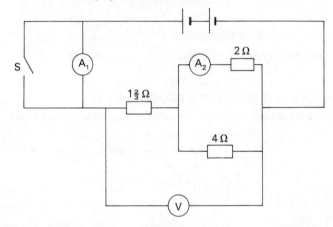

Solution to part (a):

The calculations involve applications of Ohm's Law in the form

$$\text{voltage (or p.d.)} = \text{current} \times \text{resistance.}$$

(a) (ii)   Total e.m.f. = 4V.
　　(iii) Resistance of parallel combination, $R\,\Omega$, is given by

$$\frac{1}{R} = \frac{1}{2} + \frac{1}{4} = \frac{3}{4}$$

so that $$R = \frac{4}{3}.$$

Total resistance of circuit $= 1\frac{2}{3}\Omega + 1\frac{1}{3}\Omega = 3\Omega$.

(iv) Reading of $A_1 = \dfrac{\text{applied voltage}}{\text{total resistance}}$

$= \dfrac{4}{3}$ A.

(v) Since the voltage across the parallel combination is the same for both resistors

$$2 \times \text{current through } 2\Omega = 4 \times \text{current through } 4\Omega.$$

$$\frac{\text{current through } 2\Omega}{\text{current through } 4\Omega} = \frac{4}{2} = \frac{2}{1}.$$

Therefore, current through $A_2 = \frac{2}{3}$ of $\frac{4}{3}$ A
$= \frac{8}{9}$ A.

(vi) Reading on A_1 goes to zero, that on A_2 is unchanged.
(vii) Reading on $V = 4$ volts.

EXAMPLE 2 (EM, May 74, Question 2B 3)
(This is a particularly good example of a structured question).

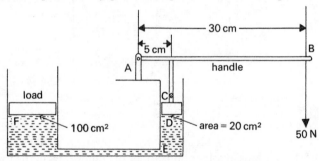

The diagram shows a simple hydraulic press which could be used to lift a load.
(a) (i)   What is meant by velocity ratio?
    (ii) What is the velocity ratio of the handle AB?
    (iii) Why is there a pin joint at C?
    (iv) If a force of 50N is applied to the handle AB, what force will act at C?
    (v)   What will be the reaction at the support A, and which way does it act?
    (vi) What is the velocity ratio of the hydraulic system?
    (vii) What force will be applied to the load? (State any assumptions made).

(b) (i)   What is meant by efficiency?
    (ii) What is meant by mechanical advantage?
    (iii) If the overall efficiency of the press is 80 per cent, what is the overall mechanical advantage?
    (iv) What is the cause of the losses?

Comment

To answer this, candidates need to know:

(a) (i)   Velocity ratio $= \dfrac{\text{distance moved by effort}}{\text{distance moved by load in same time}}$

(b) (i)   Efficiency $= \dfrac{\text{useful work done on load}}{\text{work done by effort}}$

(frequently expressed as a percentage, as here).

(ii) Mechanical advantage $= \dfrac{\text{load}}{\text{effort}}$

EXAMPLE 3 (Abbott, *Ordinary Level Physics*, p. 219, no. 10)
Some "O" Level Boards still demand treatment of the method of mixtures. The strategy involved in solving such problems is usually well drilled in physics lessons. A "heat equation" is first written out in words, then in symbols, and the remainder is mathematics. It is at this stage, however, that sometimes pupils multiply together everything in sight.

A piece of copper of mass 40 g at 200°C is placed in a copper calorimeter of mass 60 g containing 50 g of water at 10°C. Ignoring heat losses, what will be the final steady temperature after stirring?
(Specific heat capacity of water $= 4\cdot2$ J/g °C
Specific heat capacity of copper $= 0\cdot4$ J/g°C.)

Solution

Let t be the final temperature of the "mixture".
Heat gained by water and calorimeter = Heat lost by copper block

$$M_w C_w(t-10) + M_{cal} C_c(t-10) = M_{block} C_c(200-t)$$

(Here M_w, M_{cal}, M_{block} are the masses of the water, calorimeter and block; C_w, C_c are the specific heat capacities of water and copper.)

$$\Rightarrow (50 \times 4\cdot2 + 60 \times 0\cdot4)(t-10) = 40 \times 0\cdot4(200-t)$$

$$\Rightarrow \text{Final temperature} = 22\cdot16°C.$$

EXAMPLE 4 (JMB, Nov. 70, Question B28 (part))

Questions on Archimedes' Principle and on flotation have considerable notoriety. It is by no means difficult to find examples much more complex than this.

A block of wood with a volume of $200\,cm^3$ floats in a liquid of density $0.70\,g/cm^3$ with $\frac{5}{8}$ of its volume submerged. Calculate the density of the wood.

Comment

It is worth noting that the volume of the block given in the question is redundant information, but that its omission would add considerably to the difficulty of the problem.

EXAMPLE 5 (Oxford, Autumn 72, Question 3b)

When deducing an upper limit of molecular size by the surface-film method, it is assumed as a rough approximation that the molecules are small cubes. Supposing that an oil molecule is a cube of side $10^{-9}\,m$ and that the mass of a single molecule is $4 \times 10^{-25}\,kg$, estimate the mass of an oil drop which is capable of forming a circular film one molecule thick and of radius $0.2\,m$.

[Answer: $5.0 \times 10^{-8}\,kg$]

This question derives from the famous oil film experiment carried out by Lord Rayleigh which enabled him to set an upper limit to the size of a olive-oil molecule. At present a replication of this experiment is included in the first year of the Nuffield "O" Level physics course and at some stage in the two-year Nuffield Combined Science course, at which stage many pupils have great difficulty with the mathematics involved and fail to appreciate the full significance of the experiment. Its inclusion at some later point in an "O" Level course provides a very valuable experience, however.

EXAMPLE 6 (Abbott, *Ordinary Level Physics*, p. 438, no. 11 (ex JMB))

Simultaneous equations are encountered in this example but, as is usual in physics problems, these are particularly simple.

A cell is joined in series with a resistance of 2 ohms and a current of 0.25 ampere flows through it. When a second resistance of 2 ohms is connected in parallel with the first, the current through the cell increases to 0.3 ampere. What is (a) the e.m.f.; (b) the internal resistance of the cell?

Solution

Let E be the e.m.f. of the cell and r its internal resistance.

For 1st case $\hspace{3em} E = 0.25(2+r) \hspace{3em}$ (1) by Ohm's Law

Let R be the total resistance of parallel combination

$$\frac{1}{R} = \frac{1}{2} + \frac{1}{2} = 1$$

$$\therefore R = 1$$

For 2nd case $\hspace{3em} E = 0.3(1+r) \hspace{3em}$ (2)

Eliminating E gives

$$0.25(2+r) = 0.3(1+r)$$
$$\therefore 0.5 + 0.25r = 0.3 + 0.3r$$
$$\therefore 0.05r = 0.2$$
$$\therefore r = \frac{0.2}{0.05} = 4$$

Substituting in (2)

$$E = 0.3(1+4) = 1.5$$

Hence (a) the e.m.f. of the cell is $1.5\,V$
and (b) its internal resistance is 4 ohms.

EXAMPLE 7 (Oxford, Autumn 72, Question 5)

Direct and inverse proportionality are encountered in this problem involving the ideal gas laws.

A certain mass of dry air is enclosed in a graduated vessel, with arrangements to vary and measure the temperature, the pressure and the volume occupied by the air. Volumes are expressed in terms of the units in which the vessel is graduated.

The volume occupied by the air is 600 units when the temperature is $27°C$ and the pressure is $10^5\,N/m^2$. If the pressure remains constant at $10^5\,N/m^2$, find the volume occupied by the air when the temperature is

(a) $89°C$

(b) $-73°C$

(c) At what pressure will the volume be 600 units when the temperature is $87°C$?

(d) Which, if any, of these results would be affected if the air had contained just sufficient water vapour to saturate it at $27°C$? Explain.

Comment

The laws involved in this question are:

(a) *Charles' Law*: Under conditions of constant pressure the volume of a fixed mass of an ideal gas is directly proportional to its kelvin (formerly absolute) temperature.

(b) *Boyle's Law*: The pressure of a fixed mass of an ideal gas is inversely proportional to its volume provided that the temperature remains constant.

Both laws are included in the single formula

$$\frac{P_1 V_1}{T_1} = \frac{P_2 V_2}{T_2}.$$

Note that physicists employ the symbol T exclusively for kelvin temperatures.

[Answers: (a) 720 units, (b) 400 units, (c) $1.2 \times 10^5 \text{N/m}^2$.]

EXAMPLE 8 (O&C, December 70, Question II 4)

This example requires the application of the formulae $C = \pi d$ for the circumference of a circle, and $A = \frac{1}{4}\pi d^2$ for its area, and also some algebraic manipulation.

A thin wire of diameter d m and resistivity ρ in ohm-metre units is wound in a single compact layer on a cylindrical bobbin so as to make a coil of diameter D m and length l m. Write down expressions for

(a) the length of wire used;

(b) the resistance of the coil.

Deduce the effect on the resistance of the coil of using wire of half the diameter ($\frac{1}{2}d$ instead of d).

Solution

In addition to the circumference formula, the candidate needs to know that the resistance R between the ends of a wire coil of length l m, uniform cross-sectional area A m^2, and resistivity ρ ohm-metres is given by

$$R = \frac{l\rho}{A} \text{ ohms}$$

(a) Since the wire has diameter d m, and the length of the coil is l m, the number of turns is l/d.

Each turn is of length πD m, so the total length of the wire used is

$$\frac{\pi D l}{d} \text{ m}.$$

(b) The cross-sectional area of the wire is $\frac{1}{4}\pi d^2$ m^2, so the total resistance R is

$$\frac{\frac{\pi D l}{d} \cdot \rho}{\frac{1}{4}\pi d^2} = \frac{4 D l \rho}{d^3} \text{ ohms}.$$

If d is replaced by $\frac{1}{2}d$, the total resistance becomes

$$\frac{4 D l \rho}{\frac{1}{8}d^3} \text{ ohms} = 8 \times \frac{4 D l \rho}{d^3} \text{ ohms}$$

i.e. the resistance is increased by a factor of 8.

Comment

A perceptive pupil might write $\pi(D-d)$ as the length of one turn of wire. If this is not intended, it should be stated that d is very much less than D.

EXAMPLE 9 (O&C, November 73, Question I 7)

In an experiment using Young's slits, interference bands x m apart are produced on a screen D m from the slits by light of wavelength λ m coming from two slits d m apart. The formula for λ in terms of x, d and D is $\lambda = xd/D$. This formula holds also for sound waves and can be applied to the following problem.

Two posts are fixed 4·0 m apart on a line which is parallel to and 100 m away from a straight road. On each post is fixed a loud-speaker and these are connected in parallel to an a.c. supply of frequency 1650 Hz so as to emit pure tones.

An observer walking along the road notices that the sound he hears alternates from loud to quiet, the quiet positions being 5·0 m apart. With the aid of a diagram, explain this effect, and calculate the wavelength of the sounds emitted and the velocity of sound in the air.

Suggest a path along which the observer could walk so as not to hear alternate loud and quiet sounds.

Solution

Loud at L_0, L_1, $L_2 \ldots$ where $S_2 L_n - S_1 L_n = n\lambda$
Quiet at Q_1, $Q_2, \ldots$ where $S_2 Q_n - S_1 Q_n = (n-\frac{1}{2})\lambda$
$Q_1 Q_2 = L_1 L_2 = \ldots = x = 5\cdot0$ m
$S_1 S_2 = d = 4\cdot0$ m
$A L_0 = D = 100$ m

So $\lambda = \dfrac{5\cdot0 \times 4\cdot0}{100} = 0\cdot2$ m. But $\lambda = \dfrac{c}{v}$, so $\dfrac{c}{1650} = 0\cdot2 \Rightarrow c = 330$ m/s.

The sound is always loud on the path $L_0 A$.

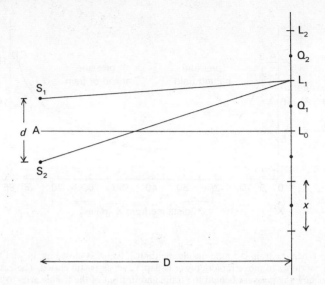

One by one the cells are reversed but kept in the circuit, and at each change the current indicated by the ammeter is noted. Which of the graphs below correctly shows how this will vary?

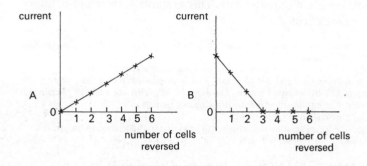

EXAMPLE 10 (London, June 74, Question II 29)

A large number of the graphical questions encountered in physics examinations require, as in this example, the determination of the general form of a graph without detailed calculation.

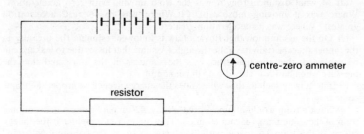

centre-zero ammeter

resistor

Six identical cells are connected in series with a resistor and centre-zero ammeter as shown above.

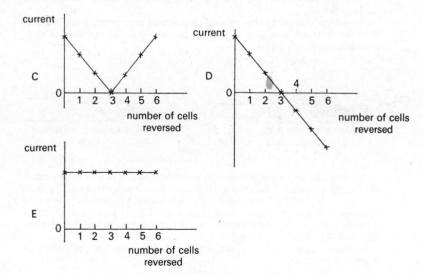

EXAMPLE 11 (O&C, July 74, Question II 3)

Little knowledge of vector methods was demanded in the recent "O" Level physics papers that were examined. The composition of vectors either at right angles or in the same straight line, and the resolution of a vector into components at right angles were the most common requirements. This example is therefore of above average difficulty.

Explain with the help of a diagram how two forces not in the same straight line may be added.

Show how to resolve a force into two components at right angles.

A uniform rigid rod AB of weight 45N is suspended from a fixed point C by strings AC, BC of equal length. The angles CAB, CBA are each 13°. When the system is in equilibrium find, by drawing or calculation

(a) the tension in each string,

(b) the forces tending to compress the rod due to the tension in the strings.

[Answers: (a) 100 N, (b) 97·4 N.]

EXAMPLE 12 (Nuffield, June 66, Question II 4)

Read the following account, look at the diagram, and answer the questions (a) to (g) below.

An underground railway has been designed to work between two cities, X and Y, 85 miles apart (see figure). It is expected to cover this distance, start to stop, in about quarter of an hour.

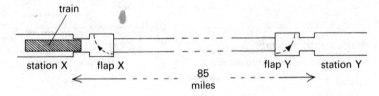

The train, shown at rest in station X, is a good fit (like a piston) in the tunnel, the clearance between it and the walls being less than an inch all round. Two flaps, at X and Y, seal off the main tunnel from the stations. Atmospheric pressure, in the station, is about 15 lb/sq in. A pump is used to reduce the pressure in the tunnel to about $\frac{1}{2}$ lb per sq in. The train at station X has one end just inside the tunnel, as shown. The flap X is then opened.

(a) What happens to the train, and why? Why may this be called an "atmospheric railway"?

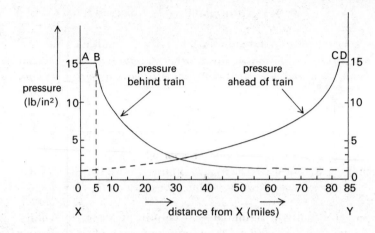

(b) When the train is 5 miles inside the tunnel, flap X is closed again, and the train continues to move rapidly towards flap Y, which is still closed. The graph shows how the pressure behind the train, and in front of the train, varies as the train travels from X to Y.

Why is the portion AB straight? Give an explanation of the rest of the graph, from B to the vertical line YD.

(c) When the train is near Y, flap Y opens and the train runs into station Y. Flap Y closes again. The graph also shows how the pressure ahead of the train varies as its distance from X increases.

Explain the graph from the start, at X, up to C, and also the horizontal portion CD.

(d) At what distance from A was the train moving with zero acceleration? Where was it moving most rapidly? Where was its forward acceleration greatest? Where was its deceleration greatest?

(e) On the assumption that Boyle's Law is followed, estimate the pressure in the tunnel after the train has gone through. (Assume that losses due to leakage can be neglected, that the temperature is the same as at the start, and that the pressure when flap X is closed is 15 lb per sq in.)

(f) In a railway such as this, where does the energy needed to propel the trains come from?

(g) Such a train would attain a speed of, say, 420 m.p.h., while a conventional train of the same mass reaches 60 m.p.h. How many times greater is the kinetic energy of this train, compared with the kinetic energy of the conventional train? What happens to the kinetic energy of an ordinary train? What happens to the kinetic energy of the train described here?

Solution

(*a*) Atmospheric pressure pushes the train into the tunnel, the small pressure inside the tunnel opposing this. The atmosphere provides the pressure.

(*b*) AB is straight (and horizontal) because, while X is open, the pressure behind the train remains constant at atmospheric pressure. When X is closed, a roughly constant mass of air fills an increasing length of tunnel behind the train, so the pressure is inversely proportional to the volume.

(*c*) The mass of air in the tunnel ahead of the train remains roughly constant while the length decreases, so the pressure rises (in inverse proportion to the volume). When Y opens, the pressure has become atmospheric, and remains at that value.

(*d*) At 32 miles from X the pressures ahead of it and behind it were equal. This was also where it was moving most rapidly since beyond this point it decelerated.

The deceleration was greatest at C, where the difference in pressure was greatest.

(*e*) Using $P_1 V_1 = P_2 V_2$
$$15 \times 5 = P_2 \times 80$$
$$\therefore P_2 = 75/80, \text{ i.e. about 1 lb per square inch.}$$

(*f*) From the atmosphere (but originally energy was needed to reduce the pressure in the tunnel—fuel for the pump).

(*g*) 49 times greater. Ordinary train's kinetic energy dissipated in its brakes, etc. This train's kinetic energy creates a low pressure behind it.

EXAMPLE 13 (Nuffield, June 65, Question I 2)

This is closely related to a standard experiment first encountered in the third year of the Nuffield "O" Level physics course. The "graph" is a step on the way towards a speed/time graph, and can virtually be considered as such.

In cutting up the paper tape to produce "tape charts" of the type shown, it is usual to work with a time interval of "one tentick" (or 0·2 s) as in this case (see p. 32). Some difficulties are encountered with the conversion of velocities from cm per tentick to cm/s and, not surprisingly, with the conversion of accelerations from cm per tentick per tentick to cm/s² ! This question adopts a more humane line.

Two boys pull a heavy trolley from rest along a bench by means of a piece of elastic, which they try to keep at constant stretch. The trolley drags a paper tape, on which marks are made by a vibrator at intervals of $\frac{1}{50}$th of a second. The tape is cut at marks 45, 55, 65, 75, 85, 95, 105 from the start, and the six lengths

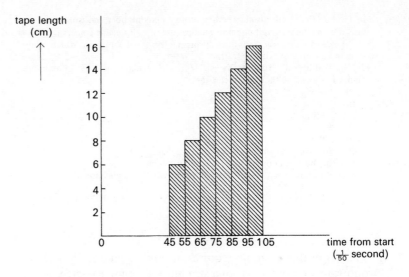

of tape are stuck on paper, as shown above. Axes are drawn showing tape lengths and times.

(*a*) Sketch on the diagram a line to indicate how the speed changed between times 1 and 2 seconds. Continue the line to show how the speed probably changed between times 0 and 1 second.

(*b*) What was the speed (cm per second) at time 1·0 second?

(*c*) What was the speed at time 2·0 seconds?

(*d*) What was the acceleration between 1·0 and 2·0 seconds?

(*e*) Did the boys apply a steady pull between 1·0 and 2·0 seconds? (Yes or No.)

(*f*) Give your reason for your answer to (*e*).

(*g*) Was the pull applied between times 0 and 1 second the same as that applied between times 1 and 2 seconds?

(*h*) Give your reason for your answer to (*g*).

[Answers: (*b*) 30 cm/s, (*c*) 80 cm/s, (*d*) 50 cm/s².]

EXAMPLE 14 (AEB, June 74, Question II 7)

This example involves graph plotting and interpolation. The graph is an exponential decay curve.

(a) Explain the terms atomic number, atomic mass number and isotope.

(b) State one medical and one non-medical use of radio-active tracers.

(c) Name and describe the three principal types of emission which may accompany radio-active disintegration.

(d) The half-life of Uranium X_1 is 24 days. Calculate the mass remaining unchanged of 0·64 g of the substance after
  (i)   24 days
  (ii)   48 days
  (iii) 72 days
  (iv)   96 days
  (v)   120 days.
  Plot your answers on a graph and hence determine
  (vi)   the mass remaining unchanged after 84 days
  (vii) after how many days there will be exactly 0·25 g unchanged.

[Answers: (d) (i) 0·32 g, (ii) 0·16 g, (iii) 0·08 g, (iv) 0·04 g, (v) 0·02 g, (vi) 0·055 g, (vii) 33 days.]

EXAMPLE 15 (AEB, November 74, Question II 5)

Part (c) of this example requires an understanding of inverse proportion, and of the use of a straight-line graph to detect it.

(a) Illustrate the modes of vibration of the fundamental and the first two overtones when a musical note of fundamental frequency 256 Hz (cycles per second) is produced by air in a tube
  (i)   open at both ends
  (ii) closed at one end.
Mark nodes and antinodes of displacement N and A respectively.
State the frequencies of each pair of overtones.

(b) Why is a musical note produced by an open tube or pipe more mellow than a note of the same fundamental frequency produced by a closed tube?

(c) While the tension of a vibrating string was kept constant, its length was varied in order to tune the string to a series of tuning forks. The results obtained were as follows:

Frequency of fork	(Hz)	256	288	320	384	512
Length of string	(cm)	78·1	69·5	62·5	52·1	39·1

By the appropriate use of the above readings, obtain a straight-line graph and hence determine
  (i)   the relationship between the frequency of vibration and the length of the stretched string.
  (ii) the frequency of an unmarked fork which was in tune with 41·7 cm of the string.

[Answers: (i) $f \propto 1/l$, (ii) 482 Hz]

Comment

Note that the candidate is not told how to obtain a straight-line graph from the data (by plotting f against $1/l$, or l against $1/f$).

"A" Level pupils might be expected to plot the logarithms of the frequencies and lengths, and deduce the relationship $f \propto 1/l$ in that way, but such an approach would certainly not be expected of "O" Level pupils. This might therefore be a very difficult question for an "O" Level pupil not familiar with the answer.

EXAMPLE 16 (Nuffield, June, 68, Question I 3)

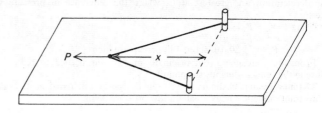

A piece of elastic is stretched across a board between two pegs as shown. The elastic is pulled back a distance x by a force P. When a spring balance is used to measure P, it is found that P is proportional to x, and that when $x = 4$ cm, $P = 8$ newtons. Show on the graph below how the force P increases with distance x.

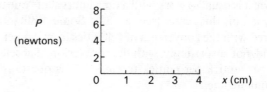

How much energy is stored in the elastic when the force is 8 newtons?
[Answer: Energy stored is represented by the area beneath the graph = 0·16 J or Energy = distance × average force = 0.04 m × 4 N = 0.16 J.]

A dynamics trolley of mass 2 kg is put on the board. It is drawn back against the elastic so that it stretches the same amount, namely 4 cm. What is the kinetic energy of the trolley as it leaves the "catapult"?
[Answer: Also 0·16 J (assuming no losses).]

What is the velocity of the trolley at this moment?
[Answer: $\frac{1}{2}mv^2 = 0·16\,J$,   where $m = 2\,kg$
   $\therefore$ $v^2 = 0·16\,J/kg = (0·4)^2\,m^2/s^2$
   $\therefore$ $v = 0·4\,m/s$]

The trolley collides with another stationary trolley, of mass 1 kg, in the middle of the runway and sticks to it. What will be the velocity of the combined mass after the collision? Assume the board is inclined slightly to compensate for friction.
[Answer: Momentum is conserved (energy is not conserved in the form of kinetic energy).

$$(2 \times 0·4)\,kg\,m/s = 3\,kg \times v$$
$$\therefore \quad v = \tfrac{2}{3} \times 0·4\,m/s$$
$$= 0·267\,m/s]$$

EXAMPLE 17

Many pupils find astronomy fascinating, so that this and the next question may have a useful motivational element, even in schools where no astronomy is taught formally.

Astronomical observers at A and B, 2·5 km apart on a horizontal baseline ABC recording the positions of meteor trails, found that for the lowest point M on one particular trail $\angle$ CBM = 61° and $\angle$ CAM = 60°. Observer A also recorded the elevation of M as 40°. Calculate the distance from A to the meteor trail and the height of the trail above the earth's surface, which you may assume is flat.
[Answer: 125 km, 81 km.]

EXAMPLE 18

Kepler's Third Law states that the square of the orbital period of a planet is proportional to the cube of its mean distance from the sun.

If the mean distance of the earth from the sun is $1·5 \times 10^8$ km and the orbital period of Jupiter is 11·9 years, calculate Jupiter's mean distance from the sun.
[Answer: $7·82 \times 10^8$ km.]

FURTHER TOPICS

3.14   Drawing Exercises in Geometrical Optics

The first three of the following four exercises (figures 3.25–3.28) involve the construction of some standard configurations of transformation geometry from the principle of reflection as formulated in optics, viz. "angle of incidence = angle of reflection"; only the latter is to be assumed when making the drawings. The closeness of the result to the standard configuration is a check on the accuracy of the drawing.

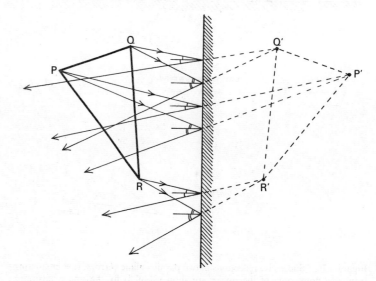

Figure 3.25.   Reflection in a single plane mirror.

3.15 Fermat's Principle in Geometrical Optics and Geography

Fermat's principle unifies the laws of geometrical optics. The mathematics involved is within the range of able pupils, and the principle has interesting applications in other fields. There is an excellent example here for showing the *polyvalence* of mathematics, i.e. the range of applicability of one mathematical idea.

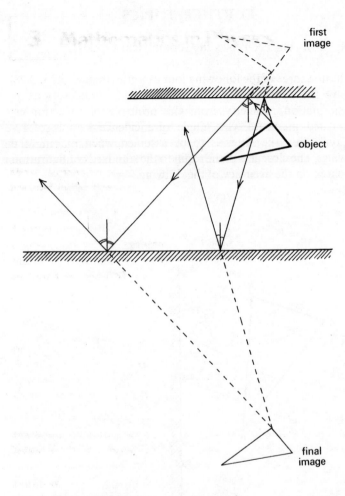

Figure 3.26. Successive reflections in two parallel plane mirrors; rays emanating from one point only of the object are shown, but to fix the image positions it is necessary to draw pairs of rays from three non-collinear points of the object.

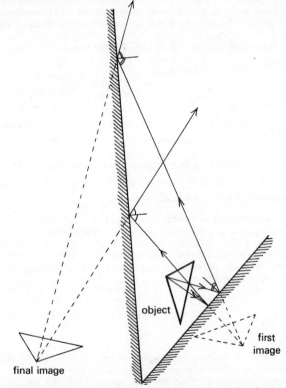

Figure 3.27 Successive reflections in two inclined mirrors; again only one pair of rays is shown.

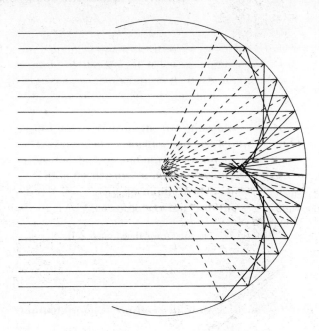

Figure 3.28   Envelope curve which can be observed on the surface of the tea in a circular cup.

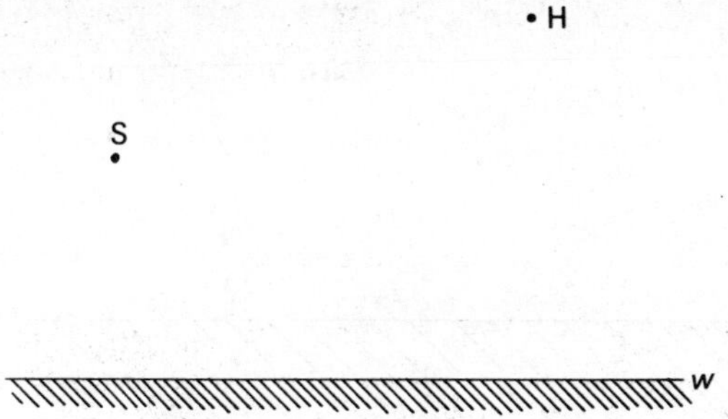

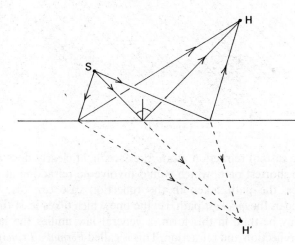

Figure 3.29.

Figure 3.30   Routes from S to H; that which starts along the straight line SH′ is the shortest, and is the only one for which angle of incidence = angle of reflection.

Suppose a child, situated at S (figure 3.29), is playing a game in which he has to touch a wall *w* and get home to H as quickly as possible. He will need to take the shortest route from S to H via a point on *w*. Figure 3.30 shows several possible routes. In each case the total journey is the same as the journey to H′, the image of H under reflection in *w*.

The shortest route from S to H is the same as the shortest route from S to H′, and this latter is obviously along the straight line SH′. The path which sets out from S to H′ but turns to H when it reaches the wall is then the route required. This is the only route which obeys the law of reflection, that "angle of incidence = angle of reflection". So the law of reflection can be re-expressed in the form of a law which states that light takes the shortest path available.

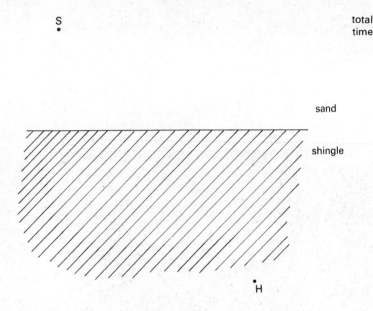

Figure 3.31.

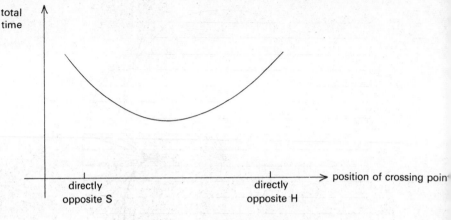

Figure 3.32   The total travel time from S to H.

In the case of refraction at an interface, light clearly does not take the shortest path, which would involve no refraction at all. However, the path taken in the reflection case can also be described as the *quickest* path, i.e. the one which takes least time. So it may be that, in this form, a general law unifies the laws of both reflection and refraction. This is called *Fermat's Principle*, and was discovered by Fermat in the seventeenth century. The application of the principle to refraction can be illustrated by another simple non-optical situation.

Suppose a child has to get as quickly as possible from start S to home H across a line dividing sand from shingle (figure 3.31). He can run faster on sand than on shingle. Where should he cross the dividing line?

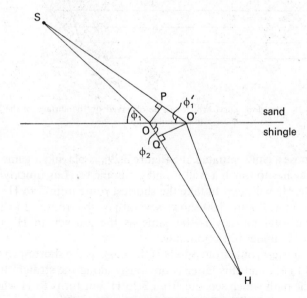

Figure 3.33   Geometrical proof of Snell's Law.

Given the positions of S and H, and the child's speed on sand and on shingle, it is possible to calculate for each possible point on the dividing line the total time taken to get from S to H via that point. If a graph is drawn, the result resembles that in figure 3.32. The point which gives the minimum journey time may be obtained from the graph.

In order to show that the result leads to the law of refraction, it is necessary either to use calculus or to appreciate the geometrical "limit" argument which follows.

At the optimum point a small movement along the dividing line makes a negligible difference to total journey time (journey times for paths via points very close to the optimum point are themselves very close to the least time). This is because the graph is "flat" at the optimum point.

Figure 3.33 shows the optimum path SOH, and another path SO'H very close to the optimum. The point P is such that SP = SO, and angle OPO' is practically a right angle. The point Q is such that HQ = HO' and angle O'QO is also practically a right angle.

The first part of the journey via O' is longer than the optimum path by a distance O'P, which takes time $O'P/s_1$ where s_1 is the speed of travel on sand. The second part is shorter by a distance OQ, which takes time OQ/s_2 where s_2 is the speed of travel on shingle.

So the extra time for the whole journey via O' is

$$\frac{O'P}{s_1} - \frac{OQ}{s_2}$$

Since this is very small,

$$\frac{O'P}{s_1} \approx \frac{OQ}{s_2}$$

the agreement being closer and closer as O' approaches O.

But in triangle OPO', $O'P = OO' \cos \phi'_1$
and in triangle OQO', $OQ = OO' \cos \phi_2$.

Hence
$$\frac{\cos \phi'_1}{s_1} \approx \frac{\cos \phi_2}{s_2}$$

with closer agreement as O' approaches O. But as O' approaches O, angle ϕ'_1 approaches ϕ_1.

Hence
$$\frac{\cos \phi_1}{s_1} \approx \frac{\cos \phi_2}{s_2}$$

If θ_1, θ_2 are the angles made with the *normal* by the first and second parts of the paths, then

$$\frac{\sin \theta_1}{s_1} = \frac{\sin \theta_2}{s_2}$$

or

$$\sin \theta_1 = \frac{s_1}{s_2} \sin \theta_2.$$

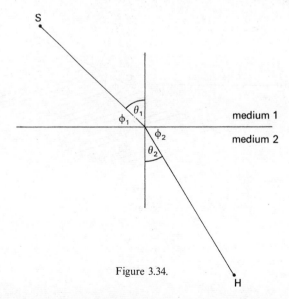

Figure 3.34.

Applied to a ray of light, this is the law of refraction (Snell's law), with the refraction index n here identified with s_1/s_2 the ratio of the speeds of light in the two media (figure 3.34).

Fermat's Principle states that light rays are *geodesics*, where this term is used in a general sense to denote a path of least effort. This idea is of use outside physics, particularly in geography. Instead of a difference of *speed* either side of the dividing line, there may for instance be different transportation costs per unit distance. This "refraction model" is discussed in Haggett and Chorley: *Network Analysis in Geography* (Edward Arnold), p. 219.

Goods are to be transported from S to D across a straight boundary (figure 3.35). Transportation costs per unit distance are c_1 on the S side and c_2 on the D side. The cheapest route is one which minimizes

$$c_1.\text{SC} + c_2.\text{CD}$$

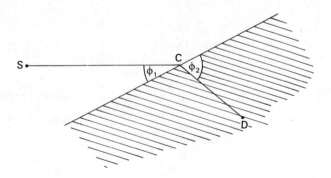

Figure 3.35.

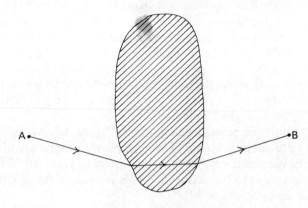

Figure 3.36.

(compare $(\text{SC}/s_1) + (\text{CD}/s_2)$ in the "shortest time" case), which is one where

$$\frac{\cos \phi_1}{\cos \phi_2} = \frac{c_2}{c_1}$$

There are many ways in which figure 3.36 can be interpreted. The path AB could represent a ray of light passing through a glass object, or the cheapest-to-build railway line from A to B tunnelling through a range of hills.

It is of interest to note that the path of a projectile under gravity can also be deduced as a geodesic using a principle known as *Maupertuis' Principle of Least Action* (see the Open University *Science Foundation Course*, Unit 29, page 17).

References
Feynmann, *Lectures on Physics*, Vol. 1, pp. 26-1 to 26-4 (Addison-Wesley).
Haggett and Chorley, *Network Analysis in Geography*, p. 219 (Edward Arnold).
Haggett, *Geography: A Modern Synthesis*, pp. 343–4 (Harper and Row).
Open University, *Science Foundation Course*, Unit 29, pp. 17 ff.

4 Mathematics in Chemistry

Although it might be expected that, as a physical science, chemistry must demand considerable mathematical skill from the student, the demand is in general at a relatively low level up to "O" Level and just beyond. But, although the demands are not on a very broad front, they are nevertheless very serious ones.

In common with physics teachers, chemistry teachers would like greater facility and experience in numerical skills (see Appendix 1, page 142). Of these the most important is the ability to handle ratio and proportion. As will be seen from the examples which follow, the sort of problem which often arises in chemistry (from about the third year onwards in an "O" Level course, and only in the fourth and fifth years of *Revised Nuffield Chemistry*) is one in which the functional relationship of proportionality is not, as it often is in physics (see pages 15–18), the focus of attention, but rather the process of obtaining single unknown values in a direct proportion. The slide rule is particularly useful in such cases.

4.1 Chemical Terminology

Teachers of mathematics may not be familiar with the chemical background and terminology of the examples which follow. In particular the idea of a *mole* is of relatively recent introduction in school chemistry courses. A brief explanation of this and other chemical terms follows.

RELATIVE ATOMIC MASS

For the type of calculation done at school, the hydrogen atom is taken as the standard of atomic mass; the relative atomic mass of an element is a number, this being the number of times an atom of that element is more massive than a hydrogen atom. For example, the relative atomic mass of magnesium is 12 (written for short as $Mg = 12$).

RELATIVE MOLECULAR MASS

The relative molecular mass of an element or compound is again measured relative to the mass of a hydrogen atom. For example, magnesium oxide, whose chemical formula is MgO, has relative molecular mass 28: each molecule consists of one atom of magnesium ($Mg = 12$) and one atom of oxygen ($O = 16$). A *monatomic* element is one whose molecules each consist of only one atom; for such an element the relative atomic and molecular masses are the same.

MOLE

Imagine that we are making two heaps of atoms, one of magnesium atoms and another of oxygen atoms. We start with one of each. The relative atomic masses are magnesium 12 and oxygen 16. Suppose that each time we add a magnesium atom to one heap we add an oxygen atom to the other. After each pair of additions, the masses of the two heaps are still in the ratio 12:16. If the magnesium heap is continued until the total mass is 12 grams, by that time the mass of the oxygen heap will be 16 grams, and *both heaps will contain the same number of atoms*. This number is actually 6×10^{23}, called Avogadro's number. This number of atoms of an element is called a *mole* of that element. The mass of a mole in grams is numerically equal to the relative atomic mass. This mass is also called a gram-atom or g-atom.

In the case of a compound or non-monatomic element, a mole

has a mass in grams numerically equal to the relative molecular mass.

If it is known from experiments that, say, 1 mole of element X combines with 2 moles of element Y, then each atom of X is linked with 2 atoms of Y, and the simplest chemical formula consistent with this (the empirical formula) is XY_2.

MOLAR, OR GRAM-MOLECULAR, VOLUME OF A GAS

A mole of gas occupies 22·4 litres at s.t.p. (standard temperature (0°C) and pressure (1 atmosphere)). Thus oxygen, for example, has relative molecular mass 32 (its chemical formula being O_2); a mole of oxygen has a mass of 32g, and occupies 22·4 litres at s.t.p.

TOPIC SURVEY

4.2   Use of Symbols

See chapter 3, page 14.

4.3   Decimal Arithmetic, Ratio and Proportion

The ways in which these topics enter into chemistry are best shown by considering some typical calculations.

EXAMPLE 1 (Holderness & Lambert, *Worked Examples and Problems in Ordinary Level Chemistry*, pp. 6–7 (adapted))

A sample of pure oxide of copper was reduced by heating to constant mass in dry hydrogen. Deduce from the data given a formula for the oxide of copper. (Cu = 63·5; O = 16.)

Mass of porcelain boat	= 10·510 g
Mass of porcelain boat and oxide	= 12·857 g
Mass of porcelain boat and copper	= 12·594 g

Solution

Mass of oxygen combined = (12·857 − 12·594) g = 0·263 g
Mass of copper used   = (12·594 − 10·510) g = 2·084 g

The proportion by atoms of copper to oxygen is thus

$$\frac{2·084}{63·5} : \frac{0·263}{16} = 0·0328 : 0·0164 = 2 : 1.$$

So the empirical formula is Cu_2O.

This calculation can also be expressed in terms of moles. The use of the mole breaks down the "ratio within a ratio" difficulty.

1 mole of copper has a mass of 63·5 g

$$\therefore 2·084 \text{ g of copper is } \frac{2·084}{63·5} = 0·0328 \text{ mole.}$$

1 mole of oxygen has a mass of 16 g

$$\therefore 0·263 \text{ g of oxygen is } \frac{0·263}{16} = 0·0164 \text{ mole.}$$

This 2 : 1 ratio of copper to oxygen by moles of atoms indicates a simplest formula for the oxide of Cu_2O.

Comment

The final ratio "came out" very easily in this example. Pupils need to be able to deal with ratios which are "approximately simple" and to extract the simple ratios from them.

The mole concept can be used in the next example, but the solution given uses proportions by atoms.

EXAMPLE 2

Calculate the empirical formula of the compound which has composition 52 per cent zinc, 9·6 per cent carbon, 38·4 per cent oxygen by mass. Relative atomic masses are: zinc 65, carbon 12, oxygen 16.

Solution

Proportions by atoms   Zn : C : O

$$\text{are} \qquad \frac{52}{65} : \frac{9·6}{12} : \frac{38·4}{16}$$

$$= 0·8 : 0·8 : 2·4 \qquad \text{(dividing by the smallest)}$$

$$= \ 1 : \ 1 : 3$$

Hence the empirical formula is $ZnCO_3$.

Figure 4.1.

The solution of Example 2 using a slide rule may be done as follows:

Set the relative atomic mass of, say, carbon (12) on the B-scale against the (percentage) mass of carbon on the A-scale (9·6).

Against the relative atomic masses of oxygen (16) and zinc (65) on the B-scale read on the A-scale masses of 12·8 and 52·0 respectively.

If the empirical formula were ZnOC, the weights would be in the proportions 9·6 : 12·8 : 52·0. Actually they are 9·6 : 38·4 : 52·0, indicating an empirical formula of ZnO_3C.

EXAMPLE 3 (JMB, June 73)

When tri-lead tetroxide (red lead) is heated, it breaks down to give lead (II) oxide and oxygen as shown in the equation

$$2Pb_3O_4 \rightarrow 6PbO + O_2.$$

Calculate (i) the mass of lead (II) oxide and (ii) the volume of oxygen at s.t.p. obtained when 27·40 g of tri-lead tetroxide are heated to constant mass.

(Relative atomic masses: O = 16, Pb, = 207. The gram-molecular volume of a gas at s.t.p. is 22·4 litres.)

Solution

Relative molecular masses are

$$Pb_3O_4 \quad (3 \times 207) + (4 \times 16) = 685$$
$$PbO \quad 207 + 16 = 223$$

(i) For mass of lead (II) oxide:

$$2 \times 685\,g\ Pb_3O_4 \rightarrow 6 \times 223\,g\ PbO$$

$$\therefore 1\,g\ Pb_3O_4 \rightarrow \frac{6 \times 223}{2 \times 685}\,g\ PbO$$

$$\therefore 27\cdot40\,g\ Pb_3O_4 \rightarrow \frac{6 \times 223}{2 \times 685} \times 27\cdot40\,g\ PbO$$

$$= 26\cdot76\,g\ PbO.$$

Alternatively,

from the equation, 2 moles $Pb_3O_4 \rightarrow 6$ moles PbO
so 1 mole $Pb_3O_4 \rightarrow 3$ moles PbO

Since 1 mole Pb_3O_4 has a mass of 685 g, 27·40 g Pb_3O_4 is

$$\frac{27\cdot40}{685}\ \text{moles}\ Pb_3O_4;\ \text{and}\ \frac{27\cdot40}{685}\ \text{moles}\ Pb_3O_4 \rightarrow 3 \times \frac{27\cdot40}{685}\ \text{moles}\ PbO.$$

Since 1 mole PbO has a mass of 223 g,

$$3 \times \frac{27\cdot40}{685}\ \text{moles PbO have a mass of}\ 3 \times \frac{27\cdot40}{685} \times 223\,g$$

$$= 26\cdot76\,g.$$

(ii) For volume of oxygen

$$27\cdot40\,g\ Pb_3O_4 = \frac{27\cdot40}{685} = 0\cdot04\ \text{moles of}\ Pb_3O_4.$$

$$2\ \text{moles of}\ Pb_3O_4 \rightarrow 1\ \text{mole}\ O_2$$
$$= 22\cdot4\ \text{litres}\ O_2\ \text{at s.t.p.}$$
$$\therefore\ 1\ \text{mole of}\ Pb_3O_4 \rightarrow 11\cdot2\ \text{litres}\ O_2\ \text{at s.t.p.}$$
$$\therefore 0\cdot04\ \text{moles of}\ Pb_3O_4 \rightarrow 0\cdot04 \times 11\cdot2\ \text{litres}\ O_2$$
$$= 0\cdot448\ \text{litre.}$$

Alternatively, using the principle of conservation of mass in the reaction, the mass of oxygen released must be 27·40 g − 26·76 g = 0·64 g.

Since 32 g oxygen occupy 22·4 litres at s.t.p.,

$$1\,g\ \text{oxygen occupies}\ \frac{22\cdot4}{32}\ \text{litres,}$$

and

$$0\cdot64\,g\ \text{oxygen occupies}\ \frac{22\cdot4}{32} \times 0\cdot64\ \text{litres}$$

$$= 0\cdot448\ \text{litres.}$$

EXAMPLE 4 (JMB, June 72, amended)

The equation for heating copper sulphate crystals gives

$$CuSO_4 . 5H_2O \rightarrow CuSO_4 + 5H_2O$$

If 2·5 g copper sulphate crystals are heated, what is the loss of mass (in the form of steam?). (Relative atomic masses: Cu = 64, S = 32, O = 16, H = 1).

Solution

Relative molecular masses are:

$$CuSO_4 = 160$$
$$5H_2O = 90$$
$$\frac{\text{Mass } 5H_2O}{\text{Mass } CuSO_4 . 5H_2O} = \frac{90}{250}$$

$$\therefore \text{Mass lost} = \frac{90}{250} \times 2 \cdot 5 \, \text{g} = 0 \cdot 9 \, \text{g}.$$

[This can also be set out in "unitary method" form.]

EXAMPLE 5 (JMB, June 72, amended)

21·0 g of gas occupy 5·6 litres at 0°C and 1 atmosphere pressure. Find the gram-molecular mass.

(Gram-molecular volume of a gas at s.t.p. = 22·4 litres.)

Solution

$$5 \cdot 6 \, \text{litres at s.t.p. have a mass of } 21 \cdot 0 \, \text{g}$$

$$\therefore 1 \, \text{litre has a mass of } \frac{21 \cdot 0}{5 \cdot 6} \, \text{g}$$

$$\therefore 22 \cdot 4 \, \text{litres have a mass of } \frac{21 \cdot 0}{5 \cdot 6} \times 22 \cdot 4 \, \text{g}$$

$$= 84 \cdot 0 \, \text{g}.$$

EXAMPLE 6 (Rogers, *Energy in Chemistry*, p. 15)

The following calculation arises in an experiment to find the heat of combustion of carbon (charcoal). This is the heat evolved in burning 1 mole of carbon. Although the calculation is here expressed in calories and kilocalories, the result may be converted to joules (1 calorie = 4·19 joules, approximately).

Heat capacity of apparatus	100 calories $g^{-1} deg^{-1}$C.
Heat capacity of 500 cm³ water in apparatus	500 calories $g^{-1} deg^{-1}$C.
Total	600 calories $g^{-1} deg^{-1}$C.
Rise in temperature of apparatus and water	5·2 deg C
Mass of dry charcoal before experiment	0·416 g
Mass of remaining ash	0·005 g
∴ Mass of carbon burnt	0·411 g

Heat evolved = 5·2 × 600 calories
$$= 3120 \text{ calories}$$
$$= 3 \cdot 12 \, \text{kcal}$$

0·411 g carbon gave, on burning, 3·12 kcal

1 g carbon would give $\dfrac{3 \cdot 12}{0 \cdot 411} \, \text{kcal}$

12 g carbon would give $\dfrac{3 \cdot 12}{0 \cdot 411} \times 12 \, \text{kcal}$

$$= 91 \, \text{kcal}.$$

Thus 1 gram-atom (mole) of carbon evolves 91 kcal on burning in oxygen.

Comment

The appeal of the unitary method in the foregoing examples lies in the fact that the unit involved is a real unit, i.e. the intermediate statement has a real meaning. The difficult subject of proportionality is discussed on pp. 7 and 15, where, amongst other applications, the gas laws are considered.

The following numerical example on Boyle's law and Charles' law is a continuation of Example 5.

EXAMPLE 5 (continued)

Calculate the volume that 21·0 g of gas would occupy at
(i)   0°C and 4 atmospheres
(ii) 273°C and 1 atmosphere
(iii) 273°C and 4 atmospheres

Solutions

(i)
$$P_1 V_1 = P_2 V_2$$
$$1 \times 5.6 = 4 \times V_2$$
$$\therefore \quad V_2 = \frac{5 \cdot 6}{4} = 1 \cdot 4 \text{ litres.}$$

(ii)   0°C = 273 K   273°C = 546 K
$$\frac{V_1}{T_1} = \frac{V_2}{T_2}$$
$$\therefore \quad \frac{5 \cdot 6}{273} = \frac{V_2}{546}$$
$$\therefore \quad V_2 = \frac{5 \cdot 6 \times 546}{273} = 11 \cdot 2 \text{ litres.}$$

(iii)
$$\frac{P_1 V_1}{T_1} = \frac{P_2 V_2}{T_2}$$
$$\frac{1 \times 5 \cdot 6}{273} = \frac{4 \times V_2}{546}$$
$$\therefore V_2 = \frac{1 \times 5 \cdot 6 \times 546}{4 \times 273}$$
$$= 2 \cdot 8 \text{ litres.}$$

Comment

Substitution into the formulae is the standard solution procedure, but its use as a routine does not encourage pupils to see the simplicity of the proportions involved in this example. They could discover something by reflecting on the answers obtained, and their relation to the data. It should be said that the arithmetic in examination questions is made artificially simpler—but the simplicity may go unnoticed and the answer be obtained by logarithms.

4.4   Algebra

The use of simple algebra is well illustrated in the two examples which follow. The solution of the resulting equations does not require any high-powered general theory of simultaneous linear equations. It is possible to use this instance in chemistry as a concrete starting point for linear algebra, but unfortunately there are no immediate returns for the study of chemistry. This topic is developed on page 65.

EXAMPLE 7

It is known that iron and water combine to give tri-iron tetroxide and hydrogen.

$$Fe + H_2O \rightarrow Fe_3O_4 + H_2$$

Let the numbers of atoms or molecules combining be w, x, y, z; i.e.

$$w\,Fe + x\,H_2O \rightarrow y\,Fe_3O_4 + z\,H_2$$

Since the numbers of atoms on each side must be equal, we have

for Fe $w = 3y$
for O $x = 4y$
for H $x = z.$

Here there are three equations, but four unknowns. Since only ratios are required, x, w, z can be expressed in terms of y, giving $w = 3y$, $x = 4y$, $z = 4y$.
Hence

$$3\,Fe + 4H_2O \rightarrow Fe_3O_4 + 4H_2$$

Comment

This problem can also be done by intelligent trial and error.

EXAMPLE 8 (JMB)

$10\,cm^3$ of a gaseous hydrocarbon were mixed with $30\,cm^3$ of oxygen and the mixture was exploded. After the mixture had cooled to room temperature, $20\,cm^3$ of gas remained. After shaking this gas with sodium hydroxide solution, its volume was reduced to $10\,cm^3$. The remaining gas rekindled a glowing splint.
   (a) Name the gas remaining at the end.
   (b) What were the reacting volumes of the hydrocarbon and oxygen?
   (c) Name the gas absorbed by the alkali.
   (d) State the volume of the gas named in (c).
   (e) Name the other product of the reaction.
   (f) Work out the formula for the hydrocarbon.

Solution

(a) Oxygen, (b) 10, $20\,cm^3$, (c) carbon dioxide, (d) $10\,cm^3$, (e) water.
   (f) Here we use the fact that carbon appears only once on each side to write in intuitively the unknowns

$$C_x H_y \quad + \quad (x + \tfrac{1}{4}y)O_2 \quad \rightarrow \quad xCO_2 \quad + \tfrac{1}{2}yH_2O$$

$C_x H_y$	$(x+\tfrac{1}{4}y)O_2$	xCO_2	
1 volume	$(x+\tfrac{1}{4}y)$ volumes	x volumes	
$10\,cm^3$	$20\,cm^3$	$10\,cm^3$	
1	2	1	

Hence $x = 1$, $x + \tfrac{1}{4}y = 2$, i.e. $x = 1$, $y = 4$.
$$\therefore \text{ Hydrocarbon is } CH_4.$$

4.5   Graphical Work

This includes an appreciation of rate of change by inspection of the gradient, as, for instance, when the gradient shows the time-rate of a chemical reaction.

Investigation of the relation between the concentration of a reagent and the rate of reaction can be carried out by finding the time T taken to reach a visible stage in the reaction (cloudiness, for example) for different concentrations C of one of the reagents. The graph of $1/T$ (which is proportional to the rate of reaction) against C, if a straight line through the origin, indicates that rate of reaction is proportional to concentration.

The interpretation of solubility curves provides an instance where the *regions* bounded by a curve bear meanings as well as the curve itself (figure 4.2). Points in the region below the

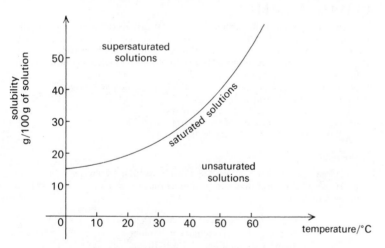

Figure 4.2   Relationship between solubility and temperature.

curve represent unsaturated solutions, and points above represent saturated solutions. Methods of growing crystals can be explained

concisely by referring to paths from one region to the other (see, e.g. Holden and Singer, *Crystals and Crystal Growing*, p. 107).

The next example illustrates how it is necessary for pupils to interpret a graph.

EXAMPLE 9 (CSE, East Anglian Board (North))

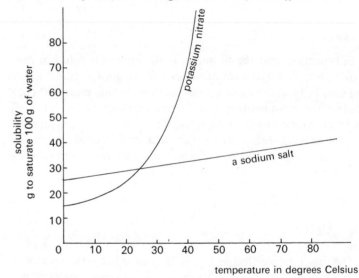

The graph gives the variation of solubility with temperature for a sodium salt and potassium nitrate. Answer the following:

(a) What would be the solubility of the sodium salt at 70°C?
(b) At what temperature are the solubilities of the sodium salt and potassium nitrate the same?
(c) What is the minimum temperature required to dissolve 45 g of potassium nitrate in 50 g water?
(d) What is the maximum mass of the sodium salt which can be obtained by evaporating 136 g of a solution of the sodium salt which was evaporated at 40°C?
(e) The sodium salt and potassium nitrate were added to water at a temperature of 21°C until it was saturated with both substances. What will be the ratio of the dissolved salt to potassium nitrate in the saturated solution?

4.6   Difference Notation

The difference symbol ΔH is used in energetics to denote the heat energy absorbed or evolved in a reaction.

The statement

$$2H_2(g) + O_2(g) \rightarrow 2H_2O(g); \qquad \Delta H = -480\,kJ$$

means that $480\,kJ$ are *evolved* when 2 moles of hydrogen gas combine with 1 mole of oxygen gas to produce two moles of water in gaseous form.

The reaction above involves a number of separate processes in which chemical bonds are either broken (energy being absorbed) or made (energy being evolved). The energy changes can be illustrated in an energy-level diagram, drawn to scale with height representing energy. See M.F.W. Rogers, *Energy in Chemistry*

(Heinemann, 1968) p. 15; or B. Cane and J. Sellwood, *Certificate Chemistry 4* (Schofield and Sims, 1974) p. 49.

4.7   Geometry and Trigonometry

The study of crystals and crystal structure provides, even at the elementary level, some interesting applications of three-dimensional geometry and trigonometry, which could provide excellent linkage material between chemistry and mathematics.

This topic, a new one in school chemistry at this level (it is an option in Stage III of *Nuffield Chemistry*), is considered in greater detail in section 4.10.

4.8   Exponential Functions

Exponential decay, its graphical representation and the associated concept of half-life are included in some "O" Level chemistry courses.

4.9   Logarithms

Calculations of pH-values are involved in "A" Level work, but difficulties arise for students who do not study "A" Level mathematics and whose "O" Level course has not included the study of logarithms.

EXAMPLE 10

(i) Calculate the pH of a solution whose hydroxonium ion concentration is $2 \times 10^{-5}\,mole\,dm^{-3}$.

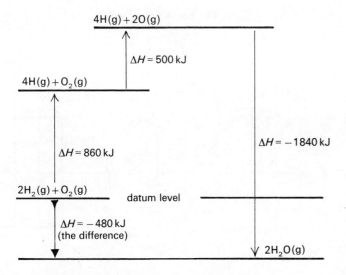

Figure 4.3   Energy level diagram.

Solution

$$pH = -\log_{10}(H_3O^+)$$
$$= -\log_{10}(2 \times 10^{-5})$$
$$= -(-5 + 0.301)$$
$$= 4.699$$

(ii) Calculate the approximate pH of a solution in which 25 cm³ of 0·1 M sodium hydroxide solution has been added to 50 cm³ of 0·1 M hydrochloric acid.

Solution

When 25 cm³ has been added, half the acid has been neutralized and there is a total volume of 75 cm³. Hence

$$(H_3O^+) = 0.1 \times \frac{(50-25)}{75} = 0.1 \times \tfrac{1}{3} = 3.33 \times 10^{-2}$$
$$pH = -\log_{10}(3.33 \times 10^{-2}) = 1.48$$

FURTHER TOPICS

4.10 Crystals and Crystal Structure

The study of crystals and crystal structure at an elementary level is a relatively new feature of school chemistry. It is part of the *Nuffield Chemistry* course, the topics discussed in this section appearing in Option 2 of Stage III. Although the mathematics described here is not demanded in that option, it should not be beyond all "O" Level students, provided that models (in the ordinary physical sense) of the three-dimensional configurations which arise are available for handling. The construction of these models is described in the *Nuffield Chemistry* book.

Early observations and measurements of crystals (in the seventeenth and eighteenth centuries) resulted in the discovery that, for crystals of a given substance,

    (i) the angles between corresponding faces is invariant from crystal to crystal;

    (ii) there is a relationship between the angles between different pairs of faces on the same crystal.

Figure 4.4 shows part of a crystal of topaz; the angles marked α and β are 24·5° and 42·3° respectively. The relationship between α and β is $\tan \beta = 2 \tan \alpha$.

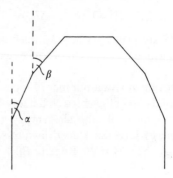

Figure 4.4   Part of a topaz crystal.

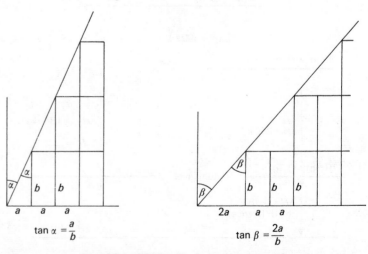

$$\tan \alpha = \frac{a}{b}$$

$$\tan \beta = \frac{2a}{b}$$

Figure 4.5   Building blocks in a topaz crystal.

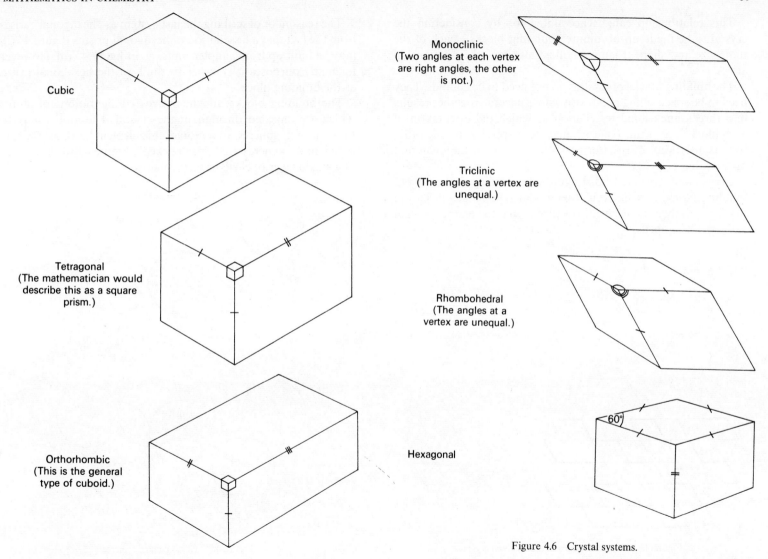

Cubic

Tetragonal
(The mathematician would
describe this as a square
prism.)

Orthorhombic
(This is the general
type of cuboid.)

Monoclinic
(Two angles at each vertex
are right angles, the other
is not.)

Triclinic
(The angles at a vertex are
unequal.)

Rhombohedral
(The angles at a
vertex are unequal.)

Hexagonal

60°

Figure 4.6   Crystal systems.

This relationship can be accounted for by considering the crystal to be made up of minute "building blocks", each of the same size and shape. Figure 4.5 illustrates how the relationship arises.

The building blocks of crystals do not need to be cuboids. They need to be space-filling polyhedra whose packing together results in a three-dimensional tessellation in which the orientation of each block is the same (i.e. each may be mapped onto any other by a translation). This latter condition is part of the definition of "building block".

Crystal systems may be distinguished according to the type of building block, or "unit cell" (figure 4.6). The names given are those generally used by chemists. All are what the mathematician calls parallelepipeds.

The reason for describing the last system as "hexagonal" arises from the fact that a tessellation of hexagonal prisms (figure 4.7(i)) may be built up from simpler units, as in figure 4.7(ii). However for many purposes it is easier to think of the hexagonal prism as the building block.

The building blocks are themselves configurations of atoms which are repeated throughout the crystal. The atoms may be thought of as spheres. In a monatomic element (such as a metal) the identical spheres are "close packed". Figure 4.8(i) shows part of a single layer of close-packed spheres.

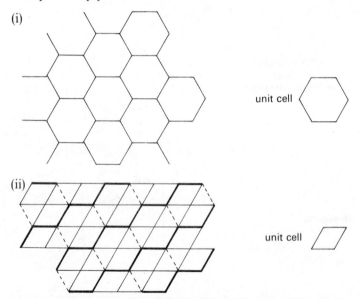

Figure 4.7   Building blocks in a hexagonal crystal.

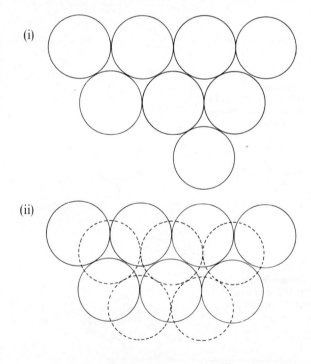

Figure 4.8   Close-packed spheres.

A second layer placed on the first looks like figure 4.8(ii). The second layer is shown dotted.

When a third layer is added, a choice of two arrangements is possible. Either the spheres in the third layer are immediately above those in the first, or they are above the gaps in the first layer. (Models are an essential aid for the exposition of these ideas.)   The first type of packing is called ABA packing, and the second ABC packing. Although there are various ways of continuing these sequences, only two appear in almost all actual structures: ABABAB....... and ABCABCABC......

To simplify the diagrams, the spheres can be replaced by dots at their centres. A view of the ABAB packing is then as shown in figure 4.9.

(i)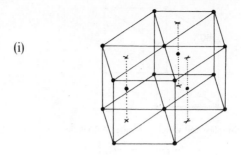

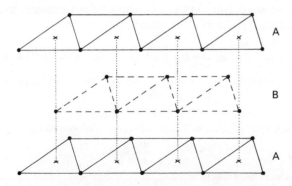

Figure 4.9   ABAB close packing.

The arrangement can be generated by repetition of the unit cell shown in figure 4.10(i), and is thus called *hexagonal close-packing*.

When counting the atoms in this cell, it is important to realize that the dots on the vertices, edges and faces of the cell represent fractions of atoms which combine (in the non-chemical sense) with

(ii)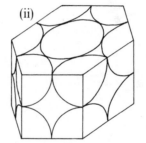

The total number of atoms in the cell is

$$3 \text{ (inside)} + 2 \times \tfrac{1}{2} \text{ (top and bottom faces)}$$
$$+ 12 \times \tfrac{1}{6} \text{ (vertices)}$$
$$= 6 \text{ atoms.}$$

Figure 4.10   Hexagonal close packing.

fractions from other cells. If the cell were drawn as made up from the spheres, it would appear as shown in figure 4.10(ii).

As explained above, the hexagonal cell is not the simplest unit cell which generates close-packing of the ABAB type. The rhomboidal prism shown in figure 4.11, which contains 2 atoms, is the simplest unit.

The other close-packed arrangement (ABC...) can be generated by repetition of a cubic unit cell. It is easiest to show this by making a model, but figure 4.12(i) shows (for those who can see it!) how parts of four layers of ABC...packing are included in a cubic cell. The layers are inclined to the faces of the cube.

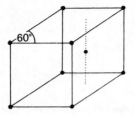

Figure 4.11   Simplest cell which generates ABAB close packing.

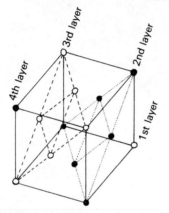

Figure 4.12(i)   ABC close packing.

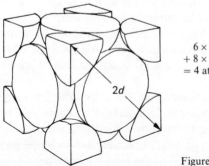

$6 \times \frac{1}{2}$ (at face-centres)
$+ 8 \times \frac{1}{8}$ (at vertices).
$= 4$ atoms.

Figure 4.12(ii)   Face-centred cubic cell.

The resulting unit, shown in figure 4.12(ii) with the spheres and fractions of spheres, is called a *face-centred* cubic unit. It contains 4 atoms.

The ABC packing is called *face-centred cubic close-packing*.

If d is the diameter of each sphere, then the diagonal of one face of the cubic unit is of length $2d$. Hence, if a is the length of an edge of the cube,

$$2d = a\sqrt{2}$$

i.e. $a = \sqrt{2}.d$

This relationship can be used to determine d, which is also the distance between the atomic centres, or nuclei (see *NC Handbook for Teachers*, chapter 13).

The calculation is carried out here for copper, known to have the face-centred cubic structure, whose relative atomic mass is 63·5 and whose density is 8·9 g/cm³.

The number of atoms included in 63·5 g of copper is 6×10^{23} (Avogadro's number).

Since the density is 8·9 g/cm³, the volume occupied by 6×10^{23} atoms is

$$\frac{63.5}{8.9} \text{cm}^3$$

Hence the volume occupied by 4 atoms (the contents of one unit cell) is

$$\frac{63.5}{8.9} \times \frac{4}{6 \times 10^{23}} \text{cm}^3$$

But each cell has a volume a^3, i.e. $(d\sqrt{2})^3$

Hence $$(d\sqrt{2})^3 = \frac{63.5 \times 4}{8.9 \times 6 \times 10^{23}}$$

from which $$d = 2.57 \times 10^{-8} \text{cm}.$$

It is also possible to calculate the percentage of the space within the unit cell (and therefore within the whole structure) which is unoccupied by atoms. The volume of the 4 atoms is $4 \times \frac{4}{3}\pi(\frac{1}{2}d)^3$, and the total volume $(d\sqrt{2})^3$.

Hence the percentage occupied is

$$\frac{4 \times \frac{4}{3}\pi \times (\frac{1}{2}d)^3}{d^3(\sqrt{2})^3} \times 100\%$$
$$= 74 \cdot 0\%$$

Thus 26·0 per cent of the space is unoccupied.

Another type of cubic unit cell, which does not generate close-packing, is the "body-centred" cubic cell shown in figure 4.13.

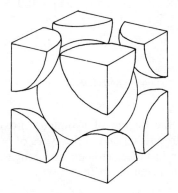

Figure 4.13   Body-centred cubic cell.

In this case the diagonal of the cube is $2d$, and a calculation on the same lines as that for the face-centred cube gives a result of 32 per cent unoccupied space.

So far the packing systems considered have been those of elements where all the spheres are identical. With compounds, the different sizes of atoms or ions have to be taken into account.

In some compounds, negative ions (cations) occupy the holes between positive ions (anions), which are themselves close-packed. There are three different types of hole, and the radius of the sphere which fits exactly into each type of hole may be calculated by trigonometry.

The holes are classified into *triangular*, *tetrahedral* and *octahedral*.

Triangular hole

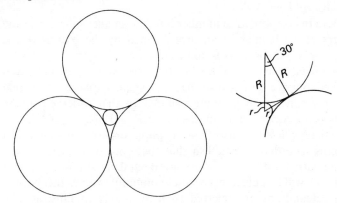

Figure 4.14   Packing in a compound: triangular hole.

A sphere which touches three others, so that the centres of all four are coplanar, is shown in figure 4.14. The *coordination number* of this arrangement is the number of spheres touched by the central sphere, i.e. 3.

If R is the radius of each large sphere, and r that of each small sphere,

$$R = (R + r)\cos 30°$$
$$R = 0 \cdot 866 R + 0 \cdot 866 r$$
$$0 \cdot 134 R = 0 \cdot 866 r$$
$$r = 0 \cdot 155 R$$

The ratio r/R, in this case 0·155, is called a *radius ratio*.

Tetrahedral hole

A sphere fitting in a tetrahedral hole has a coordination number of 4, and its centre is at the centre of the regular tetrahedron formed by the centres of the surrounding spheres. In this arrangement r/R can be shown to be 0·255.

Octahedral hole

Here the combination number is 6. The smaller sphere is at the centre of the regular octahedron formed by the centres of the larger spheres. $r/R = 0·414$ in this case.

A cubical hole is possible when the larger spheres are not close-packed, but are arranged so that each smaller sphere is touching 8 larger spheres, in a manner similar to that observed in the body-centred cubic unit. In this case $r/R = 0·732$.

In the *Nuffield Chemistry* option, pupils experiment with model spheres in order to establish that there are boundaries to the radius ratio for different coordination numbers. It is not expected that they will be able to derive these bounding values themselves. The calculations are referred to here mainly to illustrate the usefulness to chemists of certain mathematical topics, a usefulness perhaps unfamiliar to many teachers of mathematics.

THE SYMMETRY OF CRYSTALS

The foregoing account has been concerned with internal crystalline structure. A study of the relationship between internal structure and the shape of large crystals requires an understanding of the various kinds of symmetry which a polyhedron may have. A "stage A" approach to this topic is of interest in mathematics teaching, particularly if the effect upon symmetry of various ways of colouring faces or vertices of model polyhedra is investigated. For example, if opposite faces of a cube are coloured red, green and blue, the cube no longer has reflection symmetry about the plane shown in figure 4.15(i). Also the three-fold rotational symmetry about each diagonal is destroyed (figure 4.15(ii)).

The various classes of crystal may be illustrated by model polyhedra in which faces are marked with patterns (or "stri-

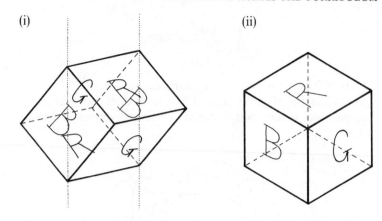

(i)   (ii)

Figure 4.15   Destruction of symmetries in a cube by colouring faces.

ations") to lessen the degree of symmetry possessed by the unmarked polyhedron (itself one of the types of building block). For details see, for instance, Holden and Singer, *Crystals and Crystal Growing* (Heinemann, 1960).

STEREOGRAMS

A stereogram is a diagrammatic representation of the axes and types of symmetry of a solid. It is derived from the solid by the following procedure:

(i)   Describe round the solid a sphere whose centre is at the centre of the solid.

(ii) Mark the points where each axis of symmetry cuts this sphere.

(iii) Take a plane through the "equator" of the sphere and map the surfaces of each of the hemispheres formed onto the plane by conical projection with vertex at the "North Pole" for points in the "northern" hemisphere, and at the "South Pole" for points in the "southern" hemisphere. The sequence of mappings is thus:

Axis of symmetry → pair of points (one on northern, one on southern, hemisphere) → pair of points in plane

Each point in the plane is marked with a conventional symbol, shown blacked in if the point was derived from the northern hemisphere but open if derived from the southern. The conventional symbols are shown in figure 4.16.

Stereograms are described in more detail in *Symmetry and Crystal Structure*, a module produced by the Nuffield Mathematics Continuation Project: Science Uses Mathematics.

4.11   Chemical Equations and Linear Algebra

In this section is considered a mathematical way of looking at the elementary problem of "balancing" a chemical equation. It is not being advocated as a method, and the returns from considering the problem in this way are for mathematics teaching, not for chemistry, in that a concrete point of departure for some linear algebra is indicated.

Consider the problem (discussed in W. W. Sawyer, *The Search for Pattern*, pp. 113–117 (Penguin, 1970)) of finding natural numbers, x, y, z, t, such that the following chemical equation "balances":

$$x\text{Zn} + y\text{HCl} \rightarrow z\text{ZnCl}_2 + t\text{H}_2$$

At "O" Level such a problem would be tackled by intelligent trial and error, although pupils who are able to solve simultaneous linear equations might appreciate a systematic approach.

The balancing of the number of atoms of each element mentioned leads to three equations:

$$
\begin{array}{lll}
\text{Zn:} & x & = z \\
\text{H:} & y = & 2t \\
\text{Cl:} & y = 2z &
\end{array}
$$

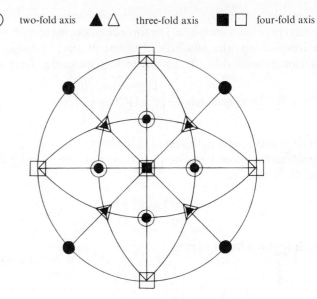

two-fold axis ▲ △ three-fold axis ■ □ four-fold axis

Figure 4.16   Stereogram showing the symmetry of a cube.

Written in this form the three equations show themselves as separate, though connected, entities. A step towards unification is made if we think of each equation as an equation in *all* the unknowns, some having coefficient zero:

$$
\begin{array}{rcl}
x + 0y & = & z + 0t \\
0x + y & = & 0z + 2t \\
0x + y & = & 2z + 0t
\end{array}
$$

A further step, the introduction of column-vector notation, exhibits more of the structure:

$$x\begin{pmatrix}1\\0\\0\end{pmatrix} + y\begin{pmatrix}0\\1\\1\end{pmatrix} = z\begin{pmatrix}1\\0\\2\end{pmatrix} + t\begin{pmatrix}0\\2\\0\end{pmatrix}$$

Here we are dealing with three-dimensional vectors, each of which represents a molecule. The three components of each vector are, respectively, the numbers of atoms of zinc, hydrogen and chlorine contained in the corresponding molecule. Thus Zn is

represented by $\begin{pmatrix} 1 \\ 0 \\ 0 \end{pmatrix}$, HCl by $\begin{pmatrix} 0 \\ 1 \\ 1 \end{pmatrix}$, etc.

The problem, originally stated in the form, "Solve the following simultaneous linear equations", can be restated, "Find a linear sum of the vectors

$$\begin{pmatrix} 1 \\ 0 \\ 0 \end{pmatrix} \text{ and } \begin{pmatrix} 0 \\ 1 \\ 1 \end{pmatrix}$$

which is also a linear sum of

$$\begin{pmatrix} 1 \\ 0 \\ 2 \end{pmatrix} \text{ and } \begin{pmatrix} 0 \\ 2 \\ 0 \end{pmatrix}$$

with the proviso that the scalars involved in the linear sum are natural numbers".

Here we have a concrete instance of linear algebra. From the mathematical point of view we could go on to ask such questions as:

Is there a solution?

Is there more than one solution? (In this case the chemist opts for the simplest—the one involving the smallest numbers.)

Recognizing that the equation(s) above can be solved for the *ratios* $x:y:z:t$, i.e. that there are only *three* effective unknowns, what happens in a case in which the number of separate linear equations is greater than the number of effective unknowns?

To focus attention on the last question, consider the chemical equation

$$x\mathrm{Ca} + y\mathrm{H_3PO_4} \to z\mathrm{Ca_3P_2O_8} + t\mathrm{H_2}$$

With components listed in the order Ca, O, H, P, this corresponds to the vector equation:

$$x\begin{pmatrix} 1 \\ 0 \\ 0 \\ 0 \end{pmatrix} + y\begin{pmatrix} 0 \\ 4 \\ 3 \\ 1 \end{pmatrix} = z\begin{pmatrix} 3 \\ 8 \\ 0 \\ 2 \end{pmatrix} + t\begin{pmatrix} 0 \\ 0 \\ 2 \\ 0 \end{pmatrix}$$

The fact that this equation is solvable for the ratios $x:y:z:t$ is due to the fact that the fourth linear equation is a multiple ($\frac{1}{4}$) of the second. In the chemical equation this corresponds to the existence of the *radical* $\mathrm{PO_4}$,

$$\begin{pmatrix} 0 \\ 4 \\ 0 \\ 1 \end{pmatrix}$$

which is exhibited in the usual way of writing this equation

$$x\mathrm{Ca} + y\mathrm{H_3PO_4} \to z\mathrm{Ca_3(PO_4)_2} + t\mathrm{H_2}$$

In the language of vector spaces we could say that, although apparently we are dealing with a four-dimensional vector space with basis

$$\begin{pmatrix} 1 \\ 0 \\ 0 \\ 0 \end{pmatrix} \begin{pmatrix} 0 \\ 1 \\ 0 \\ 0 \end{pmatrix} \begin{pmatrix} 0 \\ 0 \\ 1 \\ 0 \end{pmatrix} \begin{pmatrix} 0 \\ 0 \\ 0 \\ 1 \end{pmatrix}$$
$$\quad\ \text{Ca}\qquad\text{O}\qquad\text{H}\qquad\text{P}$$

the four vectors (molecules) in our equation belong to a three-dimensional subspace, with basis

$$\begin{pmatrix} 1 \\ 0 \\ 0 \\ 0 \end{pmatrix} \begin{pmatrix} 0 \\ 0 \\ 1 \\ 0 \end{pmatrix} \begin{pmatrix} 0 \\ 4 \\ 0 \\ 1 \end{pmatrix}$$
$$\quad\ \text{Ca}\qquad\text{H}\qquad\text{PO}_4$$

Commentary

On the face of it, we have here an example of a point of contact between chemistry and mathematics which is a genuine growing point. Much mathematics certainly grows from it, although for "O" Level pupils the mathematical discussion would be likely to stop short of the consideration of dimensionality. But how much understanding of, and application to, chemistry grows from this point? Does the mathematics return to chemistry? It would be splendid if we could say that the mathematical considerations of dimensionality lead to the identification of radicals, but un-fortunately this is not so. The chemical formulae of the molecules involved in a chemical equation are known in advance of writing down the form of the equation, as are the names of the substances which are produced. Since the interest of the chemist *qua* chemist in the mathematical treatment of his subject does not extend beyond the point at which it yields a return for him, in the topic under discussion that point is reached, certainly as far as lower school chemistry is concerned, where the ability to solve simultaneous linear equations helps in balancing awkward chemical equations.

5 Mathematics in Biology

The amount of quantitative work in 11–16 school biology varies a great deal from course to course. In most cases it is minimal, and this point should be constantly borne in mind when reading the survey below. Quantitative work features most in the original Nuffield Biology course, though the revised textbooks show some reduction of it. The fact that there is so little mathematics in biology generally at the 11–16 level is due no doubt in part to the tradition of biology as a descriptive science subject.

The range of mathematical topics occurring in biology—even in courses where mathematics figures most, such as the Nuffield Biology course and the Scottish course entitled *Biology by Inquiry* (R. A. Clarke and others, (3 vols.) Heinemann 1968–1972)—is fairly small. Graphical representation of data features most often.

Questions involving mathematics on examination papers are a minority, and are usually optional, or avoidable without dire penalty. At present it seems that only the London Board specifies the level of mathematical skill which may be required:

1. A working knowledge of such simple arithmetical processes as are necessary to perform simple calculations involving biological data, e.g. fractions, decimals, proportions, percentages.
2. Ability to construct simple graphs, histograms and "pie" charts.
3. Ability to make simple deductions from arithmetical and graphical data.

Furthermore

these do not indicate any increase in the skills which have been required in past papers and it is not anticipated that there will be any increase in the mathematical content of the examination.

However, there is evidence of some increase in the proportion of questions requiring mathematics in the papers covering the various biological subjects set by the London GCE Board in recent years.

A wide range of popular biology textbooks was examined in the process of compiling the survey which follows. The lack of examples from, or references to, many of them is itself evidence of the generally non-mathematical nature of the biology courses as taught at present.

TOPIC SURVEY

5.1 Sets, Flow Diagrams

As was stated earlier, these ideas are pre-mathematical and belong to the qualitative stage of scientific study. Nevertheless it is of interest to see how they arise in biology in the process of classifying individuals into species. Actual instances can be quite complex, but a simple non-biological example will be used here to explain the procedure.

Here is a collection of five types of geometrical figure:

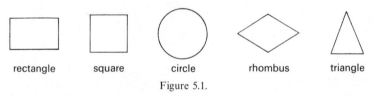

rectangle   square   circle   rhombus   triangle

Figure 5.1.

The set may be partitioned into two disjoint subsets in various ways, but the most obvious ways are those in which each member is classified according to whether it does or does not possess a certain attribute. In this example an obvious attribute for a first partition is whether or not the figure is made up of straight lines.

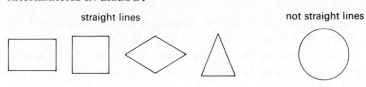

straight lines   not straight lines

Figure 5.2.

Within the left-hand subset, a further partitioning may be based upon the number of sides, or upon equality or inequality of the sides, or upon whether all angles are equal, or whether they are all right angles, etc. If the number of sides is chosen, the partitioning so far can be shown as follows.

	Given set of figures		
1st partitioning	straight lines		not straight lines
2nd partitioning	4 sides	3 sides	

Partitioning is complete when each figure belongs to only one subset. The selection of attributes for each sub-partition is not unique; one way of completing the process leads to the result below, this time illustrated by a tree diagram.

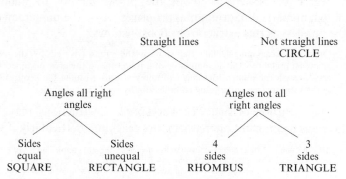

Figure 5.3.

This partitioning by attributes is the basis for a *key* for identifying the correct species for a given individual from the original collection. The key will only work when the individual to be classified is a member of the set for which the key was constructed. The key may be presented in the form of a flow diagram.

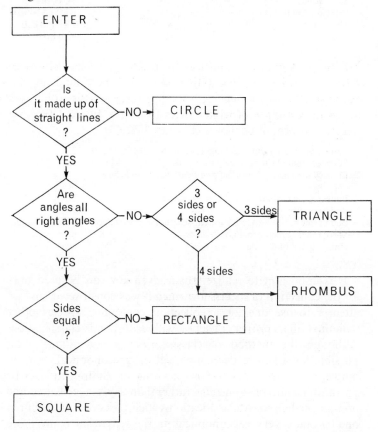

Figure 5.4.

The flow diagram format may be a little unwieldy. Another way of giving the key above is as follows:

1. Made up of straight lines   2
   Not made up of straight lines   CIRCLE
2. All angles right angles   3
   All angles not right angles   4
3. Sides equal   SQUARE
   Sides unequal   RECTANGLE
4. Three sides   TRIANGLE
   Four sides   RHOMBUS

A simple key of the kind used in biology appears below (see *NB 1* (revised), p. 263. Other keys will be found in, for example, *Biology by Inquiry*, Vol. 1, pp. 21, 28). It is to be used to sort a collection of winter twigs from five different types of tree: ash, beech, birch, horse-chestnut, lilac.

1. Buds more than 4 times as long as broad   2
   Buds less than 4 times as long as broad   3
2. Buds where cigar-shaped leaf scar nearly surrounds base
   of bud   beech
   Buds not cigar-shaped. Leaf scar much smaller birch
3. Buds smooth, green-brown or black   4
   Bud scales red-brown, sticky. Leaf scar horseshoe-shaped horse-chestnut
4. More than 2 green-brown bud scales   lilac
   Only 2 black bud scales   ash

It is important to realize that a given key can be used only for the collection of species for which it was constructed, and an attempt to use one for a collection containing species other than those in its proper collection will result in mis-classification. Although the method of classification is not unique, it is possible for a key to be economical or uneconomical. For example, it is better when sorting a group of children to start by partitioning into boys and girls rather than, say, ginger-haired and non-ginger-haired. A classification which picks out the children one by one is very uneconomical, in the sense that many more steps are necessary in the partitioning process.

Key construction can be related to binary coding and the construction of punched-card sorting systems.

Pupils studying biology, including those studying it at CSE level, are required to use given keys and to construct keys of their own.

5.2   Percentage, and Similar Calculations

The following quotation is from the *Nuffield Biology Teachers' Guide 3* (age range 13–14):

> Pupils should at this stage be able to work out the percentage composition of air samples, and then to pool results to obtain mean values for the class as a whole.[1] At first there may be some opposition from the weaker members of the class—this is an incursion of mathematics into biology periods! The sooner this attitude is dispelled the better. Mathematics is a necessary tool in all branches of science, and it would be false kindness to allow any other view to gain ground. By the end of the Nuffield biology course all pupils will be used to carrying out calculations, drawing graphs, and performing similar operations as routine.[2]

Nevertheless even in the Nuffield texts themselves there appears a degree of pessimism about the pupils' ability to handle simple numerical data in an appropriate way—the numeracy of the pupils—as this extract from *Book 4* shows:

> On each occasion, calculate the sum of the areas covered by the two growths: make this the denominator of a fraction and the area occupied by each growth the numerator. This will allow you to estimate the proportion of the total surface undergoing colonization by each kind of fungus.[3]

The inclusion of such "cookery book" instructions may be taken as a comment on mathematics teaching, particularly if we

---

[1] The "pooling" of percentages is justifiable only when the air samples used are all of the same volume. (This is not a Nuffield footnote.)

[2] *NBGT 3*, p. 19. The original Nuffield Biology course was written in the 1960s for the upper 25 per cent or so of the ability range. Since then it has been used, sometimes with adaptations, with a wider range of ability.

[3] *NB 4* (revised), p. 19.

recall that the recipe given here comes in the fourth year of an "O" Level Biology course. But however well-meaning, the "cookery book" approach cannot be justified, because all teachers, of whatever subject, who use numbers are involved in the teaching of numeracy. Teaching pupils to be numerate means helping them to understand not only *how* but *why* certain arithmetical procedures—such as calculating a fraction or percentage—are used at certain junctures to draw conclusions from data. The aim is that the pupils should learn to recognize for themselves which is the appropriate procedure in a given instance.

The topic of percentage is also considered on page 8. The two examples which follow illustrate the sort of percentage calculation which arises.

EXAMPLE 1. Human gas exchange (*NB 3*, pp. 5–9).

When potassium hydroxide solution is added to air, any carbon dioxide is quickly taken up and the air shrinks in volume. If we now add potassium pyrogallate solution to the same sample, any oxygen will be taken up too, and the gas will shrink further still. By finding out the volumes of the sample:
(*a*) originally,
(*b*) after adding potassium hydroxide solution, and
(*c*) after also adding potassium pyrogallate solution;
we can work out the percentage of carbon dioxide and oxygen in the original air samples.
For example:

Suppose that original air volume	$= 10\,\text{cm}^3$
Volume after adding potassium hydroxide solution	$= 9\cdot6\,\text{cm}^3$
Difference	$= 0\cdot4\,\text{cm}^3$ (due to uptake of carbon dioxide)
Therefore percentage of carbon dioxide	$= (0\cdot4/10) \times 100$
	$= 4$ per cent
Volume after adding potassium pyrogallate solution	$= 8\cdot0\,\text{cm}^3$
Difference	$= (9\cdot6 - 8\cdot0)\,\text{cm}^3$
	$= 1\cdot6\,\text{cm}^3$ (due to uptake of oxygen)
Therefore percentage of oxygen	$= (1\cdot6/10) \times 100 = 16$ per cent

We can assume that the remaining gas was probably nitrogen. By subtraction this gives 80 per cent of nitrogen in the original air sample.

The main precaution to be taken is to avoid altering the gas volume in any other way. If we raise the temperature of the gas burette, the gas inside will tend to expand and give too high a volume reading. So the readings will all have to be taken at the same temperature—that of a sinkful of water. If we alter the pressure on the air sample during the experiment, its volume will also alter. So all measurements must be taken at atmospheric (room) pressure.

Working out the results
(*a*) Since each burette contains a slightly different volume of air, you will have to work out the percentages of carbon dioxide and oxygen in each of your own samples before you can compare them with those of the rest of the class. Follow the example above, putting your own values into the calculations.
(*b*) You will then be able to write the following information on the board:

Name of subject	Atmospheric air		Lung air	
	Percentage of carbon dioxide	Percentage of oxygen	Percentage of carbon dioxide	Percentage of oxygen

If all groups do this, you can then work out a mean (average) value for each of the four columns of figures. Make sure you record these mean values in your notebook, as well as the number of subjects involved.
(*c*) Now examine the final class results, and draw your own conclusions.

Comment

This experiment, and the calculations involved, have been found exceptionally difficult in the biology class. The experiment has been omitted from the Revised Nuffield Biology texts, but the reason for this has been as much the practical difficulties involved as the mathematical difficulties. Note that pupils are asked to record "mean percentages", even though it is recognized that the original volumes of air in the separate experiments will differ.

EXAMPLE 2. Water loss (*Biology by Inquiry Book 2*, pp. 6–7).

We shall see later that most living organisms consist largely of water. If you leave an apple in a warm room for a few weeks, some of the water escapes and the apple gradually becomes wizened and dried up. What effect will the ratio of surface area to volume have on the proportion of water lost by an organism?

1. Select two large potato tubers about the same size, and two small ones about the same size as each other.
2. Carefully peel one large one and one small one, removing as thin a layer of peel as possible.
3. Weigh each potato and note the date.
4. Leave all four potatoes exposed to the air for a week and then reweigh.
5. Enter your results as shown in the table and work out the percentage loss of weight for each potato.

	A	B	C	Percentage Loss $\dfrac{C}{A} \times \dfrac{100}{1}$
	First weight	Second weight	Loss (A–B)	
Small whole potato	g	g	g	per cent
Small peeled potato				
Large whole potato				
Large peeled potato				

What effect has the ratio of surface area to volume on the percentage of water lost by the potatoes? What effect does the presence of the peel of the potato have on water loss?

5.3 Inverse Proportion

The DCPIP test for ascorbic acid (*NB 3*, p. 54) gives rise to a calculation involving inverse proportion. DCPIP is a dye whose colour is destroyed by ascorbic acid (vitamin C). The stronger the concentration of the acid, the smaller the amount of it necessary to decolorize a given volume of DCPIP solution. The Nuffield text explains the calculation by a worked example:

Suppose that $0.5\,cm^3$ of lemon juice just decolorized $1\,cm^3$ of DCPIP solution, and that $0.4\,cm^3$ of a given ascorbic acid solution did the same. Then the lemon juice was not as concentrated as the ascorbic acid solution—in fact it was $0.4/0.5$ times as concentrated. If the ascorbic acid solution contained $1\,mg$ ascorbic acid per cm^3, then the lemon juice must have contained $(1 \times 0.4/0.5) = 0.8\,mg$ ascorbic acid per cm^3.

This "multiplier" method is mathematically attractive, but the following explanation may be simpler to follow as it uses the "cause" of the inverse proportion, viz. the constant value of the amount of acid necessary to decolorize.

It is ascorbic acid which destroys the colour. How much ascorbic acid is there in $1\,cm^3$ of the standard solution? Answer: $1\,mg$. So how much is there in $0.4\,cm^3$? Answer: $0.4\,mg$. Thus it requires $0.4\,mg$ of ascorbic acid to decolorize the DCPIP. So $0.5\,cm^3$ of lemon juice contains this amount of ascorbic acid, i.e. $0.4\,mg$. Hence $1\,cm^3$ of juice contains $0.8\,mg$ ascorbic acid.

5.4 Compound Units: Rates

The understanding, and occasional calculation, of various rates occur throughout biology.

An example involving calculation by pupils occurs in *Nuffield Biology 4*, p. 87, where pupils are asked to measure (i) the time taken for a leaf to lose a given weight ($10\,mg$); (ii) the surface area of the leaf; and from their measurements to calculate the weight loss per cm^2 per hour.

5.5 Gradient

The idea of gradient is often involved in the mathematical modelling of biological systems. For example, the rate of passage of oxygen from air or water into an organism depends upon the difference in oxygen concentration on either side of the membrane through which gaseous exchange occurs, and also on the thickness of the membrane itself. If C_1, C_2 are the oxygen concentrations outside and inside respectively, and t is the thickness of the membrane, the rate R of passage of oxygen can be thought of as directly proportional to $C_1 - C_2$ and inversely proportional to t, i.e.

$$R \propto \frac{C_1 - C_2}{t}$$

$(C_1 - C_2)/t$ is the *concentration gradient* across the membrane.

From this formula it follows that R is increased if the concentration gradient is increased, and the latter happens if either C_1 is increased, C_2 decreased, or t decreased.

The finely divided structure of the insect tracheal system, the alveolar structure of mammalian lungs, the structure of the crustacean and fish gill systems, and the spongy structure of leaves are all examples of ways of reducing t and thus increasing R.

Ventilation mechanisms such as the mouth used as a force pump to pump water over the gills of fishes, the mammalian thorax used for "breathing", body movements in insects, fan-like appendages used to waft water over some crustacean gills, all ensure that C_1 (the concentration of oxygen outside the organism, in the respiratory medium) is kept as high as practicable, so that R is large.

Similarly the presence in internal body fluids, such as the blood, of substances with a high affinity for oxygen, especially when associated with pumping mechanisms which ensure the con-

tinual passage of body fluid through the gill or lung surface, ensures that C_2 (the concentration of oxygen inside the organism in the circulatory fluid) is kept low, so that R is large.

5.6 Enlargement, Scale Factor, Ratio, Volume, Surface Area

Biologists are interested in the effects on an organism of *enlargement* (in the mathematical sense, viz. a transformation in which every length measurement of an object is enlarged by the same factor, the so-called *scale factor*). Enlargement has different effects upon surface area and volume (and hence weight), and also affects such things as the ability of the skeleton to support an animal on land. The relation between surface area and weight is fundamental to an understanding of heat production and loss in warm-blooded animals.

Here is a point where mathematical work on enlargement and similarity links directly with biology, and leads to useful explanatory concepts in biology. In mathematics, interest focuses on the fact that if in an enlargement lengths are multiplied by a scale factor k, then areas are multiplied by k^2, volumes by k^3. (These topics occur in the *SMP* "O" Level course near the start of the second year and in the CSE course at the end of the third year. The corresponding traditional treatment, "Areas of similar triangles are proportional to the squares of corresponding sides", is usually rather later.) There is no particular reason in mathematics to introduce the idea of "Surface Area to Weight (Volume) Ratio", but the foundation is laid for this idea.

A scheme of work leading to the "Surface Area to Weight Ratio" (more properly called a *rate* than a *ratio*; the units are m^2/kg, whereas a ratio is dimensionless) and its relation to heat balance is included in a number of modern biology courses, e.g. *NB 2*, pp. 56 ff—postponed in Revised Course; *NCSTG 2*, p. 38; *Biology by Inquiry*, Vol. 2, chapter 1. When skeletal support of vertebrates on land is discussed, the corresponding ratio is that of "cross-sectional area (of bone) to weight (of animal)".

The approach in biology is through the use of a simplified model, a cube, for which the volume and surface area may be found by counting squares and cubes (or by applying formulae mechanically).

Side of cube cm	1	2	4	5	10
Surface area cm^2	6	24	96	300	600
Volume cm^3	1	8	64	225	1000
Ratio $\dfrac{\text{S.A.}}{\text{vol.}}$	$\dfrac{6}{1}$	$\dfrac{3}{1}$	$\dfrac{3}{2}$	$\dfrac{4}{3}$	$\dfrac{3}{5}$

It is observed that as size increases, the surface area to weight ratio decreases.

There is no doubt that the ideas involved here are complex, and hence quite a lot of reflection is necessary to understand exactly what is going on. Ratio, as has often been said in this book and elsewhere, is a difficult idea for children. A function relating two quantities one of which is a "ratio" (of two different measures) is of a high degree of difficulty.

It is possible to retain the powerful explanatory idea of the surface area to weight ratio for biology, whilst simplifying the approach to a semi-qualitative form. Imagine an "animal" being built up from identical cubes. A single cube has 6 faces (squares) open to the air (figure 5.5(i)). When two cubes are placed together, one face of each is joined to the other, and only ten faces are open

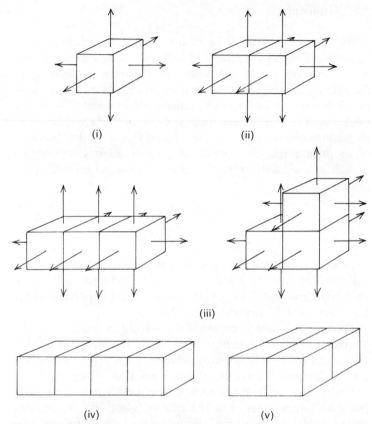

Figure 5.5   The number of faces exposed by conjunctions of various numbers of cubes.

to the air (figure 5.5(ii)). The two cubes are "huddled together for warmth".

If another is joined to these two, one of the three will have two of its faces covered (figure 5.5(iii)). Between them the three cubes are exposed on fourteen faces. Three separate cubes would expose eighteen faces.

The more cubes there are, the more they can cover one another up and leave relatively few faces open to the air. When a fourth cube is added, the differences between compact and extended structures appear. In figure (iv) 18 faces are exposed, but in figure (v) only 16.

The different relationships of surface area to volume in compact and extended structures are, in a number of cases, biologically interesting. In addition to the topic of heat balance, we may cite that of water absorption by plant roots: a large number of thin root hairs provide a greater surface area than a single root of the same total volume.

EXAMPLE 3 (JMB, November 1972, Question A3.)

A man of 25 years weighing 68 kg with a surface area of $1.8\,m^2$ has a surface area to weight ratio of $0.027\,m^2/kg$. A baby of one year weighing 10 kg has a surface area of $0.47\,m^2$.

(a) What is the difference between the surface area to weight ratio of the baby and the man?

(b) Give ONE important biological consequence of this difference.

5.7 Graphs

Graphs are to be found everywhere, and there is unlimited potential for using graphs to exhibit phenomena. Examples 4 and 5 show graphs being used to bring out certain striking features of phenomena, for which biological explanation is sought.

EXAMPLE 4 (*Biology by Inquiry, Book 1*, pp. 101–2.)

One of the first records of the growth of one person was kept by a French Count, Philibert de Montbeillard, and the figure opposite shows the growth curve of his son from 1759 to 1777.

Another way of producing a graph of human growth is to calculate the height of a large number of children of different ages, to find out the average gain in height from year to year. The next figure shows histograms* drawn from this

* This is an instance of the wrong use of a word (see page 9).

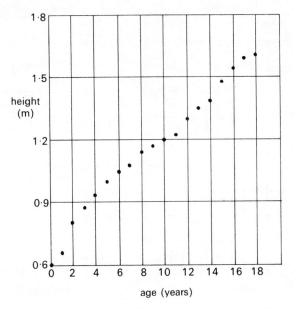

Growth curve for Philibert de Montbeillard's son (1759–77).

information. These graphs tell us a number of things about human growth. If you look at part (a), you will see that, between the age of seven and ten, girls grow at the same rate each year. Put another way, the graph tells us that an average girl gains about 53 mm in height each year from age seven to ten. As you will also see from the figure, except for one period called the *adolescent spurt*, gain in height takes place gradually, and not in bursts of growth, as many people still believe.

This adolescent spurt takes place at puberty, when the ovaries and testes are starting to produce eggs and sperms as the person becomes sexually mature.

By looking at the histograms, decide when this burst of growth usually starts in girls and boys.

Prepare growth curves of some of the animals in your laboratory. Mice are easily handled and can be used for this work. Record the weight of young mice every two days for the first three weeks after birth, every week for the next four weeks, and once a month for the next few months. Plot your results as a graph of weight against time; in other words, plot a growth curve. You should also measure at the same time the length of the mouse's tail to find its growth rate.

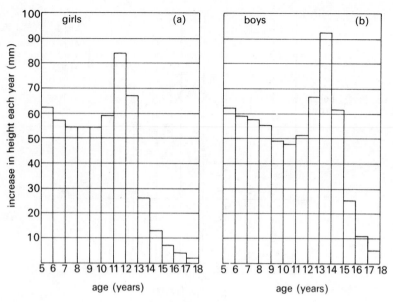

Graphs of human growth

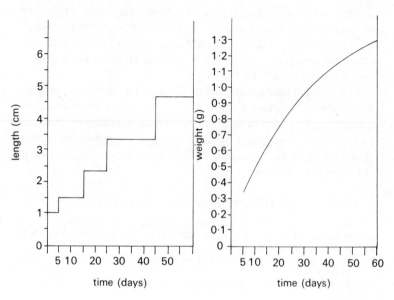

EXAMPLE 5 (East Midland, CSE)

The two graphs opposite are simplified versions of the results of a study of the growth of an insect (cockroach). The results are all for measurements of the same batch of cockroaches which were weighed and measured regularly. Like other insects they "moult" (shed their skins) at intervals as they grow. Study the graphs and consider what you have just read; then answer the questions.

(a) How many moults occurred during the time covered by the experiment?
(b) Why does the graph of length go up in such distinct steps whilst the weight graph is smoother?
(c) How can you tell from the graphs that the insects were still growing at the end of the experiment?
(d) Which is the more useful in this study of growth, the measuring of length or the weighing? Explain why you think so.

EXAMPLE 6 (JMB, June 1970, Biology Syllabus B, Question B12.)

Five cylinders of potato tissue of identical size were dried, weighed and then placed in solutions of sucrose of the following concentrations, one in 300 g/litre,

one in 240 g/litre, one in 170 g/litre, one in 100 g/litre, and one in 70 g/litre. Two hours later they were dried and reweighed and the results were as follows:

Concentration of sucrose in grams per litre	per cent change in weight
300	−10
240	− 7
170	− 3
100	+ 1
70	+10

(a) (i) Plot a graph of percentage change in weight against concentration.
    (ii) From the graph find the concentration of the solution in which the tissue would neither gain nor lose weight.*
(b) How do organisms such as (i) insects, and (ii) desert plants conserve their water?

* This is a biologically significant point.

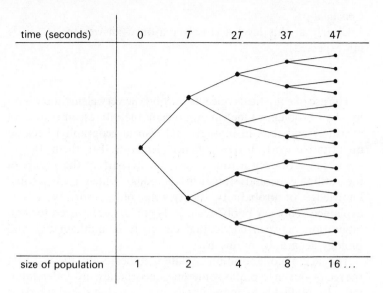

Figure 5.6 Growth of a population of bacteria.

An exponential function together with its graph arises in the course of an examination of population growth in bacteria. This idea is often used in mathematics teaching to introduce exponential growth although the word *exponential* may not be used. On the assumption that at fixed intervals of time, say every T seconds, each bacterium divides into two, the graph of the population from a single initial bacterium is as shown above.

If the initial population size is P_0 (all of the bacteria being assumed to be splitting simultaneously), the population size P at time nT seconds is given by

$$P = P_0 . 2^n$$

In the first year of the Nuffield Biology course (*NB* Revised *1*, p. 164), pupils are asked to compare the theoretical (i.e. ex-

ponential) growth curve for a colony of bacteria with figures obtained from observing a real colony, which show a rise followed by a fall, and to suggest a biological explanation for the difference.

Frequency graphs arise naturally in a study of human variation. It is worth noting that a very important distinction in biology is that between discontinuous and continuous variation. In the case of discontinuous variation, an organism may be classified according to which out of a set of discrete attributes it possesses, for example, which of two different colours it has. Discontinuous variation is the subject of Mendelian genetics, which is discussed below. Continuous variation may be exemplified by the classification of human beings by height. A continuous scale of measurement is used, and the pattern of variation may be represented by a histogram.

One of the teaching problems associated with work on frequency graphs and elementary statistics in mathematics lessons is that so often the collection and illustration of data are the endpoint of the exercise, at least at the earliest stage before any probability considerations are introduced. In biology, the investigations are carried out with a purpose, and it would appear to be better to introduce this topic, together with the elementary statistical measures of mean, median and mode (if in fact all are really useful) by way of the biological instances, or at least to do the work in close conjunction with the biology course.

5.8 Statistics

Having said that it is better to introduce elementary statistical terms through instances of scientific interest, there remains the question of how best to do this. In Revised *NB 1*, pp. 24–26, there is a section in which pupils are introduced to the ideas of range, median, mean, mode, frequency table, frequency graph, and the method of obtaining the mean from a frequency distribution. Pupils are asked to comment on the differences between some populations, using the statistical terms in their descriptions. Median and mode do not appear in the other revised texts but can arise in classwork. This chapter is intended as a reservoir of ideas to be called upon if and when required throughout the five years of the course.

Various ways of *sampling* are used in biology. The following question involving these ideas of sampling is taken from a CSE paper (West Yorkshire-Lindsey Regional Board).

EXAMPLE 7

(*a*) When a study is made of a particular area it may be necessary to do a survey of the size and distribution of the plant population. A method of sampling has to be used such as "a belt transect" or "random samples". Explain what is meant by (i) "a belt transect" and (ii) "random samples".

(*b*) The following results were obtained for ten random samples taken to estimate the population of a particular plant in an area 25 m × 10 m.

Sample station (1 m²)	1	2	3	4	5	6	7	8	9	10
No. of specimens found	2	3	5	7	14	6	2	7	13	11

(i) Calculate the estimated average population per square metre.
(ii) Calculate the estimated population of the area.
(iii) What would be the least number of samples necessary to give a valid estimate of the total population?

(*c*) Draw and label the apparatus you would use to collect small animals from the surface of the soil and describe briefly how it works.

(*d*) To estimate the size of an animal population (e.g. woodlice) in a particular area, a sample is collected and each animal is marked with a spot of white paint. The animals are then returned to the area. Several days later a second sample is collected and the number of marked and unmarked individuals are counted.

The size of the population is taken as being equal to:

$$\left(\begin{array}{c}\text{total number caught and}\\ \text{marked in first sample}\end{array}\right) \times \left(\frac{\text{total number caught (marked and unmarked) in second sample}}{\text{number of marked specimens in second sample}}\right)$$

Calculate the estimated total population of woodlice in an area if the first sample was 200, and 25 of the second sample of 200 were found to be marked.

Comment

Clearly at this level a closely reasoned answer to (*b*) (iii) is not expected!

*   *   *

The use of statistical concepts beyond the very elementary level involves problems. One can appreciate the interest in statistical measures and tests in biology (and also in geography) because quantitative work in these sciences lends itself to them. But in the absence of even a rough idea on the part of the pupils of the rationale behind statistical methods—which means some knowledge of probability theory—the only resort is to unexplained "cookery book" recipes. There is a great need for collaboration between curriculum designers in mathematics and biology/geography in this area.

The lack of collaboration to date is indicated by the fact that the recipes given to pupils sometimes incorporate misunderstandings. In Nuffield Biology, pupils are introduced to standard deviation, defined by the formula $\sigma = \sqrt{(\Sigma D^2/N)}$. The textbook states (Revised *NB 4*, p. 114):

> Since the calculation ends with a square root, we must write the standard deviation as ± 2.9 and not just 2.9.
> It is not necessary to give the standard deviation of the group separately [from the mean, 75.2]. We can write the mean of the group as 75.2 ± 2.9 showing that its true value lies somewhere between 78.1 to 72.3.

These instructions are wrong. Revised *NBTG 4*, p. 97, comments:

> When using the formula quoted in the text $[\sigma = \sqrt{(\Sigma D^2/N)}]$ the denominator $N-1$ gives a more accurate measure of variation than N, especially when small numbers are being considered. It is best to point that refinement out to students when they understand the basic computations well.

The reason given here for the refinement—greater "accuracy"—is by itself misleading.

Pupils undertake some experiments in which statistical hypothesis testing would be appropriate (testing the significance of the difference between two percentages). An outline of the background theory is supplied by the *Teachers' Guide*. The following statements occur (Revised *NBTG 4*, p. 100):

> Various statistical tests have now been devised which enable us to calculate the *probability* that a given result is due to chance.

> One of the ways of comparing two percentages is to calculate the standard error of the difference between them. This is an estimate of the probability that the difference is due to chance.

Both of these statements are false. The final remark is (Revised *NBTG 4*, p. 101):

> Whether or not tests of significance are incorporated into the work will depend, of course, on the mathematical background of the students, and the time available. It is surely important that students should be made aware of them to some extent.

There are distinct advantages, from the point of view of understanding, to be obtained by using *non-parametric* statistical tests. Two tests relevant to the work considered here are explained in Appendix 2(p. 143). Also described in that Appendix is an application of probabilty to "choice chamber" experiments.

5.9   Probability

The study of probability is not included in all mathematics courses[2], and so in introductions to genetics in biology courses the necessary simple probability theory is closely integrated with the genetic terminology. Situations in genetics can be simulated by bead models, and these are used both to facilitate understanding and to obtain results.

As the terminology of genetics may be unfamiliar to some mathematics teachers, a brief and simplified account follows.

Most characteristics of plants and animals (including human beings) are inherited. Genetics, as studied at "O" Level, deals with characteristics which are markedly discontinuous. One such

[2] It is included in *SMP* (introduced in *Book 3* and *Book E*).

characteristic is body colour (brown or black) in fruit flies (*Drosophila*). Each fly possesses a pair of *allelomorphs* (*alleles*) of the *gene* relating to this characteristic, one from each of its parents (often the word *gene* is used instead of *allele*). Each allele may be of either of two types, here denoted by *A* and *a*. Thus a fly may have *AA*, *Aa* or *aa*. Those with *AA* or *aa* are said to be *homozygous*, those with *Aa heterozygous* with respect to this genetic characteristic. *A* is the allele producing brown colour, and *a* that producing black. The brown allele is written with the capital letter to denote that it is *dominant*. This means that the *Aa* type, the heterozygote, exhibits the characteristic of the *A* rather than the *a*; so an *Aa* type is brown. The *a*-allele is *recessive*.

The three categories *AA*, *Aa*, *aa* are called *genotypes*, and the kinds of observed individual (brown or black) are called *phenotypes*.

Genotype	*AA*	*Aa*	*aa*
Phenotype	brown	brown	black

The sex cells, or *gametes*, of a fly each contain one allele of the pair borne by that fly. In the process of reproduction, one male gamete and one female gamete unite to form the offspring and establish its genotype. Each male gamete has an equal chance of contributing to the formation of any one offspring; likewise each female gamete.

If, for example, an *Aa* male mates with an *aa* female and forms an offspring, the female gamete is bound to have been *a*, while the male gamete would have been either *A* or *a* (with equal probabilities). So the genotype of the offspring can be *Aa* or *aa*.

The mating of two heterozygous parents can be simulated by using two "probability bottles", each containing equal numbers of black (*A*) and white (*a*) beads (figure 5.7). (The colours of the beads are not representing the colours of flies.)

MATHEMATICS ACROSS THE CURRICULUM

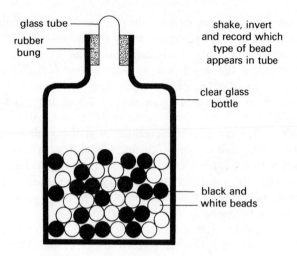

Figure 5.7   Probability bottle (from Brocklehurst and Ward, *A New Biology*, pp. 240–1).

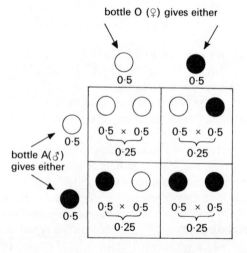

Figure 5.8   Four-way probability.

Figure 5.8 (also taken from Brocklehurst and Ward) explains how the three possible genotypes occur with probabilities $AA: Aa: aa = \frac{1}{4}:\frac{1}{2}:\frac{1}{4}$. (The example is actually concerned with pea plants rather than flies.)

A table showing the probabilities of each offspring genotype for a given mating is given below.

	Male genotype	Female genotype	Probabilities of offspring genotypes		
			AA	Aa	aa
(i)	AA	AA	1	0	0
(ii)	AA Aa	Aa AA	$\frac{1}{2}$ $\frac{1}{2}$	$\frac{1}{2}$ $\frac{1}{2}$	0 0
(iii)	AA aa	aa AA	0 0	1 1	0 0
(iv)	Aa	Aa	$\frac{1}{4}$	$\frac{1}{2}$	$\frac{1}{4}$
(v)	Aa aa	aa Aa	0 0	$\frac{1}{2}$ $\frac{1}{2}$	$\frac{1}{2}$ $\frac{1}{2}$
(vi)	aa	aa	0	0	1

Population genetics is the study of the proportions within populations of the various genotypes and genes (alleles) under different systems of breeding, conditions of selection, etc. The proportion of a particular allele in a population is usually called a "gene frequency". Population genetics lends itself to elegant mathematical modelling but is rarely found outside the Nuffield texts. (In the revised texts it is confined to the *Teachers' Guides*.) A most useful case is that of an infinite population in which the proportion of genotypes is the same for males and females, and mating is random. The distribution of offspring genotypes is the consequence of two stages of random pairing: (i) random pairing of parents; (ii) random pairing of gametes, one from each parent. The table above is concerned with the second stage.

If P, Q, R are the proportions of AA, Aa, aa in the parent generation, then among both males and females the numbers of A and a alleles in existence are proportional to $2P+Q$ and $2R+Q$ respectively. (This is because each AA contributes 2 A-alleles, etc.). Since $(2P+Q)+(2R+Q) = 2(P+Q+R) = 2$, it follows that the proportions of A and a are $P+\frac{1}{2}Q$ and $R+\frac{1}{2}Q$. If $p = P+\frac{1}{2}Q$ and $q = R+\frac{1}{2}Q$, p and q are the *gene frequencies* of A and a in the population.

The probabilities of an individual offspring receiving the A-allele or of receiving the a-allele from his father may be obtained as in the tree diagram below:

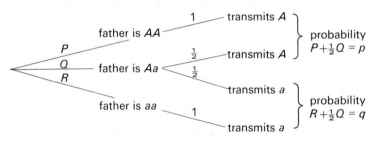

Figure 5.9.

The same probabilities apply to transmission by the mother, since it is assumed here that the genotype proportions P, Q, R are the same for both sexes. If mating is at random, then the father and mother contribute independently. It is thus possible to replace the two-stage random pairing process referred to above by a single-stage random pairing between male genes (A or a) and female genes, with given proportions p, q of A, a within each. A collection of A and a genes available for inheritance is called a *gene pool*.

Random mating may be simulated by a bead model (NB 5, p. 164 ff) in which beads represent male and female genes. Beads of two colours are placed in a container in the proportions $p:q$ to represent the A and a male genes. Another similar container represents the female gene pool. The genotype of an offspring individual is determined when a pair of beads is drawn at random, one from each container. (The model can be modified to take account of selection as when, for example, 80 per cent of a certain genotype do not reach maturity owing to poor adaptation to environment.) (NB 5, p. 185 ff.)

The probabilities of the offspring individual being each of the three genotypes may be calculated in terms of p and q. The results are given in the table below.

Male gene	Female gene	Offspring genotype	Probability
A	A	AA	p^2
A	a	Aa	pq
a	A	Aa	pq
a	a	aa	q^2

The proportions of each genotype in the offspring generation are thus

$$AA:Aa:aa = p^2:2pq:q^2. \tag{1}$$

(Probabilities are equated with proportions in a (large) population.)

In the offspring generation the proportion of A-genes is $p^2 + \frac{1}{2}.2pq = p(p+q) = p$. Similarly the proportion of a-genes is q. Since these remain unchanged, and the genotype proportions in (1) are functions of them, these proportions are constant from the first filial generation onwards, given the conditions of the model. This is the Hardy-Weinberg law.

The Hardy-Weinberg proportions can be used in gene frequency calculations; an example follows from *Biology by Inquiry*, Vol. 3, pp. 132–3. Another example is in *NB 5*, p. 168.

About 60 per cent of the population of this country can roll their tongues, because of the presence in their genotypes of a dominant allelomorph R, and 40 per cent cannot roll their tongues because they have the double recessive allelomorph r for non-tongue-rolling.

Since R is dominant, the tongue-rollers may be either RR or Rr; it is required to find the percentage of each.

If p, q are the frequencies (proportions) of R,r then $RR:Rr:rr = p^2:2pq:q^2$.

But $q^2 = 40$ per cent $= 0.4$

Hence $q = \sqrt{0.4} = 0.6325$

Since $p+q = 1$, it follows that $p = 0.3675$.

Thus the frequency of RR is $p^2 = (0.3675)^2 = 0.135 = 13.5$ per cent

and that of Rr is $2pq = 2 \times 0.3675 \times 0.6325 = 0.465 = 46.5$ per cent

Comment

Note the appearance in this example of the square root of a decimal, and the conversion from percentage to decimal and vice versa. These are mathematical stumbling blocks.

5.10 Field Work

The elementary surveying involved in field work (for example, finding the height of a tree) leads to further mathematics, such as scale drawing and trigonometry, and also to ingenuity in the design of easy-to-use measuring instruments. The instrument shown in figure 5.10 could be calibrated by the pupils them-

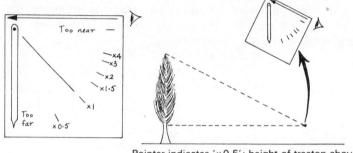

Pointer indicates '×0·5'; height of treetop above level of observer = 0·5 × distance from base.

Figure 5.10   Elementary surveying instrument (from Bishop, *Outdoor Biology*).

selves with the aid of some measured height marks on a vertical wall.

6 Mathematics in Geography

In many quarters geography teaching has been undergoing radical changes in the past few years, and new developments are still being made. Part of the change has been the greater use of quantitative methods, and the study of certain geographical features, such as transportation networks and market regions, which recur all over the globe and are amenable to abstraction from particular context. These form possible elements for model-building with the aim of understanding and, if possible, controlling geographical processes.

It is not part of the purpose of this survey to go into greater detail about the newer thinking behind geography and its teaching. It is hoped that the unfamiliarity of many of the mathematical applications described here will prompt teachers of mathematics to inquire further, and a bibliography is therefore given at the end of the chapter. It must be borne in mind, however, that at present the majority of school geography courses do not include most of the topics described in this survey.

Abbreviations used in chapter 6
OGP   Oxford Geography Project (OUP)
SIG   Science in Geography (OUP)
ITC   Introducing Towns and Cities (Briggs) (ULP)
ITN   Introducing Transportation Networks (Briggs) (ULP)

TOPIC SURVEY

6.1   Scale

The importance of an understanding of scale in the reading and drawing of maps is obvious. The scale of a map is often expressed as a fraction or ratio, and this is referred to as the *representative fraction*. (It is equivalent to the term *scale factor*.) Examples are the ratio 1:50000, where the fraction is $\frac{1}{50000}$, for the Metric O.S. maps (2 cm represent 1 km), and 1:63360, where the fraction is $\frac{1}{63360}$, for the 1 inch to 1 mile O.S. maps.

6.2   Coordinates

The grid-reference system for specifying the location of a place is an example of a Cartesian coordinate system. The origin of the coordinate system on the 1:50000 O.S. maps is situated somewhere near the Scilly Isles; so on any given O.S. map the point in the bottom left-hand corner is not the origin (0,0). This may cause initial difficulty for children whose only experience of coordinate systems has been of those with visible axes, and origin placed in the bottom left-hand corner.

The two coordinates are *eastings* and *northings*. On the 1:50000 maps grid lines occur at 1-km intervals (on the ground); tenths of a kilometre have to be measured or estimated separately. A point whose grid reference is 363242 has easting 36·3 km and northing 24·2 km. Grid references are given as six-figure numbers (or, occasionally, four-figure numbers, where tenths of a kilometre are omitted and all points of a square of side 1 km are specified by the reference) and thus contain no note of *hundreds* of kilometres. The point 363242 could be at (536·3, 224·2) or (936·3, 724·2), etc. Although the hundreds are printed on the edges of the maps, the normal method of giving a reference if the region under discussion is not clear from the context, is to give the grid letters of the map. Thus Trafalgar Square has full reference TQ 301805.

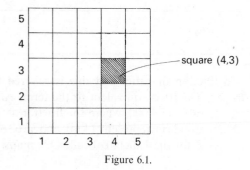

Figure 6.1.

It is worth noting that the Ordnance Survey Grid is a coordinate system in the proper sense in that it specifies points rather than squares. Children are often introduced to coordinate systems by means of examples which use coordinates to specify squares, as in figure 6.1

This system is used in, for example, the "A to Z" maps and town guides. Four-figure O.S. grid references are often used to refer to squares rather than points.

6.3   Bearings

The use of bearings in specifying relative locations occurs particularly in surveying, which is a component of some geography courses. The difference between compass bearings and polar coordinate bearings can cause confusion. (The relationship between them gives an interesting graph.)

6.4   Spherical Geometry: Great Circles, Latitude and Longitude, etc.

These topics, formerly of great importance in geography, are

comparatively neglected nowadays, although they are included in some mathematics syllabuses.

The calculation of the distance between two points on the same circle of latitude, measured along the circle (parallel) of latitude, compared with the distance between the corresponding pair of points on the equator (i.e. with the same longitudes as the first pair), aids the understanding of the distortion involved in Mercator's Projection, in which these two distances are represented as equal (figure 6.2).

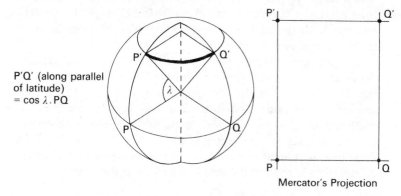

$P'Q'$ (along parallel of latitude) $= \cos \lambda . PQ$

Mercator's Projection

Figure 6.2   Mercator's map projection.

6.5   Map Projections

The general principles and problems of map projection are an interesting mathematical topic (also now neglected in "O" Level geography) but the detailed working out of the transformation equations for points, local angles, local distances and local areas often involves trigonometry beyond the scope of an "O" Level course.

The curved surface of a cone or cylinder can be flattened out. In the case of the cone, a sector of a circle is formed, and in the case of the cylinder a rectangle. Map projections are classified as zenithal, conical or cylindrical, according as the points of the spherical earth are mapped onto a plane, a cone, or a cylinder. In the last two cases the map is obtained when the surface is developed (flattened out).

Mercator's projection (widely used but highly distorting) is a cylindrical projection. A cylindrical surface is placed round the globe touching it round the equator. The meridians are represented by parallel lines at right angles to the equator. As shown opposite, at latitude λ the scale of the map in the direction parallel to the equator is such that the true distance is $\cos \lambda$ times that shown on the map. The latitude (vertical) scale at this height is chosen so that the distortion factor in this direction is the same. (It follows that the true area at this point is $\cos^2 \lambda$ times that shown on the map.) The consequence of this choice is that the angle on the map between a path and a meridian at their point of intersection is the same as the true angle on the globe. For this reason maps employing Mercator's projection are useful in navigation.

From the mathematician's point of view, map projections are interesting as practical examples of transformations. By the term *transformation* is meant a one-to-one correspondence between points in one set (say the earth's surface) and points in another (a map of that surface). Certain properties of the original set of points are also properties of the corresponding points in the map. Any such properties are said to be *invariant* under the transformation. The angle between a path through a point and the meridian through that point is an invariant under the transformation known as Mercator's projection. Other types of map may have different invariants: for example, the relative sizes (ratio) of any two areas may be invariant.

6.6 Contour Maps, Gradient

Pupils who are introduced to gradients in the form "1 in n" often continue to use this form in later mathematical work where it is not appropriate. It would be an advantage if the method of expressing a gradient as a fraction or decimal were introduced at the same time.

Pupils need to be able to "read" a contour map, to be able to determine the (average) gradient between two points represented on such a map and to be able to draw the profile of a vertical section. In drawing such profiles it is necessary to use a larger scale for vertical distances ("vertical exaggeration"). Contour maps are a special case of a more general class of map, called *isopleth maps*, considered below.

6.7 Statistical Tables, Graphs and Diagrams

There is no limit to the potential use of graphs to illustrate statistical data in geography. The percentage protractor for constructing pie charts has been mentioned before (p. 10), and is clearly useful in this context. Familiarity with percentage is needed early in geography courses. Pie charts, whether representing percentages or otherwise, involve some quite difficult mathematical concepts such as proportion, and teachers often try to introduce them too early.

Circles of different sizes are often used to represent quantities for comparison, with, possibly, each circle broken down as a pie chart. In order that the area of the circle should be proportional to the quantity represented, it is necessary for the quantity to be proportional to the square of the radius, i.e. the radius has to be proportional to the square root of the quantity.

Sometimes it is a circle and a surrounding annulus which

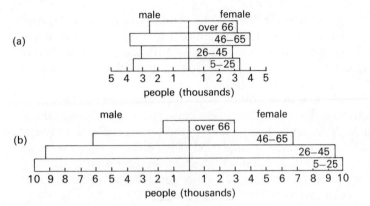

Figure 6.3   Age-sex pyramids for (a) Hemel Hempstead, (b) Christchurch (Rolfe *et al.*, *Oxford Geography Project*, *Book 1*, p. 102).

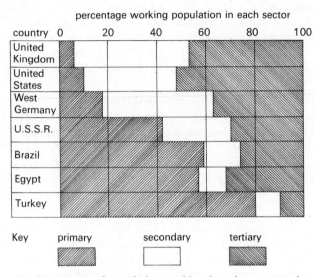

Figure 6.4   Percentages of population working in primary, secondary and tertiary sectors of industry (primary industries provide materials for secondary, or manufacturing, industries; tertiary industries comprise services) (Rolfe *et al.*, *Oxford Geography Project*, *Book 3*, p. 24).

represent two quantities, for example the population of a city and that of its surrounding hinterland.

An understanding of the proportionalities involved is necessary for the construction of such diagrams, but also for the criticism of misleading diagrams, which are not unknown in the literature (see, for example, W. J. Reichmann: *Use and Abuse of Statistics* (Penguin 1964)).

Figures 6.3 and 6.4 are examples of statistical diagrams.

6.8   Use of Graphs in Formulating a Model

In the early nineteenth century, von Thünen put forward a model for land use round a market centre. The understanding of the derivation of the model from certain stated assumptions is aided by the use of graphs of certain functions involved.

The profitability of a certain crop and therefore the price or rent which one is prepared to pay for land to grow it, depends to

some extent on the type of crop and how it is affected by the distance it has to be transported to the market. For instance, perishable products might be highly profitable near the centre, yet not worth producing a long way away from the market. Von Thünen considered the highly simplified model of an isolated state with one market centre in land of uniform productivity, where cost of transportation is proportional to distance. For each type of crop, the graph of profitability against distance from centre would in a simple case be a downward sloping line (figure 6.5(i)). Some crops will be highly profitable near the centre, but with profitability very sensitive to distance; others less profitable, but not

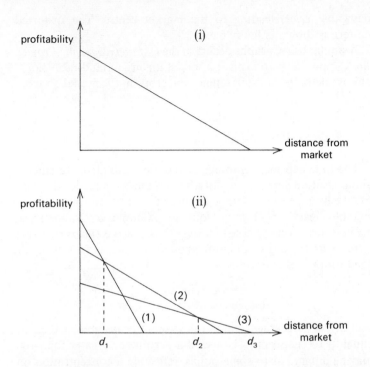

so sensitive. The resulting composite graph for, say, three crops, would then be as in figure 6.5(ii) (which is a graph of a type familiar from linear programming).

Assuming that it is the most highly profitable crop (i.e. the one which bids the highest price for land) which is actually grown at any given distance from the market, it follows that up to distance d_1, crop (1) will be grown; from d_1 to d_2, crop (2); from d_2 to d_3, crop (3). So the pattern of land use will be as in figure 6.5(iii).

It is of interest to note how the basic pattern derived from the model is likely to be altered by the existence of one superior channel of communication (such as a good road, or a

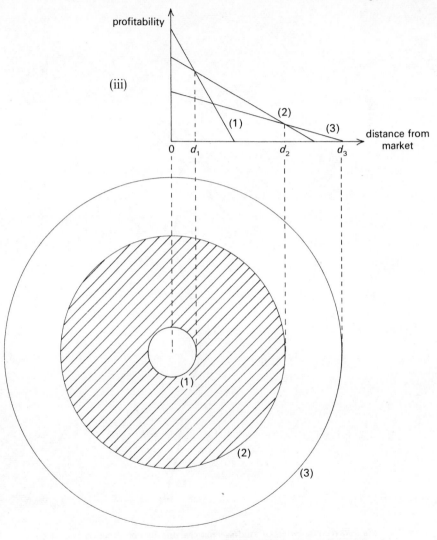

Fig. 6.5   Pattern of land use round a market centre (von Thünen's model).

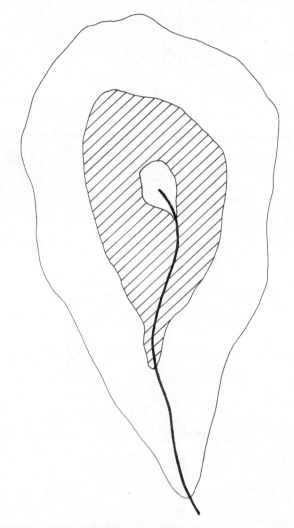

Figure 6.6   Distortion of land-use pattern due to one superior line of communication.

navigable river) leading to the market centre. The distorted
pattern is shown in figure 6.6.

A similar use of graphs occurs in the *Oxford Geography Project*,
Book 3, pp. 68–9, to explain a model for urban land-use; shops/
offices, factories, housing replace the crops in the model above.

6.9   Indices, Percentage

The first step in attempting to replace qualitative statements
about relationships by quantitative statements is to decide what
to take as a measure of some feature of interest. In some cases a
suitable measure is fairly obvious: for example, geographers use
a *detour index* (in the case of a river, it is called a *sinuosity index*)
to measure the degree of indirectness of a route, say a railway or
road route. It is defined as

$$\frac{\text{distance via route}}{\text{distance in a straight line}} \times 100,$$

is clearly a percentage, and in this case is always greater than or
equal to 100 per cent. (The use of a percentage greater than 100
may be unfamiliar to some pupils, reflecting a concentration on
percentages as "fractions" in mathematics lessons.) For a straight
journey over hill terrain a *relief index* (Howling and Hunter,
Mapping Skills and Techniques, Oliver and Boyd) may be defined
as

$$\left(\frac{\text{surface distance}}{\text{straight-line distance}} \times 100\right) - 100.$$

This index is difficult and time-consuming to use in practice, a
simpler one being defined by

$$\frac{\text{number of contour intervals } (=\text{number of contour lines crossed}+1)}{\text{length of section}}$$

To obtain a relief index for a given region it is possible to average the indices for three sections of the region chosen at random or in some other way.

In studies of the location of industry, a *location quotient* (see e.g. *OGP 2*, pp. 90–1) for a given industry is used, defined as

$$\frac{\text{percentage of local population engaged in the industry}}{\text{percentage of national population engaged in it}}$$

In *Geography for the Young School Leaver* the *job ratio* of an area is defined by

$$\frac{\text{number of people working in the area}}{\text{number of people living in the area}} \times 100\%$$

In other cases the problem of defining a suitable index may be more complex, and may lead to several different suggested indices. Where the feature to be measured does not involve conceptual difficulties, it is an interesting exercise to ask pupils to devise their own indices, and then compare and criticize results. This can be done for an *index of compactness* of a shape (e.g. the shape of a county or country). The indices already mentioned are not above criticism. For instance, the relief index based on contour intervals may not be a good one for undulating country.

Several *indices of compactness* have been used in geography. Among them are*:

(1) $$\frac{\text{area of shape}}{\text{area of smallest circle enclosing shape}} \times 100\%$$

(2) $$\frac{\text{lenght of longest axis of shape}}{\text{length of axis which bisects longest axis at right angles}} \times 100\%$$

The first of these takes the value 100 per cent for a circle alone, the most compact shape, whereas the second is 100 per cent for many non-circular shapes, including a square.

*(1) R. Walford (ed.), *New Directions in Geography Teaching*, p. 141.
(2) W. V. Tidswell & S. M. Barker, *Quantitative Methods*, p. 61.

An *index of scatter* for the major towns or cities in a region or country is defined by Briggs in *Introducing Towns and Cities*, pp. 57–8 as follows:

First the mean centre of the locations of the towns is calculated by averaging eastings and northings based on a grid, superimposed if necessary, on a map of the region. The distance of each town from the mean centre is obtained by measurement on the map. (It may also be obtained using Pythagoras' theorem.) From these distances a mean distance is obtained. The index of scatter is defined by

$$\frac{\text{area of circle whose radius is mean distance of towns from mean centre}}{\text{area of region}} \times 100\%$$

These are only some of many indices which have been used in school geography. Others arise in connection with topics dealt with below, and are mentioned in context.

6.10 Functions of Location, Spatial Distributions, Isopleth Maps, Loci

Geography is very much concerned with the variation in certain measures over the earth's surface, or over limited regions of it. The variation of height above sea-level and the resulting contour maps have already been referred to. Other well-known examples of functions of location are annual rainfall, average seasonal temperature, average atmospheric pressure for a given month. Each of these functions can be represented by, or thought of as, a surface, drawn above a map of the region of definition in such a way that its height represents the value of the measure at a particular location. The contour lines corresponding to such a surface are called *isopleths*; each isopleth goes through points of the region for which the function value is the same. (In the case of temperature, the isopleths are called *isotherms*, for pressure *isobars*.) The purpose of an isopleth map is to give a two-dimensional representation of a function of location which draws attention in particular to the regions of high and low values, and the gradient, or rate, at which the function changes with change of location.

An interesting case of an isopleth map results from a consideration of the journey time saved when a motorway is constructed. If it is supposed that journeys from a certain point A to surrounding points may either be along ordinary roads or a fixed length of motorway followed by ordinary roads, then (given certain assumptions about the mode of travel in each case) it is possible to plot the function "time saved when travelling from A using the motorway". One such set of assumptions used by Briggs in *Introducing Transportation Networks* is this:

(*a*) Travel on the motorway is at 100 km/h; on ordinary roads at 50 km/h.
(*b*) Travel on ordinary roads may be considered to be in a straight line from start to finish.

In figure 6.7, A is the starting point for journeys, and AB is a straight motorway of length 50 km. The continuously drawn circles show the points reached from A in 30, 45, 60 min, etc., using ordinary roads only, whilst the dotted circles show points reached from A using the motorway, followed by ordinary roads. The motorway has no exits between A and B.

The zero isopleth (equal journey times) has been drawn. (The isopleths are hyperbolae). Other isopleths, representing different values for the time saved by using the motorway may also be plotted.

Briggs gives several interesting examples of variations of this basic scheme, including a map showing the contribution of the M6 motorway to accessibility in part of the North Midlands (*ITN*, pp. 43–48).

One particular type of function of location which merits special consideration is much used in geography. Given a spatial distribution of points (representing, say, farms, or road-junctions) it

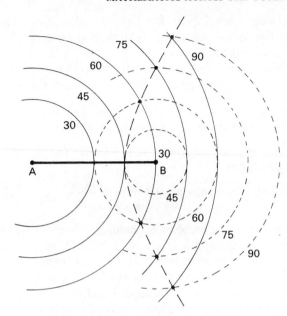

Figure 6.7   Travel times using and not using a motorway.

is possible to ask how the *areal density* (measured in points per unit area) varies in the region under examination. The problems involved in mapping densities in two-dimensional spatial distributions are a natural extension of the problems raised by one-dimensional distributions, which are here considered first.

As a first stage towards constructing a histogram of, say, the heights of 20 boys, we may mark the heights on a linear scale.

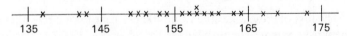

If the class-interval chosen is too large (in the extreme case 40 cm!), the obvious concentration of points in the centre of the interval does not appear in the distribution. If a very small class-interval is chosen (say 1 cm), the point distribution is merely replaced by a distribution of small rectangles exactly reproducing the point-distribution.

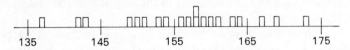

If a class-interval of 10 cm is decided upon, the histogram appears as below.

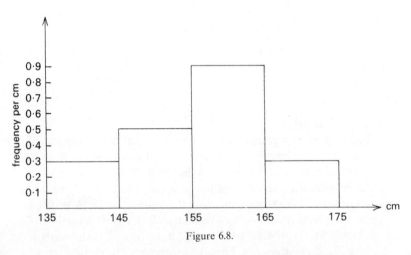

Figure 6.8.

In a histogram the *area* represents frequency, and hence the unit on the vertical scale is "frequency per cm", or "number of crosses per cm" if reference is made to the original representation of heights as crosses on a line.

If it is now supposed that the crosses on the line represent starlings sitting on a telephone wire, the vertical scale of the histogram represents population density in birds per unit length.

However, in the geographical case (in which the only difference is that the distribution of crosses or dots is a two-dimensional one), it is required to plot the density as a function defined at a *point*, rather than over an interval. For the one-dimensional example above, two ways of doing this suggest themselves:

(*a*) Plot a cumulative-frequency graph first. For the distribution of starlings it would appear as below.

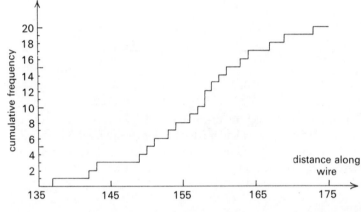

Draw a continuous graph through the vertex-points of this graph, and use the gradient of the resulting graph as a measure of population density (see page 92).

This method, particularly its two-dimensional version, is prohibitively difficult and time-consuming, and is not used.

(*b*) It is misleading to regard the population density (as shown by the histogram above) as being constant for 10 cm, then constant, but at a higher value for another 10 cm, and so on. To find the population density at a given point on the line, take

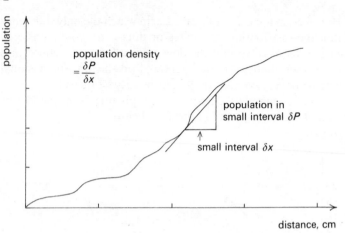

Figure 6.9.

One simple way of plotting this moving average is to make a cardboard "window" whose length is that of the interval chosen, and move it along the line, recording above it on a graph the population density as a function of the position of the midpoint of the window.

It is now necessary to consider how this method is to be adapted to deal with a two-dimensional distribution of crosses.

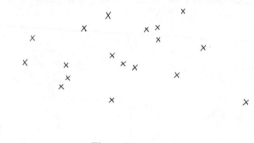

Figure 6.11.

that point as the centre of an interval (not too large, not too small; say 5 cm) and calculate density for the interval. The density function thus obtained is a "moving average": the interval corresponding to one point will overlap others for nearby points.

The density is measured in "crosses per unit area", instead of "crosses per unit length", so we need a window of a suitable area. One consideration is the shape of the window. In one dimension an interval is used centred on the point at which the density is being measured. The two-dimensional analogue is a circle centred upon the given point; being symmetrical, it covers exactly the same region no matter which way it is turned. (Although a square window does not have this property, it is simpler to construct and use.)

If a circular window is to be used, its radius needs to be chosen in such a way that the area it represents is a convenient one for the density calculation. This clearly involves an application of $A = \pi r^2$ in reverse.

It is impossible in the case of a spatial distribution to find the density at every point. A grid is drawn and the density found at grid points. From the results isopleths may be drawn. (If it has

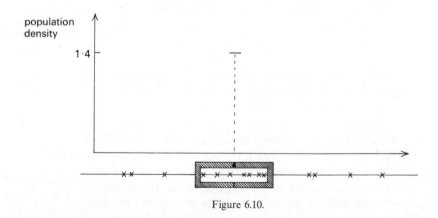

Figure 6.10.

been decided to use a square window, the squares of the grid itself are taken as successive positions of the window, giving density values at the centres of the squares.)

An example of the use of the circular window is to be found in *Introducing Transportation Networks*. A suggested measure of road density is "the number of road junctions per km^2" (*ITN*, pp. 27–9), it being prohibitively time-consuming to find the length of road per km^2. The radius of the circle is chosen so that it represents an area of 500 km^2. (The counting system proposed by Briggs is open to objections. A junction like $+$ counts 1, but one like $\vdash$ counts 2, even though the connecting link between the two junctions in the latter case may be minute.)

6.11 Time-Distance and Cost-Distance Maps

Often the distance between two places is of less importance than the time taken to cover the journey—as is the case, for example, on a railway system. It is then of interest to draw a map in which the distance between two points on the map represents (is proportional to) the journey time. Such a map emphasizes the relative remoteness of certain places, insufficiently brought out by an ordinary map. A similar procedure can be carried out for journey costs.

Figure 6.12 is reproduced from B. P. Fitzgerald: *Science in Geography*, Vol.1, p. 49. It shows a time-distance map of Britain using British Rail fastest train times from London as the basis (for the year 1968).

This map is drawn in such a way that the *bearing* of each town from London is correctly represented, but the distance represents travel time. As a result the map is not correct as a representation of either travel times or bearings from any starting point other than London.

In the case of a railway line with intermediate local stations,

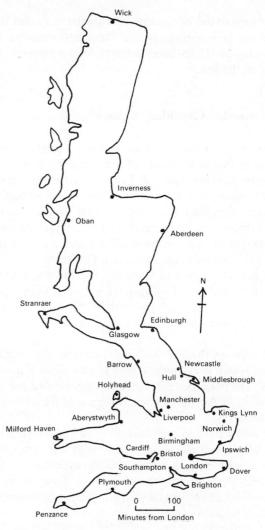

Figure 6.12   Time-distance transformed map of Britain using the fastest train times from London.

the travel time to one of these may be greater than that to a more distant main-line station. Hence the transformation from an ordinary map to a time-distance map does not preserve the order of points on the line.

Figure 6.13   A network with three components.

6.12   Networks: Graphical Aspects[1]

In *Introducing Transportation Networks*, Briggs explains the terminology used in the study of networks. With one exception this introductory material will be familiar to those acquainted with *SMP*, where it is to be found in *Book 2* and in *Book C*. The equivalence of graphs is dealt with, and the various elements in a network: vertices (or nodes; classified as 2-nodes, 3-nodes, etc.); edges (links, arcs); regions (faces). The departure from the treatment in *SMP* occurs in the restriction that there may be at most one link between a pair of vertices. (The interest is in whether vertices are linked or not—not in the nature or number of links.) A *circuit* is defined as a closed path starting and ending at the same vertex; a *fundamental circuit* as a circuit not containing any other circuits.

The discussion throughout is restricted to *planar* graphs, i.e. graphs for which every intersection of two edges is a vertex (no "flyovers" are permitted). A network may be *directed* and may contain *components* (figure 6.13). (Briggs uses the term *subgraphs* for *components*.)

Other terms defined and used are: *null graph* (one with no links at all), *connected graphs* (one with no vertex isolated), *complete graph* (one with a link between every pair of vertices), *tree* (a connected graph without circuits), *spanning tree* (a tree which connects all vertices leaving no disconnected components).

The *matrix* corresponding to a given network is defined. Because of the restriction on links mentioned above, all network matrices will be binary matrices (i.e. contain 1s and 0s only). It follows that if M is a network matrix, M^2 will not necessarily be one as well; the information contained in M^2, M^3, etc., is not used in Briggs's book, but geographers have made use of it (see, e.g., Haggett and Chorley: *Network Analysis in Geography*, pp. 38–40.)

Two rules connecting the numbers of edges and vertices are required for an understanding of some of the indices used in the study of networks. The first states that the minimum number of edges for all vertices to be linked (either directly or indirectly) is $V-1$, where V is the number of vertices. The network is then a spanning tree (*minimum spanning tree* in *SMP*). Any more edges than $V-1$ would lead to a circuit somewhere. The second rule states that the maximum number of edges is $3(V-2)$. Both formulae are illustrated by examples in Briggs's book, but not proved.

CONNECTIVITY

Geographers are interested in the degree of connectedness in a network, and several indices of connectivity have been used to measure connectedness. It would be a worthwhile exercise to pose to pupils the problem of how to measure connectivity before introducing the standard formulae.

[1] *Graphical* is the correct term, although the word *topological* has been used both in mathematical and graphical texts. For a fuller discussion of networks and graph theory and possible applications to geography and other subjects, see *Counting and Configurations*, a book in this series.

Indices of connectivity

1. Beta Index

$$\text{Beta index} = \frac{\text{number of edges } E}{\text{number of vertices } V}$$

The Beta index is less than 1 for a tree and equal to 1 for a connected graph with one circuit.

2. Cyclomatic Number

The cyclomatic number is the number of fundamental circuits. Since the number of edges needed to form a spanning tree is $V-1$, the difference between the actual number of edges E and $V-1$ is the number of fundamental circuits.

Thus the cyclomatic number is

$$E-(V-1) = E-V+1$$

Each fundamental circuit encloses a region. If we add to the number of regions so formed the region outside the graph, we obtain the total number R of regions. It follows that the cyclomatic number is equal to $R-1$. Equating this with the formula $E-V+1$ given above, leads to Euler's formula $V+R-E=2$. In the case of a network with G separate components the formula for the cyclomatic number is $E-V+G$.

3. Alpha Index

$$\text{Alpha index} = \frac{\text{cyclomatic number}}{\text{maximum possible cyclomatic number for the given number of vertices}}$$

The maximum number of edges, given V vertices, is $3(V-2)$. So the maximum cyclomatic number is $3(V-2)-V+1$ or $2V-5$. Hence

$$\text{Alpha index} = \frac{E-V+1}{2V-5}$$

ACCESSIBILITY

A study of accessibility of vertices within a connected non-directed network starts from the *shortest-path matrix*, in which the entry (P,Q) is the number of links in the shortest path (measured in links) from P to Q. In this approach no account is taken of the *distance* between vertices, distance (whether measured as actual distance, time-distance or cost-distance) being a non-graphical concept.

The *König number* (Briggs uses the term *associated number*) of a vertex P is the greatest "distance" (measured in links) to another vertex. It is thus the largest entry in row P (or column P) of the shortest-path matrix.

Briggs uses the mean König number, defined as

$$\frac{\text{total of all König numbers}}{\text{number of vertices}}$$

as a measure of the general level of accessibility. For a given network drawn on a map it is possible to exhibit the pattern of accessibility by isopleths—in this case contours of equal accessibility (König number). Care must be taken in the interpretation of such a diagram (see figure 6.16). Accessibility is not defined for points other than the vertices of the graph.

The *Shimbel index* (called the Vertex Accessibility Number by Haggett and Chorley, *Network Analysis in Geography*, p. 46) for a given vertex P is defined as the row-total of P in the shortest-path matrix. Other measures of general accessibility are the *dispersion index* (the total of all entries in the shortest-path matrix, and hence equal to the sum of all the Shimbel indices), and the mean Shimbel index, defined as

$$\frac{\text{dispersion index}}{\text{number of vertices}}.$$

An index very similar to the Shimbel index described here has been used to measure the centrality of a position in a network of communication links between individual people. In *Human Groups* (Penguin, 1958), pp. 125–6, W. J. H. Sprott considers the four networks illustrated in figure 6.14.

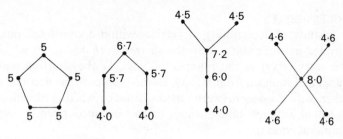

Figure 6.14.

The index used (the values are shown on the diagram) is

$$\frac{\text{total of all entries in shortest-path matrix}}{\text{row total in matrix}}, \text{ i.e. } \frac{\text{dispersion index}}{\text{Shimbel index}}.$$

(*a*) Shortest-path matrix, König numbers, Shimbel indices.

	A	B	C	D	E	F	K.N.	S.I.
A	0	3	1	2	2	3	3	11
B	3	0	2	1	2	2	3	10
C	1	2	0	1	1	2	2	7
D	2	1	1	0	1	1	2	6
E	2	2	1	1	0	1	2	7
F	3	2	2	1	1	0	3	9
Totals							15	50

$$\text{Mean König number} = \frac{15}{6} = 2 \cdot 5$$

$$\text{Mean Shimbel index} = \frac{50}{6} = 8 \cdot 3$$

(*b*) Isopleth Map (Shimbel indices) (figure 6.16)

WORKED EXAMPLE

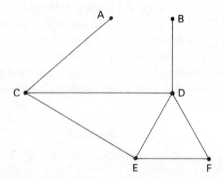

Figure 6.15.

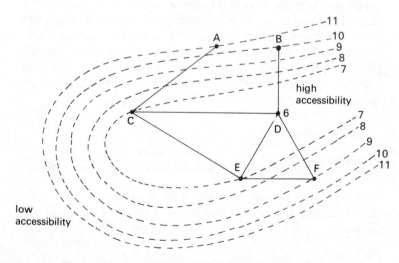

Figure 6.16   Accessibility within a network—an isopleth map.

Briggs also discusses the effect on accessibility of adding further edges to a network, and the relative importance of edges in relation to shortest paths. (One edge may be a part of many shortest paths, and hence be particularly important to the general accessibility of the network.)

6.13   Matrices

In addition to the binary matrices described above, geography makes use of matrices to show distances, journey times, journey costs, traffic flows, etc., between pairs of places. It is possible to construct examples in which two matrices whose entries are both, say, journey times, are subtracted (for example, to find the change in journey time between 1876 and 1976, or before and after the construction of a motorway) or added, but matrix multiplication has not as yet found any significant application at the school level. Much more common is the division of corresponding entries in two matrices to yield a matrix of quotients, rates or indices. For example, this operation applied to the distance-by-road matrix and the straight-line-distance matrix (except for the zero entries on the diagonal!) yields a matrix of detour indices.

6.14   Mathematical Models: Algebraic Models

The degree of interaction (e.g. traffic flow, volume of telephone calls, etc.) between two towns would appear to depend positively on the populations of the towns, but be affected inversely or negatively by the distance between them. The analogy between this situation and the law of gravitation in physics has led geographers to experiment with "gravity models" for interaction. In such a model the interaction I between towns with popula-tions P_1 and P_2, whose distance apart (or journey time, or journey cost) is d, is given by a relation of the form

$$I \propto \frac{P_1 P_2}{d^n}$$

Two particular cases are of special interest, and are easy to compute, namely $n = 1$, $n = 2$, but the question whether either of these, or indeed any, values of n results in a model which to a reasonable degree of accuracy represents some real-life situation can only be answered empirically.

One of these models, if accepted as accurate, may be used to calculate theoretical values of the relative interactions between real towns in place of actual measurements, which may be difficult to collect. The calculated "data" may then be used as a basis for geographical discussion. Alternatively, the model can be used to aid the planning of new transport networks—for example, in allowing an order of priority for road building to be established. It is exercises of these two kinds, rather than the checking of the model against known data for traffic-flow, which figure in school geography (e.g. Briggs *ITC*, pp. 59 ff; *OGP 2*, pp. 114–5.). The computation involved can be heavy unless shared out or done on an electronic calculator. The interactions between towns may be represented on a map by flow bands whose widths are proportional to the flow.

WORKED EXAMPLE

Distances are given in units of 10 km and populations (in brackets) in 1000s. The model

$$I = \frac{P_1 P_2}{d^2}$$

is used to calculate interactions.

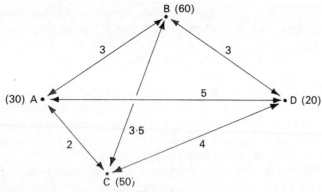

Figure 6.17.

Interaction Matrix

	A	B	C	D
A	—	200	375	24
B	200	—	245	133
C	375	245	—	63
D	24	133	63	—

(The interaction between a town and itself is not covered by the model).

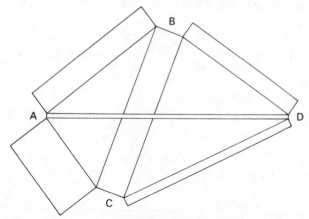

Figure 6.18   Traffic-flow diagram.

One particular deduction from the inverse-square law is known as Reilly's Law of Retail Gravitation.[1] This law has been used to delineate the boundary of the trade areas of two neighbouring towns.

On the gravitational-model assumption that the *pull*[2] of a town at distance x from it is proportional to P/x^2, where P is the population of the town, then there is a point somewhere on the line joining two towns, of populations P_1 and P_2, where the "pulls" of the two towns are equal. If x is the distance of this point from the town with population P_1 and d is the distance between the two towns, then x satisfies

$$\frac{P_1}{x^2} = \frac{P_2}{(d-x)^2}$$

$$\therefore \quad \frac{(d-x)^2}{x^2} = \frac{P_2}{P_1}$$

$$\therefore \quad \frac{d-x}{x} = \sqrt{\frac{P_2}{P_1}}$$

$$\therefore \quad \frac{d}{x} - 1 = \sqrt{\frac{P_2}{P_1}}$$

$$\therefore \quad \frac{d}{x} = 1 + \sqrt{\frac{P_2}{P_1}}$$

$$\therefore \quad x = \frac{d}{1 + \sqrt{\dfrac{P_2}{P_1}}}$$

This formula states Reilly's Law.

[1] This has so far, to our knowledge, appeared only in books for sixth form use and beyond, in each case without any algebraic derivation from the gravity model.
[2] This falling off with distance is a case of what geographers refer to generally as the "friction of distance".

6.15 A Geometrical Model: Central Place Theory
(due to W. Christaller)

If it is assumed that each of several towns acts as a "service centre" for a surrounding region—its "market region"—and that the radius of each region is the same for each town, the "packing" shown in figure 6.19(i) is not as good as that in (ii), since the latter leaves a smaller area unserved.

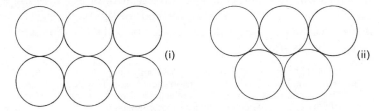

Figure 6.19 Two "packings" of equal circles.

In order that the gaps in (ii) may be filled, the circles may be overlapped as in figure 6.20(i). If each area of overlap is bisected, the final theoretical configuration of market regions is a hexagonal tessellation (figure 6.20(ii)).

Each side of a hexagon is the perpendicular bisector of the line joining two centres. Each hexagon includes that part of the plane

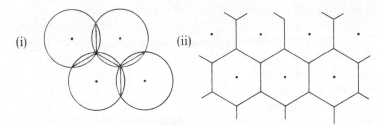

Figure 6.20 Hexagonal tessellation of market regions.

which is nearer to one service centre than any other.

In central place theory, service centres are classified according to the levels of services provided. Higher-level services, such as legal services, in order to be viable require greater market regions than lower-order services, such as food shops. The hexagonal tessellation may be used as the basis for other hexagonal tessellations using larger hexagons. Figure 6.21 shows the theoretical boundaries of market regions for centres of orders 3, 2, and 1, which may be called *cities*, *towns* and *villages*. Note that a town also serves as a village, and a city also serves as a town and village.

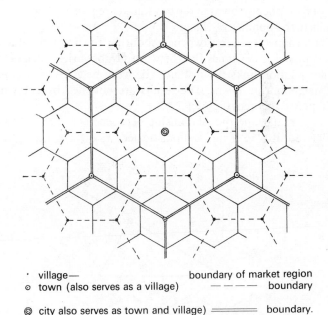

- · village—
- ⊙ town (also serves as a village)
- ◎ city also serves as town and village)

- boundary of market region
- - - - - boundary
- ═══ boundary.

Figure 6.21 A hierarchy of market centres and regions.

The areas served by each type of centre are (using the smallest hexagon as a unit)

Village: 1 hexagon
Town: 3 hexagons (1 hexagon + 6 × $\frac{1}{3}$ hexagon)
City: 9 hexagons (7 hexagons + 6 × $\frac{1}{3}$ hexagon).

The numbers of each type in a large area would be in the proportions 9:3:1. This may also be obtained by direct counting, and the procedure is analogous to the atom-counting procedure for a crystal building block (see page 61). The market region of the city in figure 6.21 contains 1 city; this city also counts as a town. Another six towns are on the boundary, but for each of these only $\frac{1}{3}$ of its market region is included in the city region. Hence the total number of towns in the city market region is $1 + 6 \times \frac{1}{3} = 3$. Similarly the number of villages is $7 + 6 \times \frac{1}{3} = 9$.

The distance between two neighbouring towns in this theoretical model is $\sqrt{3}$ times that between neighbouring villages. A similar relation links the distances between neighbouring cities and neighbouring towns. The results are obtained by applying Pythagoras' theorem (figure 6.22).

These results, and the relationship between market areas, may be derived also in a more sophisticated way. Each hexagonal

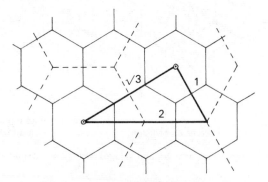

Figure 6.22 Inter-centre distances.

tessellation is constructed from the tessellation of immediate lower order in the same way. Thus the area factor of 3 is preserved: the areas increase in geometrical progression. It follows that the distance between corresponding points increases each time by a factor of $\sqrt{3}$.

When the central place model and the deductions drawn from it are to be compared with reality, some way has to be found of identifying the villages, towns and cities of the model among the settlements in the real region being investigated. Briggs in *Introducing Towns and Cities* gives two methods of allotting *centrality indices* to actual centres, prior to an attempted classification into villages, towns, etc.

(1) Centrality Index = number of shops + (5 × number of professional services).
(2) First decide which establishments (stores, gas board showrooms, etc.) are to be used as basis of index. From telephone directory obtain for each a *centrality value* = 100/number of occurrences in region.
    For each settlement, centrality index = sum of centrality values for establishments represented.

(There is a degree of arbitrariness involved in the construction of a centrality index. If the model turns out to fit the real data well, this may be because of the particular choice of index. In fact the conclusions reached by Briggs in his example of Anglesey's central places are very little affected by changing the factor of 5 in his first index to 10.)

The model predicts discontinuities in the distribution of centrality indices; according to it, central places fall into a number of discrete "orders"—villages, towns, cities, and possibly higher orders. In order to see whether such discontinuities occur in the distribution of the observed centrality indices, a graph of centrality index against rank order may be plotted. If the model is obeyed, there will be jumps in this graph of the type shown in figure 6.23. The jumps can then be used to partition the places into centres of decreasing orders. Another method of partitioning is to calculate the percentage jumps in centrality index as we

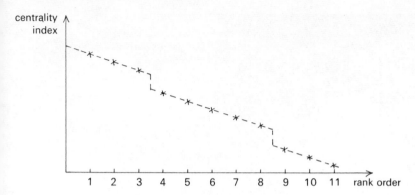

Figure 6.23   Distribution of observed centrality indices.

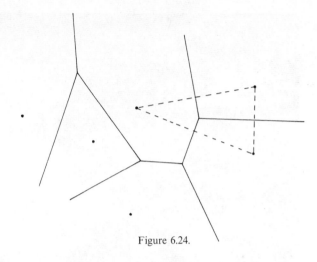

Figure 6.24.

move up the list from lowest to highest index. Large percentage jumps can be used to mark off the boundaries of the groups.

The next prediction of the model which may be checked against reality concerns the proportions of centres of each order. The model predicts that there are 3 times as many centres of order $n-1$ as there are of order n. (It has to be remembered at this stage that each centre of a given order also counts as a centre of every order less than its own.)

A third prediction of the model is the configuration of the centres and the boundaries of market regions (figure 6.21). This is harder to check, as it is difficult if not impossible to delineate the actual boundaries of market regions in a real country or county. Recourse may be had to some simplifying theoretical technique, of which the easiest is to delimit as the market region for each centre the region of points nearer to that centre than to any other. This results in an interesting locus problem, and the resulting configuration exhibits the fact that the three perpendicular bisectors of the sides of a triangle are concurrent (figure 6.24).

6.16   Optimization Problems: Linear Programming

Linear programming has been of interest to economic geographers for many years. In fact the first applications of the technique were to the problem of minimizing transportation costs between a set of suppliers of components and a set of users. The topic has not so far been in evidence in school geography, even though it is included in some "O" Level mathematics courses (including *SMP*). It is true that the graphical solution of linear programming problems—and this is the method of solution most easily understood and hence used in schools—necessitates restricting the problems discussed to those with only two variables. This results in artificiality, but even so an appreciation of the method and the type of problem solvable by it is a worthwhile objective.

Another optimization problem and its relation to Snell's law in optics are discussed on page 48.

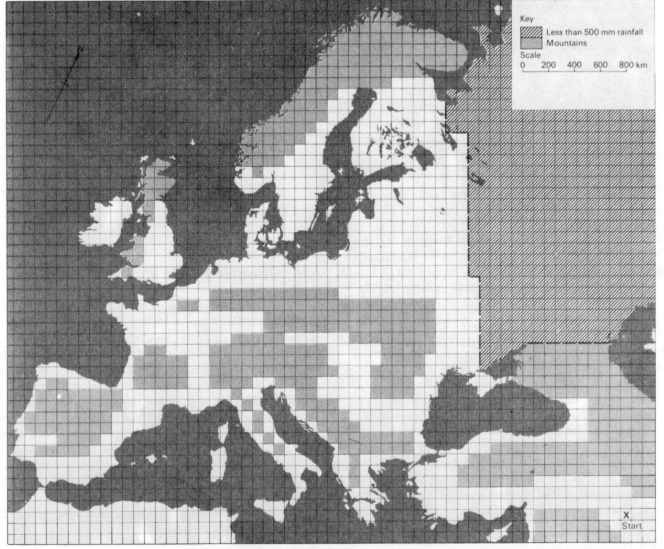

Figure 6.25   Base map for the Neolithic Game (from Rolfe *et al.*, *Oxford Geography Project*, *Book 2*, p. 16).

6.17 Arithmetic and Geometric Progressions

In the study of population growth an important place is held by the theory of Malthus, which states that population tends to increase in geometrical progression, whilst the supply of food tends to increase in arithmetical progression. These progressions, and their corresponding graphs, are dealt with in *Oxford Geography Project*, *Book 3*, chapter 2.

6.18 Random Numbers: Simulation

Random numbers can be used in the simulation of processes in which the transition from one stage to the next is not determined but is governed by probabilities (a *stochastic process*). An instance of such a process is the gradual spread of men or tribes (or ideas) over a region. A number of games which simulate diffusion using random numbers have been designed for use in schools. The example outlined here (the "Neolithic Game") is to be found in *Book 2* of the *Oxford Geography Project* (p. 16). It simulates the spread of people across Europe.

The map of Europe is covered by a grid of squares. (Some other games use a hexagonal grid.) Some of the squares are characterized as mountainous, or particularly dry in climate, and this affects the consequences of landing on them (figure 6.25). In other games each square may be ascribed a total "score" representing the overall effect of desirable and undesirable features it has; deciding which features are desirable or undesirable, and how they should be scored, may in fact be part of the game. In the Neolithic game, transition from a given square X on the map to another square is governed by the throw of a die, according to the pattern shown in figure 6.26. The starting square for the whole game is already marked on the map. Each throw counts as 50 years of time.

If any of the squares to which transition is possible from a

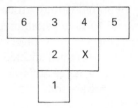

Figure 6.26

Figure 6.27

given square is dry, it does not count. Thus in the presence of such squares the transition probabilities are altered. In the case of a mountainous square, a transition to it is counted as 5 throws (equal to 250 years in terms of the game rules).

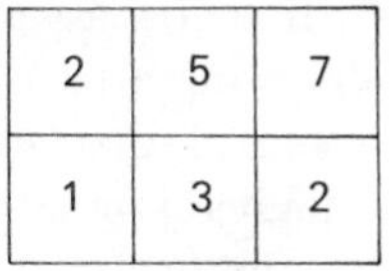

The purposes of this game are educational rather than research-orientated. Nevertheless it is worth noting that because of the modifications introduced by the "mountainous" and "dry" squares, the stochastic process is made very unamenable to direct mathematical treatment. For example, in order to obtain a value for the mean time taken to reach Britain, the only available method would be to derive an empirical value from a large number of realizations of the process. (Each actual run of the game, obeying the laws, is a *realization* of the process.) For this a computer would be the only fully adequate means, but playing the game in class shows in principle what needs to be done. If thirty children each do the game, the thirty realizations also teach something about what the computer does.

Geography teachers have suggested other simulation games in which the purpose of the simulation is not clear. An example is provided by a "settlement game", in which a map of a region is covered by a grid of squares and each square is assigned a "desirability" score, based on an assessment of the advantages and disadvantages of the various geographical features of the country within that square. A simplified grid showing desirability scores is shown in figure 6.27.

It is now assumed that the probability of an individual settler choosing a particular square is proportional to the desirability score of that square (and that the desirability scores of the squares as far as subsequent settlers are concerned are not affected by the fact that settlement has taken place—a more dubious assumption). Individual settlers' choices of square are to be represented by random numbers read from a table; allocation of settlers to squares as shown below ensures that the probability of choosing a square is proportional to the desirability score. Numbers beyond 19 are ignored.

00, 01	02, 03, 04, 05, 06	07, 08, 09, 10, 11, 12, 13
14	15, 16, 17	18, 19

The purpose in carrying out this simulation is not clear, because the result of a long run of this allocation procedure is theoretically predictable—that the numbers of individuals in squares should be in proportion to the scores of the squares. If the actual distribution of settlers in the region under examination is to be compared with the theoretical distribution based on desirability scores, the comparison might just as well be made with the proportions indicated by the scores themselves without any intervening simulation.

The only interest which attaches to a short-run simulation is in seeing how far the expected proportions are departed from. But even these departures are not surprising to anyone who has some probability theory background. (For additional discussion of simulations see *Mathematics in the World*, a book in the present series, and the publications of the Schools Council Project *Computers in the Curriculum*.)

6.19   Statistical Methods

The movement towards quantification in geography involves the need for statistical methods. Two particular instances of statistical ideas have appeared in recent school geography: correlation, and point patterns.

(a) CORRELATION
In chapter 1 of the *Oxford Geography Project, Book 3* pupils are introduced to scatter graphs and lines of best fit[1] (the latter drawn by eye). In order to measure the degree of correlation, Spearman's rank correlation coefficient R is used. The formula

$$R = 1 - \frac{6\Sigma d^2}{n^3 - n}$$

is stated and used, but not justified. (The procedure for coping with equal ranks is given wrongly.)

Kendall's coefficient has an advantage for teaching purposes over Spearman's, in that it is more easily explained as a reasonable measure. An explanation of Kendall's coefficient which is in the spirit of the geographers' approach to the construction of indices can be found in Appendix 2 (p. 143).

(b) POINT PATTERNS IN AN AREAL DISTRIBUTION
Geographers are often interested in examining a distribution of individual points in a region of the earth's surface, so that some conclusion can be reached as to the degree of regularity in the arrangement or the extent of clustering, or as to whether the distribution is a random one. The individual points may be, for example, settlements or farms.

The method used to study point patterns is known as *nearest*

[1] The term *residual* is used to refer to a point a long way from the line of best fit (normally called an *outlier*). The word *residual* is properly applied to the difference between a data value and the value indicated by the regression line, irrespective of whether this is large or small.

neighbour analysis. The base of the nearest neighbour index is the expected average distance of a point from its nearest neighbour given a *random* distribution of points. The formula for this expected distance is $1/(2\sqrt{D})$ where D is the point density in the region

$$\text{i.e.} \quad D = \frac{\text{number of points}}{\text{area of region}}$$

From the actual distribution being studied, the mean nearest neighbour distance is calculated. The value of the index for the distribution is then

$$\frac{\text{observed mean nearest neighbour distance}}{1/(2\sqrt{D})}$$

An index 0 corresponds to clustering (possibly only as point pairs); 1 indicates a random distribution. The maximum value of the index can be shown to be 2·1491 (2·15 approximately) and corresponds to an equilateral triangular lattice of points.

The statistical theory underlying nearest neighbour analysis is well beyond the scope of a school course, and even the concept of the mean nearest neighbour distance for a random distribution of points has its difficulties. However the number 2·1491 is relatively easily explained, even though no attempt is made to do so in any school geography textbook.

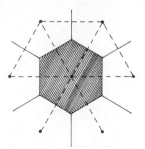

The diagram shows a regular pattern of lattice points forming equilateral triangles of side 2 units. Each point "occupies" the area of a regular hexagon as shown (shaded).

The shaded hexagon is made up of six equilateral triangles, each of height 1 unit and therefore of side $2/\sqrt{3}$. The total area of the shaded hexagon is thus

$$6 \times \tfrac{1}{2}\left(1 \times \frac{2}{\sqrt{3}}\right) = \frac{6}{\sqrt{3}} \text{ square units.}$$

The point density is thus

$$\frac{1}{6/\sqrt{3}} = \frac{\sqrt{3}}{6}.$$

For a random distribution with this density the formula $1/(2\sqrt{D})$ gives

$$\frac{1}{2\sqrt{[(\sqrt{3})/6]}} = \tfrac{1}{2}\sqrt{\frac{6}{\sqrt{3}}}$$

for the expected nearest neighbour distance. The actual mean distance is 2 units. So the index in this case is

$$\frac{2}{\tfrac{1}{2}\sqrt{[6/(\sqrt{3})]}} = 4\sqrt{\frac{\sqrt{3}}{6}} = 2\cdot1491.$$

A problem which accompanies the use of this and other sophisticated statistical techniques with pupils at this level is this: if the difference between, say, extents of clustering of two point distributions is apparent to visual discrimination, then the statistical analysis is not necessary. If on the other hand a measurement of fine differences is required, then one is dealing with small differences in index whose *significance* needs to be tested. The significance test is likely to be very difficult to understand and not easy to apply.

Bibliography

(1) *Teaching Geography*
R. Walford (ed.), *New Directions in Geography Teaching*, Longman 1973.
New Thinking in School Geography, HMSO 1972.
R. Walford, *Games in Geography*, Longman 1969.

(2) *Primary and Early Secondary*
J. P. Cole and N. J. Beynon, *New Ways in Geography*, Basil Blackwell 1968.

(3) *Secondary (11–16)*
J. Rolfe and others, *Oxford Geography Project*, Books 1–3, OUP 1974.
K. Briggs, *Introducing Transportation Networks*, ULP 1972.
—— *Introducing Towns and Cities*, ULP 1974.
E. A. Walker, *Location and Links*, Book I, Basil Blackwell 1972.
P. H. Howling and L. A. Hunter, *Mapping Skills and Techniques: A Quantitative Approach*, Oliver and Boyd 1974.

Schools Council, *Geography for the Young School Leaver*, Nelson 1974.
D. C. Money, *Patterns of Settlement*, Evans 1972.

(4) *Sixth Form and University*
W. V. Tidswell and S. M. Barker, *Quantitative Methods: An Approach to Socio-Economic Geography*, UTP 1971.
B. P. Fitzgerald and others, *Science in Geography* (4 Books), OUP 1974.
J. A. Everson and B. P. Fitzgerald, *Settlement Patterns*, Longman 1969.

(5) *University Textbooks*
J. P. Cole and C. A. M. King, *Quantitative Geography*, John Wiley 1968.
P. Haggett, *Geography: A Modern Synthesis*, Harper and Row 1972.
P. Haggett and R. J. Chorley, *Network Analysis in Geography*, Arnold 1969.
R. Abler, J. S. Adams and P. Gould, *Spatial Organization: The Geographer's View of the World*, Prentice-Hall 1971.

(6) *General*
M. Chisholm, *Human Geography, Evolution or Revolution?*, Penguin 1975.
P. Gould and R. White, *Mental Maps*, Penguin 1974.
D. M. Smith, *Patterns in Human Geography*, Penguin 1977.

7 Mathematics in Economics and Social Studies

The mathematical work which occurs in CSE and "O" Level economics and social studies courses is mostly arithmetic, particularly percentage, together with simple cases of graph-reading and an understanding in some cases of functional dependence (such as the dependence of quantity bought upon price). Numerical work need not figure very much, either in the course or the examination. The survey of mathematical topics which follows is based largely on two school textbooks (one for CSE and one for "O" Level) which make quite extensive use of numerical data and graphs. They are: J. Nobbs and P. Ames: *Daily Economics*, McGraw-Hill, 1975 (CSE) and J. Nobbs: *Social Economics*, McGraw-Hill, 2nd edn., 1975, (GCE).

Economics and social subjects provide considerable scope for the exercise of numeracy. This is made more interesting by the presence so often of political allegiances, causing people to select those numerical relationships which support their own point of view. Often this can lead to the production of misleading graphs, with unclear origins or scales.

An interesting exercise is to set pupils the task of producing from a given set of figures a numerical relationship or a diagram favourable to upholders of one point of view. Having done this they can then be asked to use the same data to produce a relationship or graph favourable to the opposite point of view. For example, the numbers 20, 25, 31 can show "increasing jumps" 5, 6, or "decreasing percentage jumps" 25 per cent, 24 per cent.

Much of the arithmetical content of economics courses is also covered in one or other of the CSE (Mode 1) syllabuses in Civic Mathematics. A matrix showing the topic-by-topic breakdown of these syllabuses is given in the Schools Council Examinations Bulletin No. 25 (*CSE Mode 1 Examinations in Mathematics*). The following list contains all topics which occur in at least one of the syllabuses:

Wages	Insurance
Percentage	Endowments
Simple Interest	Stocks and Shares
Compound Interest	Ready Reckoners
The Budget	Trade and Cash Discount
Taxes	Foreign Exchange
Income Tax	Comparative Costs
Savings	Timetables
Home Budgets	Bank Statements
Hire Purchase	Bankruptcy
Life Assurance	Invoices
Loans	Rent

The *Bulletin* comments that Civic Mathematics is one of the more popular options of the eleven boards which offer it.

TOPIC SURVEY

7.1 Arithmetic and Simple Graphs

The following CSE questions are reprinted in *Daily Economics*. They indicate the scope of arithmetical work required.

EXAMPLE 1 (East Midlands CSE, 1972)

	Number of stoppages	Number of workers involved	Number of working days lost
Official strike	82	84 700	643 000
Unofficial strike	2 125	663 300	1 857 000

(Figures are an annual average for the period 1964–67).

(a) Which was the most frequent type of strike during these years?

(b) Explain the difference between the two types of strike.

(c) How many men, on an average, were involved in each official strike?

(d) Of the total working days lost through strikes, what proportion was lost because of unofficial strikes?

EXAMPLE 2 (West Yorkshire and Lindsey CSE, 1972)

An £80 television set may be obtained from a certain dealer in three ways:
  (i) *Cash purchase*. This entitles the buyer to a $12\frac{1}{2}$ per cent discount. The dealer will maintain the set at a charge of £8 per annum, increasing by £2 per annum after each complete year.
  (ii) *Hire purchase*. This involves a payment of a 10 per cent deposit. To the balance, the dealer adds an interest charge which is equal to 10 per cent per annum simple interest for 3 years on the balance. The balance and the interest charge is to be paid in 36 equal monthly instalments. During this time no charges are made for maintenance.
  (iii) *Rental*. For the first year the monthly rent is £2·40. The monthly rent is reduced by 5p after each complete year. No charges are made for maintenance.
      (a) If the set is bought on hire purchase:
          (i) What is the amount of each monthly instalment?
          (ii) After how many complete months will the buyer have paid $\frac{1}{3}$ of the total hire purchase price?
      (b) Calculate the total cost of each of the above three methods for the first three years (including maintenance).

EXAMPLE 3 (West Yorkshire CSE, 1972).

Calculate the time required for £400 to become £449 at $3\frac{1}{2}$ per cent per annum simple interest.

EXAMPLE 4 (East Midland CSE, 1972)

Advertising and Sales Promotion by Media, UK.

Media	Expenditure 1956	1965
	(£ million)	
Press	159	282
Television	11	106
Poster and Transport	15	18
Outdoor signs	11	15
Cinema	6	6
Radio	1	2
Catalogues	35	45
Free samples and gifts	11	20
Total	249	494

(a) Draw a histogram[1] to show the increase in press and television advertising between 1956 and 1965.
(b) Which of these two methods of advertising has increased most during this time?
(c) What other forms of advertising have grown rapidly during this time?
(d) If the present development of radio continues, what will happen to the level of radio advertising?

Comment

Note that in part (b) of this question no clue is given as to whether it is more appropriate to compare absolute or proportional changes, but the graph drawn in (a) will suggest the latter.

EXAMPLE 5 (East Anglian CSE, 1972).

You are the secretary of your village fete committee which is organizing a function on August Bank Holiday. If the day is wet, you stand to lose £200. The Pluvius Insurance Company offers your committee a policy to cover this possible loss in return for a premium of £20. How does the company fix this premium?

Comment

Some very simple probability theory is involved in the understanding of insurance.

*   *   *   *   *

The remaining topics considered in this chapter are from "O" Level economics courses.

7.2 Percentage

Price indices

There are several types of price index, among them the Index of Retail Prices (Cost of Living Index) and the various indices of Stock Market Prices. In each case a particular year is selected as a base year and the level of prices in that year is denoted by

---

[1] *Histogram* is not used here in its correct sense as graph with an area scale showing frequencies or relative frequencies.

100. The price index for a subsequent year shows the level of prices as a percentage of the level in the base year.

In the case of, for example, the Index of Retail Prices, a weighting scheme is used to take account of the varying degrees of importance amongst the items whose prices contribute to the index.

There is obviously an inverse relationship between the general level of prices and the value, or purchasing power, of money. Calculation of the latter given the former provides a useful application of percentage, but computation of this kind is not demanded of pupils taking economics. The graph in figure 7.1 (from *Social Economics*, p. 20) shows the value of the £ taking 1915 as base year.

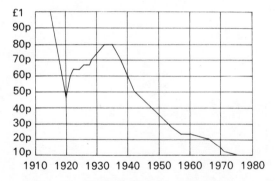

Figure 7.1   The declining value of the £, 1915–75.

Investment yield

The percentage dividend on a share is calculated on the basis of its nominal value. However, the price paid for the share in the market may be different from its nominal value, and to the potential buyer its yield is measured in relation to his own out-

lay if he were to buy it, i.e. the market value of the share. For example, for a 5 per cent share whose nominal value is £5 the dividend paid would be £0·25. If this share is currently valued at £8, the yield is $(0·25/8) \times 100$ per cent $= 3\frac{1}{8}$ per cent. The yield is obtained in the general case from the formula

$$\text{yield} = \frac{\text{nominal value}}{\text{current market value}} \times \text{dividend per cent}$$

7.3   Use of Graphs in Formulating a Model

Supply and demand schedules and graphs

In order to understand how the price of a commodity is determined, it is necessary to bring together the different points of view of buyer and seller. The account given here is simplified so that the mathematical points may be brought out. For each party, buyer and seller, there is a functional relationship between a suggested price for the commodity and the quantity which he is prepared to buy or sell. It is universal practice in economics textbooks to plot price on the *y*-axis and quantity on the *x*-axis, even though it seems more natural to think of quantity as a function of price rather than vice versa. When expressed in tabular form, these functions are called *schedules*.

Generally speaking, from the point of view of the buyers in a market, the lower the price the more they will be prepared to buy. (This may not be simply that each individual buyer wants to buy more, but that when the price gets low enough more potential buyers become interested in buying.) The graph of the buyers' schedule (or *demand schedule*) slopes down from left to right (figure 7.2(i)). Note that continuous models are used, although price and quantity may be discrete.

The sellers' schedule has the opposite characteristic: the higher

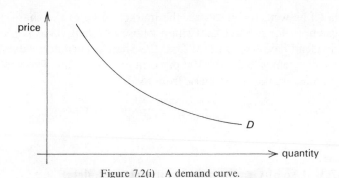

Figure 7.2(i)   A demand curve.

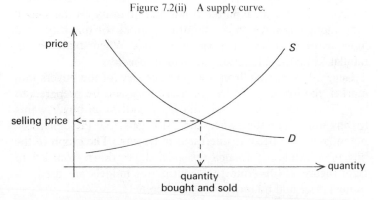

Figure 7.2(ii)   A supply curve.

Figure 7.2(iii)   Determination of the equilibrium price.

the price, the more there is offered for sale. The *supply schedule* graph slopes up (figure 7.2(ii)).

Superimposing the two graphs leads to the determination of the price and the quantity sold (figure 7.2(iii)).

The determined selling price is called the *equilibrium price*.

The composite graph can be used to illustrate the consequences of an *increase in demand*. By this is meant an alteration to the demand schedule whereby the quantity demanded *for a given price* is increased. Because of the roles of the *x* and *y*-axes, an increase in demand corresponds to a *horizontal* shift of the demand curve D to D′ (figure 7.3).

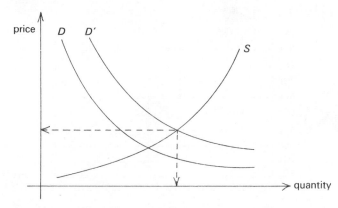

Figure 7.3   Consequence of an increase in demand.

On either a demand curve or a supply curve the area of the rectangle shaded in figure 7.4 represents the total value of sales or total revenue (quantity × price).

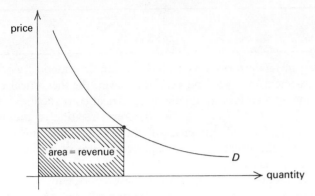

Figure 7.4   Area representing total revenue.

7.4   Note for Mathematics Teachers on Elasticity of Demand

Demand is said to be highly *elastic* if a small change in price P leads to a large change in quantity Q demanded. Elasticity of demand can be measured by the ratio of the percentage change in quantity to a *small* percentage change in price. It is not necessarily constant along any given demand curve.

If continuity (and differentiability) of demand curves is assumed, elasticity of demand may be defined as the limiting value of

$$-\frac{\delta Q/Q}{\delta P/P} \quad \text{as} \quad \delta P \to 0.$$

The negative sign is included so that the result should be positive. It follows that elasticity can be defined by

$$-\frac{P}{Q}\cdot\frac{dQ}{dP}$$

(If F is any point on the demand curve, the elasticity of demand is numerically equal to

$$\frac{\text{gradient of curve at F}}{\text{gradient of OF}}$$

where O is the origin).

From this definition it can be shown that total revenue PQ increases with a decrease in price if the elasticity of demand is greater than 1, remains constant if it equals 1, and increases with an increase in price (or decreases with a decrease in price) if elasticity is less than 1.

Bibliography

J. Nobbs and P. Ames: *Daily Economics*, McGraw-Hill 1975.
J. Nobbs: *Social Economics*, McGraw-Hill, 2nd edn. 1975.
A. Battersby: *Mathematics in Management*, Penguin Books 1966.

8 Mathematics in Technical Subjects

The following subjects are covered under the heading of technical subjects: technical and engineering drawing, woodwork, metalwork, design and technology.

The interest of teachers of technical subjects in the mathematical content of their subjects is naturally enough practical rather than theoretical. It is often the case that the bias of mathematical content depends on the teacher. For instance, if technical drawing is taught by a mathematician, the emphasis may be on theory, with a possible lack of practical examples; whereas a technical teacher may teach drawing methods by rules, but may be able to use engineering experience to provide realistic examples.

It is essential for a pupil studying technical subjects to have a good level of ability in the four rules of number, particularly applied to decimals,* and to be accurate in measurement and careful in presentation. The dominant role of geometry in technical drawing is evident from the syllabus outlined below, and this has implications for the student, depending on the nature of his mathematical background. The student who has followed a traditional mathematics course including Euclidean geometry will have a good theoretical background for understanding (if he wishes to and is encouraged to) the rationale of most of the constructions needed in technical drawing.

Many modern mathematics texts largely ignore straight-edge-and-compass constructions as not being central to their concern. Many of the most simple of these are applications of symmetry, and this idea has a much larger place in modern approaches. The concepts of scale and similarity are dealt with in some detail in modern projects with, for example, practical work on enlargement in *SMP* (2nd year). However, the theoretical background is often lacking for the geometrical constructions whose rationale is to be found in the theorems relating to the angle, tangent and chord properties of the circle. Three-dimensional work on the other hand (including the use of projections in sketching) has a larger place.

The adoption of the various modern courses in mathematics requires a re-appraisal of the relationship between technical drawing and mathematics. Technical drawing has lost the advantages of a syllabus which teaches explicity many of its basic techniques in the language which it uses itself. Even where an explanation of the techniques is still available in the concepts taught in a modern mathematics course, the language has changed. Liaison between departments is vital.

SYNOPSIS OF SYLLABUSES FOR DRAWING COURSES IN BUILDING, ENGINEERING, METALWORK, WOODWORK AND GEOMETRICAL DRAWING

CSE

Parallel lines. Compass and ruler constructions.
Division of a line into equal parts.
Perpendicular to and from a point.
Perpendicular bisector of a line.
Angle bisector.
Construction of 30-degree angles and multiples thereof.
Construction of tangents and normals to circles.
Enlargement and reduction. Scale.
Orthogonal, isometric and oblique projections.
Sectional views. Plans and elevations of prisms, pyramids, cylinders and cones.
Loci and the construction of the ellipse and simple helix.
Construction of triangles, the circumscribed and inscribed circles, quadrilaterals.

* The addition and subtraction of fractions in the $\frac{1}{2}, \frac{1}{4}, \ldots, \frac{1}{64}$ series may still be required in practice.

Regular polygons constructed within a circle.
Ellipse, focal points, construction of tangent and normal.
Curve parallel to ellipse. Parabola.
Areas of plane figures.
Use of instruments, calipers, micrometer, vernier.

GCE

Graphical solution of point, line and plane problems.
Orthographic drawing.
British Standards engineering drawings.
Principles of plane and solid geometry for solution of problems in true length and shape.
Division of a line into proportional parts.
Circles, angles and tangent theorems.
Reduction and enlargement.
Loci, ellipse, focal points, tangent and normal.
Planes; projections of simple plane figures.
Projections of right geometrical figures and solids—spheres, cylinders, cones, prisms and pyramids.
Linear helices.
Isometric and oblique projections.
Developments of surfaces of right prisms, pyramids, cylinders and cones.

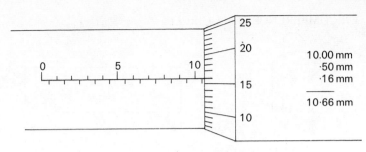

Figure 8.2   A micrometer reading in hundredths of a millimetre.

TOPIC SURVEY

8.1   Decimal Arithmetic, Mensuration, Ratio

Proficiency in the four rules is necessary for pupils studying technical subjects. Some simple applications of arithmetic, mensuration and ratio are illustrated below.

ADDITION

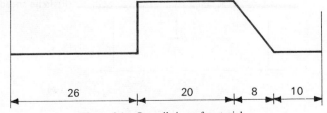

Figure 8.1   Overall sizes of material.

SUBTRACTION AND DIVISION

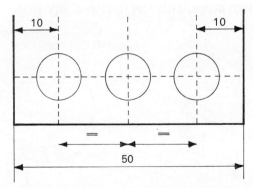

Figure 8.3   Spacing out.

CIRCUMFERENCE OF A CIRCLE

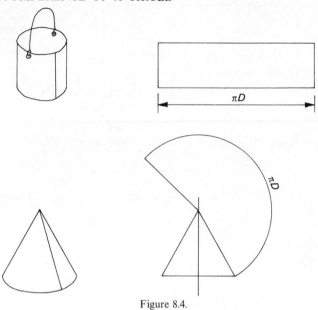

Figure 8.4.

AREA, PERIMETER, MULTIPLICATION, DIVISION

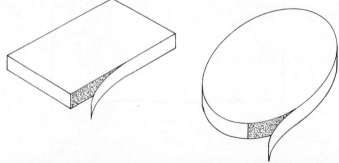

Figure 8.5   Calculation of length or area of veneer, or of adhesive required.

RATIOS

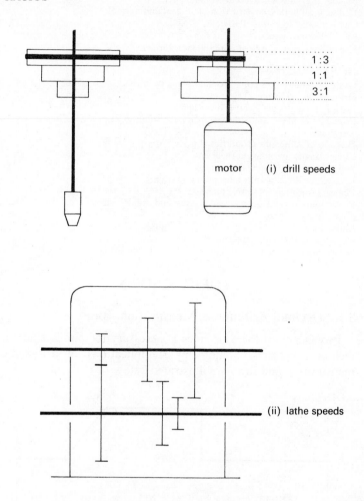

Figure 8.6   Drill and lathe speeds.

8.2 Scale

The importance of an understanding of scale in technical drawing needs no emphasis. As in geographical mapwork, scales are often stated as representative fractions or ratios: $\frac{1}{100}$ or 1:100.

Scaling down (or up) of dimensions for the purpose of a drawing may be done by calculation, or by using a special scale ruler, or by first constructing a scale. The latter involves proportional division, which is considered next.

8.3 Properties of Parallel Lines: Proportional Division, Enlargement

Much use is made in geometrical constructions of the property of equally spaced parallel lines.

The standard construction for dividing a given length AB into, say, 5 equal parts is shown in figure 8.7(i).

Figure 8.7(ii) shows a method of dividing a piece of timber of awkward width into four equal strips: the geometry involved is the same.

Figure 8.8 is a diagram of a *diagonal scale*. The representative fraction is 1/20 000 (i.e. 50 mm represents 1 km). Dividers placed across the points A and B would mark out a distance representing 1·75 km.

If the scale shown in figure 8.8 were bent into the form of a cylinder (the axis being across the page), the diagonal lines would form a "screw thread". This is the basis of the micrometer screw gauge shown on page 113.

The proportional division construction is also used in conjunction with enlargement using a centre. Figure 8.9 shows the construction of a figure whose dimensions are enlarged from those of a given figure in the ratio 3:5.

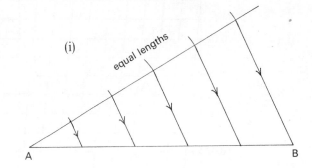

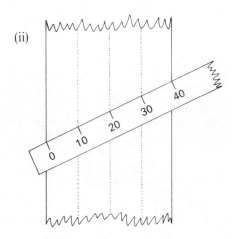

Figure 8.7 Dividing a given length into equal parts.

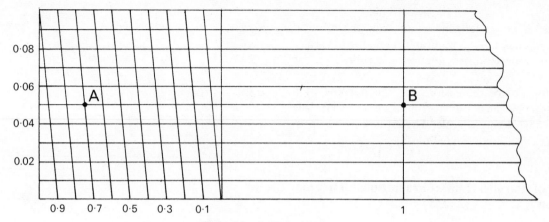

Figure 8.8   A diagonal scale.

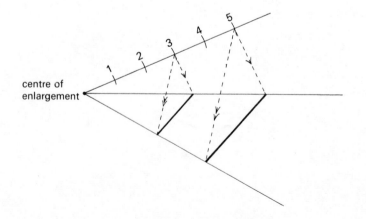

Figure 8.9   Enlarging a figure in a given ratio.

8.4   Geometrical Constructions

ELEMENTARY CONSTRUCTIONS

The standard elementary constructions using straight-edge and compasses are a familiar topic in traditional geometry courses. The most important of them are:

   (i) copying an angle (and the particular case of constructing parallel lines) (see figure 8.10).
  (ii) bisection of an angle;
 (iii) construction of a right angle at a given point;
  (v) dropping a perpendicular from a point to a line;
 (vi) construction of an angle of 60° (equilateral triangle construction).

The validity of the constructions (except for (vi)) is proved in the traditional type of course by the method of congruent triangles.

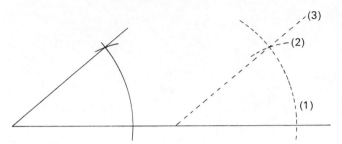

Figure 8.10 Copying an angle.

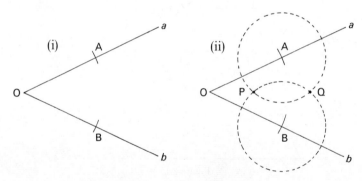

Figure 8.11 Bisecting an angle.

In the different approaches to geometry embodied in modern mathematics courses, the constructions (except (vi)), and the method of proof by congruent triangles, often do not appear. However, many of the constructions (ii) to (v) can be seen as applications of symmetry, a topic which is common to the new geometry courses.

Consider the construction for bisecting an angle, and its justification in terms of symmetry.

The given angle is that between lines a, b which meet at O. The marking off of the points A, B on a, b at equal distances from O (figure 8.11(i)) can be seen as an instance of *whatever you do to one side (arm) you do to the other*. This is true also of the next step, the drawing of equal circles (in practice circular arcs) centred on A, B (figure 8.11(ii)).

The points P, Q lie on the axis of symmetry of a, b. The point of intersection O of the two lines a, b must also lie on the axis of symmetry of a, b. Hence OPQ is a straight line which bisects the angle between a and b.

Similar arguments justify constructions (iii), (iv) and (v) in the list above.

The "copying" construction (i) hardly needs a justification. The proof by congruent triangles turns out to be simply a statement that a triangle is completely specified when its three sides are given.

OTHER CONSTRUCTIONS

The elementary constructions are used in more complicated constructions. The following geometrical theorems are the basis for constructions appearing in technical drawing courses:

(1) Tangent properties of a circle.
    (*a*) Tangent is perpendicular to radius. (Construction of tangent from given point, using (2).)
    (*b*) Alternate segment property. (Construction of triangle when given vertical angle, base and altitude.)

(2) Angle in a semicircle is a right angle. (Construction of right angle in certain circumstances, e.g. in drawing tangent from point to circle.)

(3) Intersecting chords property of circle, in particular $ab = c^2$ in figure 8.12.

(4) Tangent case of (3): $PT^2 = PA \cdot PB$ in figure 8.13 (used in conjunction with "mean proportional" construction to construct a circle through two given points touching a given line).

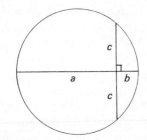

Figure 8.12 Intersecting chords property: $ab = c^2$.

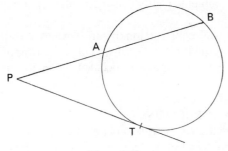

Figure 8.13.

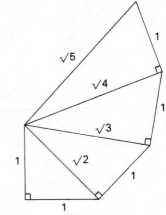

Figure 8.14.

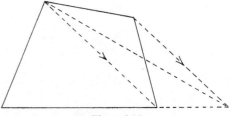

Figure 8.15.

(5) Pythagoras' Theorem. (Construction of right angle from 3, 4, 5 triangle; geometrical determination of some square roots as illustrated in figure 8.14. The 1, 1, $\sqrt{2}$ triangle can be used to draw a figure similar to a given figure and of double its area.)

(6) Area Theorems: triangles on same base and between same parallels equal in area; area of triangle equals that of rectangle with same base, half height. (Construction of triangle, then rectangle, then (using (3)) square, equal in area to given polygon) (figure 8.15).

(7) Similar Figures: areas are proportional to squares of corresponding sides (used in conjunction with (3) to construct similar polygons with areas in given ratio).

Two constructions which may be of interest to the mathematics teachers are given in figures 8.16 and 8.17.

8.5 Loci

In addition to the loci traced out by points on simple linkage mechanisms, certain standard loci are included in courses of geo-

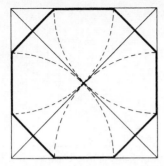

Figure 8.16   Constructing an octagon inside a square.

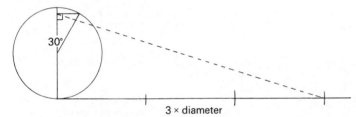

Figure 8.17   Constructing a line whose length is approximately equal to the circumference of a given circle. The required line (dotted) has a length equal to that given by taking $\pi = 3.1417$ (to four decimal places).

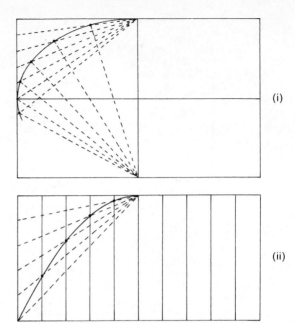

Figure 8.18   Constructing (i) an ellipse, and (ii) a parabola.

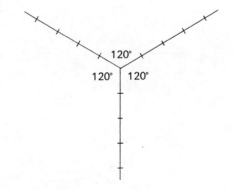

Figure 8.19   Isometric scales.

metrical drawing. These can include ellipse, parabola and hyperbola, and loci derived from circles, such as involute curves, and the cycloid and hypocycloid.

Of the various methods used to construct the ellipse, the one shown in figure 8.18(i) is of interest. The ellipse is obtained as the locus of points of intersection of two pencils of lines, one of which cuts off equal intercepts on a horizontal axis, the other equal intercepts on a vertical axis. When the vertex of one of these pencils is "moved to infinity" (i.e. the pencil becomes a set of equally spaced parallel lines) a standard construction for the parabola (Figure 8.18(ii)) results.

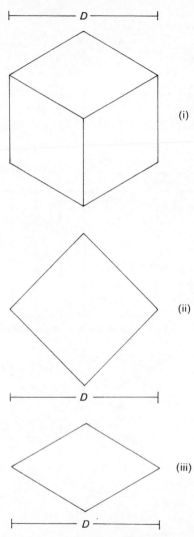

Figure 8.20   True isometric projection of a cube.

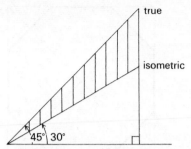

Figure 8.21   Relationship between true length and that marked on an isometric axis.

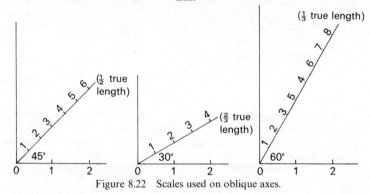

Figure 8.22   Scales used on oblique axes.

ISOMETRIC AND OBLIQUE PROJECTION

In isometric projection the scales used on the three axes are the same (figure 8.19). However, in *true* isometric projection these scales do not show true distances. In the true isometric drawing of a cube shown in figure 8.20(i) the distance D is correctly drawn. The square top of the cube is in reality as in (ii), but is shown as in (iii).

The relationship between true length and lengths as marked on an isometric axis is thus as shown in figure 8.21.

In oblique projection, the scale used on the oblique axis follows a rule of thumb (figure 8.22).

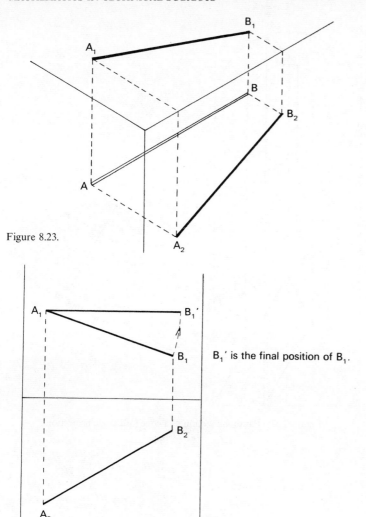

Figure 8.23.

B₁′ is the final position of B₁.

Figure 8.24.

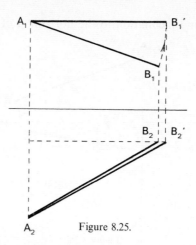

Figure 8.25.

8.6   Orthographic Projection

An understanding of orthographic projection is the central requirement of technical and engineering drawing. Even simple constructions require an ability to think in three dimensions whilst working in two.

Consider, for example, the problem of finding the true length and inclination to the horizontal of a line whose two projections are given (3rd angle projection).

In figure 8.23, AB is a line, A_1B_1 its plan (projection onto horizontal plane), A_2B_2 its elevation (projection onto vertical plane). This subscript notation for plans and elevations of points is used throughout the following description.

If A is fixed and B moved *horizontally* to B′ so that AB′ (equal in length to AB) is parallel to the vertical plane, this movement can be recorded on the horizontal plane as in figure 8.24.

Since B_1 has moved horizontally, its elevation on the vertical plane remains on the same level. Hence the construction for B'_2, shown in figure 8.25.

The length and inclination to the horizontal of A_2B_2' are the

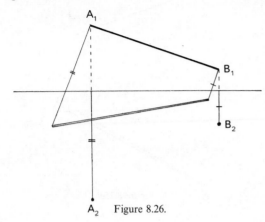

Figure 8.26.

true lengths and inclination of AB.

Another solution to the same problem uses an auxiliary projection on the vertical plane through A_1B_1. It is known how far A and B are below A_1 and B_1—this is recorded in the vertical elevation A_2B_2. Using these two known depths the auxiliary projection is drawn. Its length and elevation to the horizontal (i.e. to A_1B_1 in the auxiliary projection) are true (figure 8.26).

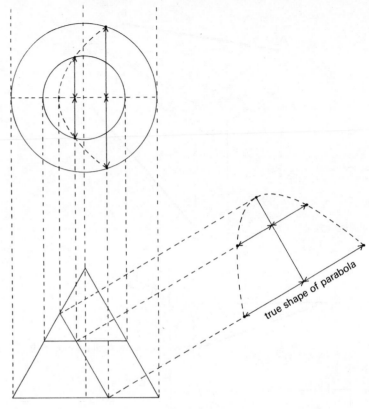

Figure 8.27   Parabolic section of a cone (3rd angle projection).

Amongst items of possible interest to mathematics teachers are conic sections (figure 8.27), and the helix (figure 8.28).

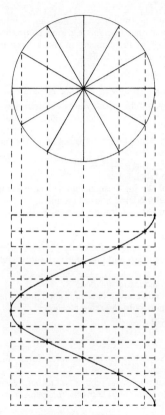

Figure 8.28   Helix.

9 Mathematics in Domestic Subjects

The heading Domestic Subjects refers to home economics, including cookery and needlework.

The link between home economics and mathematics is already well established. The Schools Council Curriculum Bulletin on Home Economics Teaching (*Bulletin 4*, p. 13) includes arithmetic in its list of intellectual skills basic to the subject:

Arithmetic is needed for shopping, budgets, time-plans, calorie calculations, quantities of food, fabric, and decorating materials.

In some cases topics are common to syllabuses in home economics, economics and practical or civic mathematics (see chapter 7, p. 107). Among such topics are:

Wages, tax deductions, bank accounts and loans, interest, hire purchase, insurance.

There is considerable scope for linking work in home economics with mathematics (and other subjects). The Schools Council Bulletin reports:

One school has a team teaching approach to a fourth-year leavers' course, part of which is on setting up a home. Visits are paid to furnished show houses and to salesrooms...Calculations for curtains, carpets, wallpaper, etc., are worked out in mathematics lessons, and methods of purchase—cash, accounts, hire purchase, etc.—are discussed (*Bulletin 4*, p. 65).

In an appendix, the Bulletin gives an extract from a scheme in the integration of mathematics and home economics (*Bulletin 4*, pp. 150–1).

Money management
Budgeting, personal allocation of pocket money.
Wages, wage slips; deduction for NHS, income tax, hospital fund; basic wage, hourly, weekly, piece work.

Savings, national savings, building societies, banks, interest, bank charges.
Average amount spent on main items, e.g. food, comparison of the cost of meals at home / at school / in the canteen / in snack bars / in restaurants / packed meals, cost of the family food bill.

Housing
Choice of house, bungalow, flat, bearing in mind the needs of the family group, e.g. elderly, handicapped, young children.
Relative merit of renting and buying, mortgages, rental, purchase, insurance, private loan.
Rates, ratable value, water rate, rate papers, how the rates are spent.

Services
Gas, electricity, solid fuel, water.
Relative methods of heating, cost, cleanliness, convenience.
Measurement of fuel used, methods of payment.
Water supply, water rate, sanitation, drainage.

Household budgeting
Hire purchase, credit buying, credit cards, bankers' orders.
Choice of furniture, fittings and furnishings, quality, style, cost, suitability.

Household cleaning and labour involved
Comparison of cost and convenience of home laundry/laundrette/commercial laundry/dry cleaners/coin-operated cleaner.
Daily help/home help.

Care of the family
National Health Service benefits, hospital fund, Private Patients Plan, maternity grants and allowances.
Nurseries and play groups, cost related to mother's earnings.
Welfare services for the elderly, meals for pensioners, pensions and supplementary pensions.

Holidays
Passports, insurance.

Good grooming
Hairdressing, cosmetics costs.

The family car
Running costs compared with travel by public transport.

Independence
Cost of bed-sitting room, flatlet, shared flat.
Responsibilities of living alone, shopping, cooking, cleaning, laundry, illness.
Cost of living alone, compared with family, deductions for living-in, e.g. nurses.

The main mathematical demand of domestic subjects is for competence in measuring and in arithmetic. The main advantage of these subjects to the teacher of mathematics is in providing realistic and practical applications of arithmetic drawn from everyday life, without the attendant conceptual difficulties which so often arise in science.

The rest of this chapter is devoted to topics which illustrate the uses of mathematics in the field of domestic subjects.

9.1   House Purchase

The mathematics involved in the calculation of mortgage repayments is too advanced for pupils at the level being considered, but the graph in figure 9.1 is instructive. (See G. T. Bone and A. O. Hone, *Setting Up Your Home. Design for Living* Series No. 3, (Mills and Boon, 1964), p. 38.)

The graph shows the approximate breakdown between interest and capital repayment in each year, and the total areas show the overall ratio of interest to capital. (The loan is £10 000 repayable over 25 years at 12·25 per cent p.a. Annual repayments are approximately £1300.)

9.2   Consumer Education

In the field of Consumer Education there is scope for data collection (for example, the prices of goods in different shops, or

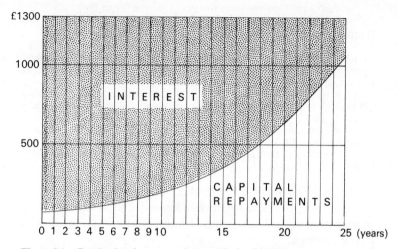

Figure 9.1   Graph showing approximate relationship between interest and capital repayment on a mortgage of £10 000, repayable over 25 years @ 12·25% p.a.

consumers' preferences for competing brands or shops) with subsequent graphical display. Also involved is the comparison of prices by unit cost: 100 g of toothpaste costs 20p; 175 g costs 29p. Which is cheaper?

9.3   Cookery

The mathematical aspects of cookery are of two kinds. First there is the arithmetic involved in calculating quantities and costs of ingredients, cooking times, nutritional values, etc. Secondly, there is the business of planning the production of a meal—the order in which jobs are best done and the times at which they should be started and finished. This aspect is one which cookery has in common with many other instances of work-planning; building a house and servicing a vehicle are two other examples.

As examples of the arithmetic of cookery the following are typical:

(1) Roasting lamb takes 25 minutes per lb plus an extra 25 minutes. If the joint weighs 2 lb 12 oz, how long will it take to roast? If it is to be finished by 1.15 p.m., at what time should it go in the oven?

(2) The recipe says "6 oz flour". What is that in metric units? (At present 25 g will be used as the metric equivalent of 1 oz, so an ability to count in 25s is useful).

(3) The quantities given in this cake recipe are for use with a 7″ cake tin. If I want to use a 10″ tin, but not alter the depth of the cake, how should I alter the ingredients? Here is a very practical example of scale, area and volume factors.

The planning involved in cookery can be represented in the form of a network. The network in figure 9.2 illustrates one way of preparing a meal consisting of roast joint and potatoes with boiled cabbage.

The figures are the times in minutes for each job. This kind of planning network is amenable to Critical Path Analysis. Each arrow is drawn in such a way that the starting point has to be reached before the job denoted by the arrow is possible. For example, the oven must be heated, the potatoes peeled and the joint prepared before roasting can begin. The critical path is shown by heavy lines: this is the longest path through the network. If it is desired to save time, then it must be by cutting down the time required by one of the jobs on the critical path. As shown, the whole process takes 110 minutes. The latest starting times for the various jobs (measured from the start) are:

Peeling potatoes and preparing joint	0
Heating oven	3
Roasting joint and potatoes	13
Preparing cabbage	97
Boiling cabbage	100
Putting plates in oven to heat	102
Carving joint	103
Serving joint	107
Serving cabbage	108
Serving potatoes	109

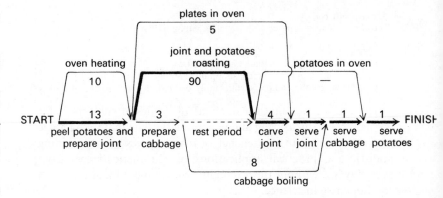

Figure 9.2   Critical path diagram for the preparation of a meal.

9.4   Furnishing a Room

The problem of furnishing a room involves questions of convenience and taste, but also problems of size and shape. Scale drawing of plans on graph paper is of assistance, particularly when items of furniture are represented by movable pieces of card. It is also necessary to show as sectors of circles the space taken up by opening doors.

9.5   Needlework

Scope for geometrical ingenuity is provided in needlework by the problem of fitting pattern shapes into a piece of material to obtain the most economical use of cloth. Other geometrical ideas which arise are: symmetry (in embroidery and tapestry design, and in dress patterns), the construction of polygons (various types of patchwork and embroidery), and enlargement (of scaled-down patterns). Needlework also provides instances of measurement: linear measurement (personal measures, measurement of material), area measurement (comparison of wastage when using various standard widths for the same pattern), and the classification of materials by mass (weight) per unit area. The making of garments with pleats and tucks requires careful measurement and accurate division.

10 Mathematics in Games and Physical Education

This chapter describes ways in which mathematics enters the fields of Games and Athletics, Orienteering, and Educational Dance.

GAMES AND ATHLETICS

10.1   Geometrical Construction and Mensuration

The marking out of pitches and tracks, and the construction of scale diagrams of pitches are obvious instances of geometrical work. The relationship between circumference and radius of a circle enters into the problems of constructing a running track and marking staggered starts in the lanes.

10.2   Geometrical Problems

In many games appreciation of tactics involves an understanding of geometrical configurations. Some examples are given below.

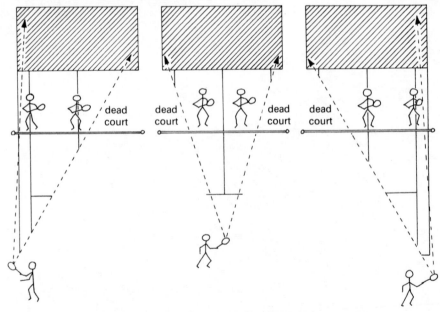

Figure 10.1   Net coverage in tennis.

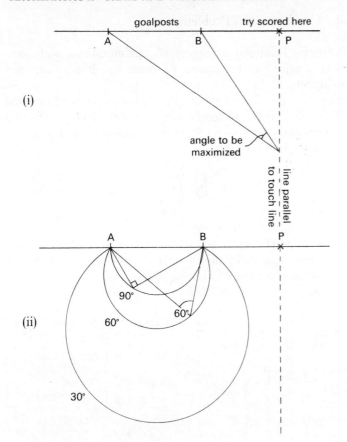

(i)

(ii)

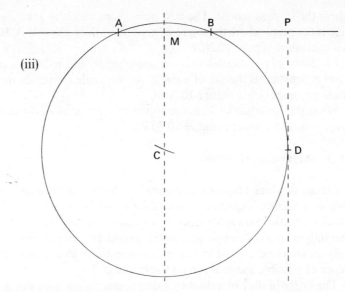

(iii)

To find C, the centre of this circle, draw a line through M, the midpoint of AB, parallel to the touchlines. With centre B and radius equal to PM, draw an arc to cut this line at C.[1] Make PD = MC.

Figure 10.2   Determination of the optimum position from which to convert a try in rugby.

NET COVERAGE IN TENNIS

A full understanding of this aspect of tennis requires a knowledge of the motion of projectiles. However, a plan view showing the consequences of the laws of motion is instructive. If the ball is hit from a given position on the base line, there are parts of the opponents' court over which the ball cannot travel without probably going "out". These parts constitute "dead court". They are shown for three positions of the player hitting the ball in figure 10.1.

Because there is no need for the opposing players to cover the "dead court" areas, they can position themselves for maximum coverage of the remaining "live court".

A PROBLEM IN RUGBY UNION FOOTBALL

When a try is scored, the conversion may be attempted from any point on a line parallel to the touch lines through the point P

[1] It is a simple matter to show that the locus of points of maximum angle as P varies is the rectangular hyperbola $x^2 - y^2 = a^2$, where AB = 2a, the origin is at M and the x-axis is MB produced.

where the try was scored. The best point from which to take the kick is the point where the angle subtended by the goalposts A, B, is a maximum (figure 10.2(i)).

The locus of points such that the angle subtended by the goal posts is constant is the arc of a circle. As the angle decreases the circle becomes larger (figure 10.2(ii)).

When the circle just touches the dotted line, the point of contact gives a maximum angle (figure 10.2(iii)).

10.3 Algebraic Structure

Games in which players are required to change position and/or role in a regular sequence exhibit (like some forms of country dancing) mathematical structures. An understanding of these is certainly no part of competence in the game! They are of interest only as concrete embodiments of mathematical ideas, and are hence of possible use in teaching those ideas.

The order of play in a doubles table-tennis match provides an example (see J. F. Ling and C. P. O'Donoghue: *Modern Exercises in Ordinary Level Mathematics*, pp. 73–4). In each pair the partners take it in turn to play the ball and to serve. Service changes from pair to pair after each player's turn to serve. Figure 10.3 shows the sequence of a game (arrows indicate service).

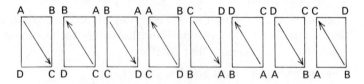

Figure 10.3 Service in table-tennis.

There is a correspondence between these positions and the elements of the symmetry group of a square.

10.4 Combinatorial Problems

Problems involving arrangements, permutations and combinations arise in the course of planning fixture lists and tournaments.

In an American Tournament with five teams in one section and one court it is required to arrange an order of play such that each team plays every other. If no two teams play in consecutive games, a solution is as follows:

(1) A v B	(5) D v E	(9) C v D
(2) C v E	(6) A v C	(10) B v E
(3) A v D	(7) B v D	
(4) B v C	(8) A v E	

The scorecard for such a section takes the form of a 5×5 matrix, with the points scored by each team in the *rows*, and consequently the points scored *against* in the columns.

	Team A	Team B	Team C	Team D	Team E	Points	Place
Team A		0 / 4 8	2 / 6 4	2 / 5 4	1 / 6 6	5	
Team B	2 / 8 4		2 / 4 3	0 / 3 6	0 / 3 7	4	
Team C	0 / 4 6	0 / 3 4		1 / 3 3	2 / 5 2	3	
Team D	0 / 4 5	2 / 6 3	1 / 3 3		2 / 5 2	5	
Team E	1 / 6 6	2 / 7 3	0 / 2 5	0 / 2 5		3	

The table opposite shows an example of a tennis championship. Since the number of players involved is not a member of the 2^n series, byes are necessary. The total number of games played is 11. In general it will always be one less than the number of players. In this table seeded players are in capitals.

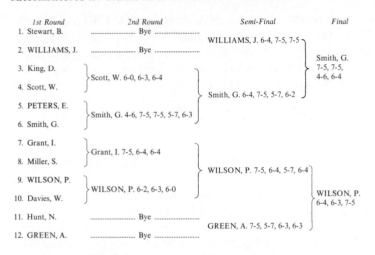

1st Round	2nd Round	Semi-Final	Final
1. Stewart, B.	.... Bye		
		WILLIAMS, J. 6-4, 7-5, 7-5	
2. WILLIAMS, J.	.... Bye		
			Smith, G. 7-5, 7-5, 4-6, 6-4
3. King, D.			
4. Scott, W.	Scott, W. 6-0, 6-3, 6-4		
		Smith, G. 6-4, 7-5, 5-7, 6-2	
5. PETERS, E.			
6. Smith, G.	Smith, G. 4-6, 7-5, 7-5, 5-7, 6-3		
7. Grant, I.			
8. Miller, S.	Grant, I. 7-5, 6-4, 6-4		
		WILSON, P. 7-5, 6-4, 5-7, 6-4	
9. WILSON, P.			
10. Davies, W.	WILSON, P. 6-2, 6-3, 6-0		WILSON, P. 6-4, 6-3, 7-5
11. Hunt, N.	.... Bye		
		GREEN, A. 7-5, 5-7, 6-3, 6-3	
12. GREEN, A.	.... Bye		

The arrangement of the fixture list for 5 teams in a football tournament can be obtained with the aid of a 5-sided regular polygon. The sets of "parallels" in figure 10.4 indicate the matches.

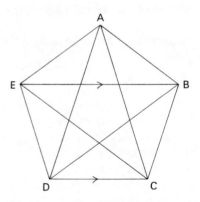

Figure 10.4   Generation of a fixture list.

First matches	B v E	C v D	A bye
Second matches	A v C	D v E	B bye
Third matches	B v D	A v E	C bye
Fourth matches	C v E	A v B	D bye
Fifth matches	A v D	B v C	E bye

This diagram assists in the compilation of the order of games in the American tournament described above.

The case in which there are 6 teams is dealt with by placing five of the teams, A, B, C, D, E, on the pentagon as in figure 10.4 and pairing the sixth team F with each of the "bye" teams in the list above.

First matches	B v E	C v D	A v F	
Second matches	A v C	D v E	B v F	etc.

The method can be extended to any number of teams, odd or even (see E. H. Lockwood, *Mathematical Gazette* Vol. 20, p. 333 and *Counting and Configurations*, a book in this series).

10.5   Scoring and Ranking Systems

The calculation of the *goal average* for a team, defined as the quotient

$$\frac{\text{goals for}}{\text{goals against}}$$

involves some simple division. It is worth pointing out the effect upon goal average of a scored draw as opposed to a non-score draw, or of, say, a 3–2 win as opposed to a 1–0 win. A comparison may be made with the effects of these scores upon *goal difference*, defined as (goals for − goals against).

If the outcome of a single game is either win or loss with no differentiation between scores, the overall result may be that several individuals have identical numbers of wins. One way of discriminating further between players is to take into account the number of *second-order dominances* of each player. A player A has a second-order dominance over another player B if he has beaten another player who has beaten B.

The results of the games between, say, four players can be shown in a directed network: An arrow indicates a win (figure 10.5); e.g. A beat B.

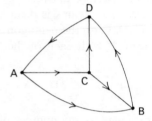

Figure 10.5   Results displayed on a directed network.

The matrix associated with this network is

$$
\begin{array}{c c c c c}
 & A & B & C & D \\
A & 0 & 1 & 1 & 0 \\
B & 0 & 0 & 0 & 1 \\
C & 0 & 1 & 0 & 1 \\
D & 1 & 0 & 0 & 0
\end{array}
$$

The total scores of A,B,C,D are 2,1,2,1 respectively.

The second-order dominances may be obtained by inspection of the network or by squaring the matrix above. They are

$$
\begin{array}{c c c c c}
 & A & B & C & D \\
A & 0 & 1 & 0 & 2 \\
B & 1 & 0 & 0 & 0 \\
C & 1 & 0 & 0 & 1 \\
D & 0 & 1 & 1 & 0
\end{array}
$$

Totalling these second-order dominances for each player is equivalent to the following procedure:

  (i) Give each player a weight equal to his total number of wins.
  (ii) Calculate an overall score for each player by adding the weights of the players he has beaten.

The second-order dominance scores are: A:3, B:1, C:2, D:2. They may be used to discriminate between players with equal first-order scores. Alternatively, from the first and second-order scores a composite score may be obtained by using some previously agreed rule, e.g. "First-order score + ½ second-order score."

Work on dominance matrices is included in *SMP Book* 3.

ORIENTEERING AND EXPEDITION

In many schools orienteering is now an accepted part of the physical education programme, with competitions arranged locally and nationally for junior, intermediate and senior pupils.

The Duke of Edinburgh's Award Scheme has also become very popular in schools. One of the essentials of the Award Scheme is for every candidate to have a knowledge of navigation with map and compass. Candidates are expected to plan and carry out expeditions unaccompanied by adults. Their route cards provide the necessary link for checking on safety and assessing proficiency. Training for this aspect of the Award often starts at the age of 13.

Mathematical requirements for Orienteering and Expedition are:

(1) *A knowledge of circular measure.*

Orienteers make use of a type of compass which enables them to obtain their line of travel directly from a map without having to note a bearing as a number of degrees. The compass of this kind most commonly used in Britain is the "Silva" compass, illustrated in figure 10.6.

When a compass bearing is being taken, the longer edge of the compass base plate is first placed along the line of intended travel on the map. The compass housing is then rotated until

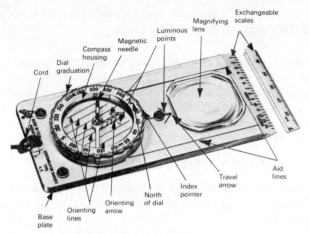

Figure 10.6 "Silva" compass.

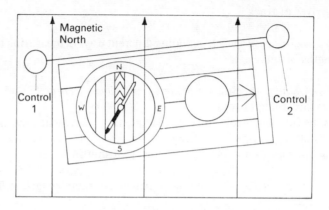

Figure 10.7 The line of travel is from Control 1 to Control 2.

the orienting lines (which rotate with the housing) are parallel to the magnetic north lines on the map, and the arrow indicating north points in the direction representing (magnetic) north on the map (see figure 10.7).[1]

The compass is then removed from the map and held flat in the palm of the hand. The orienteer turns his body until the arrow on the compass housing coincides with the magnetic north-pointing needle. In this position (shown in figure 10.8) the line of travel arrow is pointing along the actual bearing of Control 2 from Control 1.

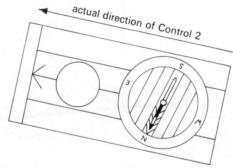

Figure 10.8 Actual bearing of Control 2 from Control 1.

(2) *A realization that the effects of an error in determining a bearing are magnified as distance from starting point increases.*

The effects of (unavoidable) errors in angle can be allowed for by "aiming off". If the landmark to be reached lies on some easily followed continuous feature, such as a river or track, and the orienteer aims directly at it, he is likely to arrive some distance away either side of the landmark without knowing when he arrives which side it is. If he purposely aims so that even given the greatest possible error he will certainly arrive, say, left of the

[1]J. D. Watson: *Orienteering*, pp. 18, 19. ("Know the Game" series, published by EP Publishing Ltd; 3rd Edition, 1975.) The "Silva" compass is manufactured by Silva Compasses (London) Ltd.

landmark, then he will know which way to turn when he meets the river or track.

(3) *Length measurement*, including different ways of measuring the lengths of curves.

(4) *An ability to estimate distance and times accurately* and to compare different routes.

One rule for calculating approximate travel time when walking is to allow 1 hour for 3 miles on the level, plus an additional half hour for every 1000 feet climbed (Naismith's Rule).

(5) *Understanding of scale* (maps, plans), coordinates (grid refer-

ences, see page 83). Much use is made of displacement vectors, though they may not be described as such.

(6) *Ability to interpret contours*, and to relate these to gradients.

(7) In addition to the skills above, the planning of an expedition involves some of the skills already described as necessary in home economics—costing, planning meals.

MODERN EDUCATIONAL DANCE

Modern Educational Dance is established on the principles of Rudolf Laban. In his book on the subject (R. Laban: *Modern*

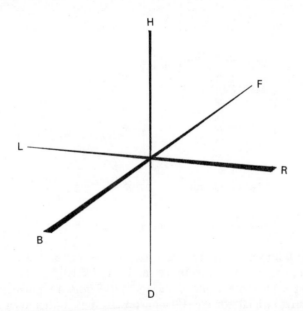

Figure 10.9   The dimensional cross.

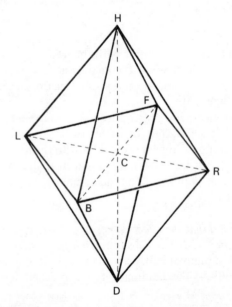

Figure 10.10   The set of peripheral transitions.

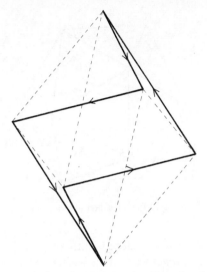

Figure 10.11   Six-ring closed peripheral path.

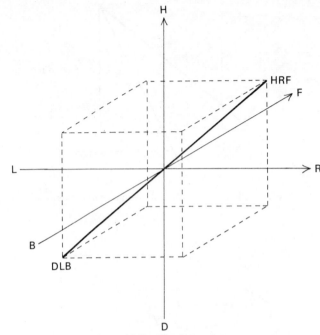

Figure 10.12   The diagonal cross.

Educational Dance, Macdonald and Evans, 1948.) Laban described sixteen basic movement themes, of which Theme XI is concerned with "orientation in space". In her *Handbook for Modern Educational Dance* (Macdonald and Evans, 1963) Valerie Preston bases her exposition upon Laban's sixteen themes. The section devoted to orientation in space shows how certain configurations of solid geometry are of importance in describing movement.

The three dimensions of bodily movement can be represented as axes drawn through the centre of the body. This set of axes is called the *dimensional cross*, and the six directions radiating out from the centre are high (upward), deep (downward), left, right, backward, forward (figure 10.9).

A movement in one of these directions, starting or finishing at the centre, is called a *central transition*. Transitions may also be made *peripherally*, and the whole set of all possible peripheral transitions is the set of edges of an octahedron (figure 10.10).

Of particular interest are closed peripheral paths, of which the *six-ring* shown in figure 10.11 is important.

Movement through the centre can also take place on each of four diagonal lines, which together form the *diagonal cross*. One of these diagonals is shown in figure 10.12.

The associated peripheral transitions take place on a cube. They may be "over edge" or "over plane" transitions (figure 10.13).

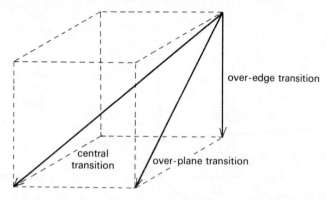

Figure 10.13   Over-edge and over-plane transitions.

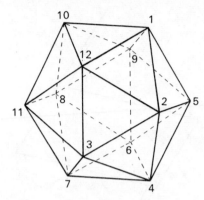

Figure 10.15   Icosahedral movements.

Figure 10.14 shows a closed path of peripheral transitions called an *equator*, together with its associated *axis*.

Also associated with the original set of axes are three planes (which mathematicians will recognize as the $x = 0$, $y = 0$, $z = 0$ planes). If these three planes are drawn as rectangles, the peripheral transitions between vertices form an icosahedron, and the corresponding movements are sometimes referred to as icosahedral movements (figure 10.15). (The icosahedron will be regular only if each of the rectangles has its sides in a certain ratio). As in the cases of the octahedron and cube, circuits or rings of transitions can be made.

In a suggested scheme of work for secondary schools, Theme XI, which includes all of the foregoing material, would be worked at each year between ages 12 and 16 (see Valerie Preston's book, p. 157).

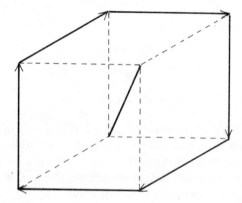

Figure 10.14   Equator: a closed path of peripheral transitions.

11 Mathematics and Art

It is a debatable point as to whether this chapter should be about mathematics in art, or about art in mathematics, hence the ambivalent title. Many mathematicians speak of the beauty of mathematics, and even though they may be thinking of the beauty to be found in the order and inter-relatedness of abstract mathematics, the more concrete manifestations of order, in

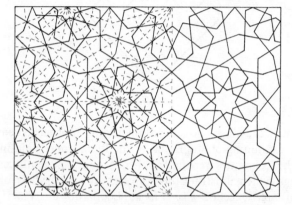

Figure 11.1   An Arabic geometric design.

geometry, can also be objects of aesthetic appreciation. Because of a shared interest in two-dimensional and three-dimensional space, inter-relationships between art and mathematics can be looked for in the area of geometry.

In some cultures, geometrical patterns have been the basis of flourishing decorative art: this is particularly true of the Arabic civilization. The ordered complexity which can be created out of essentially simple elements is often breathtaking. The pattern in figure 11.1 is from a book containing two hundred examples

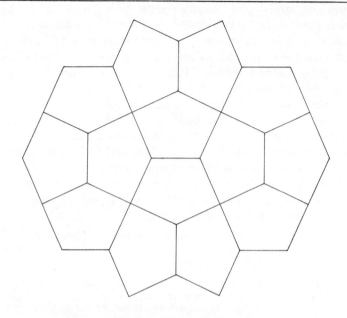

Figure 11.2   Pentagonal tessellation.

(J. Bourgoin: *Arabic Geometrical Pattern and Design*, Dover 1973). The book is well worth having for the school mathematics library.

The geometrical tradition lives on in Arab countries: even ordinary pavements in Cairo are tessellated with pentagonal paving stones (figure 11.2).[1]

---

[1] For further discussion of pentagonal tessellations see *Geometry*, a book in the present series, chapter 8 and also *Mathematical Gazette* 394, December 1971, pp. 366–369 for a note by J. A. Dunn.

The geometrical designs of the Arabic civilizations were often interlaced. Figure 11.3 shows a simple interlacing pattern.

The pattern is made up of two closed paths, but on each of them the "overs" and "unders" as the path crosses either the other path or itself are alternate. Is it possible to interlace any pattern in this way; if not, what conditions have to hold for interlacing to be possible? These questions are the subject of an article on "Celtic Interlacing Patterns and Topology" by H. A. Thurston in *Science News* No. 33, 1954 (Penguin).

Among art teachers in general there is not at present a great deal of interest in those aspects of two-and three-dimensional space which are amenable to mathematical treatment. Crown Woods School, London, operates a Mode III CSE Mathematics with an option entitled "Mathematics and Art", for which the syllabus is given below. The choice of topics did not involve the art department and the teaching is currently the responsibility of the mathematics department.

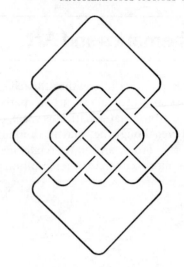

Figure 11.3   Interlacing pattern.

Crown Woods School "Mathematics and Art" syllabus

Loci	Cardioid, cycloid, limaçon, spirals, hyperbola, parabola, ellipse. Use of spirograph, linkages, pantograph, etc.
Graphs	Parabola, hyperbola. Meaning of asymptotes. Cubics.
Envelopes	Cardioid, cycloid, limaçon, nephroid, astroid.
Sine Curve	Drawing; using apparatus; plotting on a graph. Lissajous' figures—by cathode-ray oscilloscope and by using apparatus
Tessellations	Regular and semi-regular. Artistic tessellations.
Solid Geometry	Construction of all platonic solids and one other regular solid. Some Archimedean solids; some Archimedean duals. Six pyramids to make a cube. Rhombic dodecahedron. Solid tessellations.
Golden section	Use; equiangular spiral.
One-sided figures	Moebius strip; Klein bottle.
Ruled Surfaces	Hyperboloid, paraboloid, hyperbolic paraboloid, etc.

It was once a major concern of artists to represent reality pictorially, and it is possible to trace the history of the discovery of the rules of perspective in the Renaissance. Nowadays perspective is taught to architects and engineers as a branch of technical drawing. The subject can also be approached empirically by examining photographs, or the Renaissance paintings in which the techniques were first applied. Amongst fifteenth-century paintings which illustrate the convergence of parallels on the horizon are Uccello: *The Flood*; Leonardo da Vinci: *The Adoration of the Kings*; Ghirlandaio: *The Adoration of the Magi*. The location of the vanishing point affects the structure of the picture: it may be central and in a position unoccupied by any feature of the painting, or it may be located in or near the central subject.

The construction of a pictorial representation of a square-tiled pavement involves the use of a second vanishing point. This is the point to which diagonals of the squares which are in fact parallel appear to converge (figure 11.4).

The pavement in Raphael: *Disputa* is a clear example of this technique. Once a method for drawing a square grid is

STUDY FOR THE ADORATION OF THE MAGI. Florence, Uffizi.

THE FLAGELLATION OF CHRIST.   Urbino, Gallery.

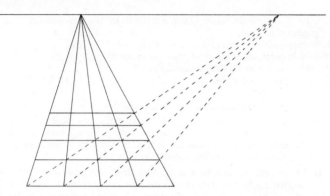

Figure 11.4   Pictorial representation of a square-tiled pavement.

available, the representation of other shapes becomes possible if they can be related to the grid. The tiling of the floor in Piero della Francesca: *The Flagellation* shows this.

A study of perspective[1] leads into projective geometry, in particular to Desargues' theorem. Also of interest is the way in which the ambiguity inherent in perspective and other systems of projection (e.g. isometric) can be exploited to produce representations of impossible three-dimensional structures. The ambiguity arises from the fact that the mapping from a point in space to its image on the picture plane is many-to-one. All points on a line of sight (in perspective projection) or on a line perpendicular to the picture plane (in isometric projection) are represented in the picture by the same point.

Figure 11.5(i) is an isometric view of the following configuration: A is 1 metre north of B on horizontal ground; C is 1 metre vertically above B; D is one metre east of C on the same level as C. In the picture A and D coincide. The ambiguity of the point AD is exploited in the well-known diagram of figure 11.5(ii).

[1] Some lessons in perspective are described in *Geometry*, a book in the present series.

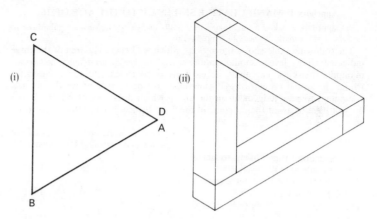

Figure 11.5   Ambiguity in an isometric projection.

Perspective views of impossible structures are a speciality of M. C. Escher, whose work in general has many features which appeal to the mathematically minded.

This chapter draws attention to certain mathematical topics which, while perhaps not at present felt to be important by many art teachers, might nevertheless be found of interest to some, as well as to teachers of mathematics.

Bibliography

H. Osborne (ed.): *Oxford Companion to Art* (articles on "Perspective" and "Proportion") OUP 1970.

M. Holt: *Mathematics in Art*, Studio Vista 1971

J. Bourgoin: *Arabic Geometrical Pattern and Design*, Dover 1973.

H. A. Thurston: "Celtic Interlacing Patterns and Topology" (article in *Science News* 33, Penguin 1954).

M. C. Escher: *Graphic Work of M. C. Escher*, Pan/Ballantine 1972.

R. Arnheim: *Art and Visual Perception*, Faber and Faber 1956.

E. H. Gombrich: *Art and Illusion*, Phaidon Press, 4th Edn. 1972 (especially chapter VIII: Ambiguities of the Third Dimension.)

F. Dubery and J. Willats: *Drawing Systems*, Studio Vista 1972.

Appendix 1: MANIPULATIVE SKILLS UP TO THE AGE OF 16

This appendix is taken from *Manipulative Skills in School Mathematics* published by the School Mathematics Project, 1974 (pp. 11–13).

The following table shows the ages by which we believe children of the three indicated ability levels, should acquire a *high degree of proficiency* in various manipulative skills. The ability levels correspond roughly to the children for whom the whole range of SMP materials have been written; we do not feel competent to pass judgement on the group which does not attempt CSE and we will have to await the outcome of the 7–13 Project before attempting to do so.

	By age of about 13	By age of about 14	By age of about 16
The most able: those likely to get a good grade at "O" Level	1–13	14–18	19–21
The able: those likely to get a pass at "O" Level or Grade 1 CSE	1–7	8–13	14–19
The average: those likely to be graded at CSE	1–3	5–8	4, 9–12

The numerals in the table refer to mathematical processes as follows:

1. Recall and use of the addition and multiplication of integers up to 10.
2. Manipulation of simple* arithmetic fractions.
3. Simple problems involving percentages.
4. Simple mental arithmetic with integers, involving "carrying" one number in the head, using $+$, $-$, $\times$ and $\div$.
5. Addition, subtraction, long multiplication and division, normally of numbers with up to three significant figures (including decimals).
6. The four arithmetic operations of directed numbers.
7. Simple use and applications of units of length, area, volume, mass and decimal money.
8. Simple ratio calculations.
9. Estimation of size of answers to numerical calculations (including decimals) using "rounding".
10. Solution of simple linear equations, e.g. $ax+b=c$; $px+q=rx+s$. etc., where the coefficients are numbers.
11. Manipulation of simple formulae involving $+$, $-$, $\times$, $\div$ and use of brackets.
12. Use of slide rule or calculator for multiplication and division.
13. Use of standard form, with positive indices, in simple multiplication and division.
14. Use of standard form, with negative indices, in simple multiplication and division.
15. Squares and square roots using slide rule and tables.
16. Simple applications of sin, cos, tan and the use of the corresponding tables.

*It is difficult to avoid using the word "simple" in such a list. It is also difficult to define the levels of simplicity appropriate on each occasion. Broadly, by "simple" we mean "*very* simple"!

17. Solution of simultaneous linear equations in two unknowns by a non-graphical method.
18. Interpretation of the graph of $y=ax+b$.
19. Simple examples of the applications of proportion.
20. Use of log tables for simple calculations.
21. Interpretation of graph for $y=ax^n+b$, and use of linear graphs for non-linear relations.

Some further remarks need to be made about this table:

(i) Many of the skills 1–13 should have been first acquired at primary school (i.e. before the age of about eleven), though more practice may be needed to achieve and retain the "high degree of proficiency" which we deem desirable at the age of 16.

(ii) As to item 20, we believe that a high degree of proficiency in the use of logarithms for calculations is no longer relevant to most children and that "long" methods, slide rule, electronic calculators and approximate calculations provide adequate alternatives. There remain some applications, however, for which the use of log tables is still needed and, in these cases, training in their use would be better included in the relevant course.

(iii) The items in the table should be read in conjunction with the published set of *SMP Elementary Tables*. It is the intention that this set of tables should be freely used as an aid to performance at all times.

(iv) Most of the requirements of this table are consistent with the timing and placing of topics in the SMP's pupil materials. But teachers should always be flexible in their use of the published books, and be on the lookout for variations—such as re-ordering of topics, further simple introductions, or more practice examples—which would help their pupils.

(v) This table does NOT represent any SMP examination syllabus. For example, the GCE "O" Level syllabus for "SMP Elementary Mathematics" (obtainable on request to the SMP Office) includes a great deal more material. But for this additional material, we do not think that such a high level of manipulative expertise is necessary.

(vi) The needs of other school subjects (notably physics, economics, chemistry) have been taken into account.

Finally, we wish to stress the need for continuous attention, week by week and term by term, being given to these key topics during previous years. Not everything can be provided by textbooks. Teachers themselves must be prepared to devise means of maintaining their pupils' interest and skill in these topics. They will be helped by the suggestion made here and there in the Teachers' Guides. Also, some of the responsibility for securing this continuing level of skill should be accepted by science teachers and others who use mathematics as a service subject. It is therefore vital that, within any one school, there should be good understanding between teachers of related subjects in regard to the timing of topics, the language to be used and the methods to be employed.

12 Some Statistical Topics

A2.1 Non-Parametric Statistical Tests

Some non-parametric statistical tests have, from the teaching point of view, certain advantages in that it is possible to understand their rationale on the basis of only simple probability theory.

Described below are an application of the binomial distribution to a type of experiment used in the study of animal behaviour, and two statistical tests used in circumstances where we may wish to decide whether two different treatments applied to individuals such as animals, plants, cars, etc., give significantly different results.

CHOICE CHAMBERS IN ANIMAL BEHAVIOUR STUDIES

The simplest form of apparatus in this type of experiment consists of a divided chamber which is set up so that a single physical or chemical factor difference exists between the two chambers, e.g. light/dark or humid/dry. In order to determine the sensitivity of an animal to the factor, resulting in a directional response, animals are placed at the interface between the two conditions and allowed to "choose".

If the animals "choose" entirely at random, then we would expect to get approximately equal numbers of them opting for the left-hand and right-hand chambers. Large departures from equality are associated with the greater plausibility of the hypothesis that some factor-influenced response is present. If out of, say, 8 animals, 2 choose the left and 6 the right chamber, it is necessary to determine the probability of getting a distribution as unequal as or more unequal than this on the basis of purely random choice. The random choice may be represented by the

tossing of a coin, and the question to be answered then becomes: What is the probability that when 8 coins are tossed the numbers of heads and tails differ by at least 4? There are $2^8 = 256$ ways in which 8 coins may fall. In 74 of these ways the numbers of heads and tails differ by at least 4. (The number 74 may be obtained using Pascal's triangle.) So the probability of such a divergence from equality is $\frac{74}{256} \approx 0.29$, and this is not sufficiently low to warrant rejecting the hypothesis of random choice.

THE SIGN TEST

The experimental data in this case are obtained by giving each of two treatments to each of several individuals. It is assumed that the effects of the two treatments are independent (if this is thought not to be so, then pairs of individuals as nearly identical as possible ("matched pairs") have to be used). As an example, suppose that eight pairs of new-born animals are chosen, each pair being of comparable weight and from the same litter. One of each pair is fed on diet A, the other on diet B. The gain in weight after 1 week is recorded for each animal.

Pair number	1	2	3	4	5	6	7	8
Diet A	26	31	28	29	35	22	29	27
Diet B	28	34	28	26	39	26	30	24
B − A	2	3	0	−3	4	4	1	−3

Since in all other respects the two animals in each pair are identical, the difference in weight-gains $(B - A)$ in each pair arises from differences between the effects of the diets. For each diet it is assumed that its effect (measured as a gain in weight) is symmetrically distributed about a central value (which is thus both mean and median).

The test is based on the numbers of positive and negative differences (zero differences being ignored). On the hypothesis that there is no median difference between diet effects, each difference is equally as likely to be positive as negative. A large number of positive differences is associated with the greater plausibility of the alternative hypothesis that the diet B has a greater median effect than A. Given seven non-zero differences, there are $2^7 = 128$ different arrangements of $+$ and $-$, all equally likely under the hypothesis of no diet difference. The probability of getting 5 (as in the example given) or more $+$ signs may be found by counting the arrangements concerned. There are 29 of them. So the probability of 5 or more $+$ signs is $\frac{29}{128}$. This probability is not so low as to lead to a rejection of the hypothesis of no diet difference.

(Note that the probability of 6 or more $+$ signs is $\frac{8}{128} = 0.0625$, and even this not sufficiently small if we wish to operate at the 5 per cent significance level. One of the drawbacks of this test lies in the fact that the level of significance of any conclusion drawn is restricted to a range of discrete values such as $\frac{29}{128}, \frac{8}{128}, \frac{1}{128}$.

This problem is alleviated by having more pairs of experimental data.)

THE WILCOXON TWO-SAMPLE TEST

The experimental data in this case are obtained by giving the two treatments to two different random samples of individuals. Once again each treatment effect is assumed to be symmetrically distributed about a central value (median and mean). Suppose that a random sample of 3 animals is fed on diet A, and another random sample of 4 is fed on diet B. As before, the gain in weight is recorded for each individual.

The observed values (of weight gain) are arranged in rank order, the diet in each case being noted.

Individual	1	2	3	4	5	6	7
Diet	A	A	A	A	B	B	B
Weight gain	13.2	16.5	14.9	12.7	18.3	14.2	13.9

Rank	1	2	3	4	5	6	7
Diet	B	A	A	B	B	A	A

The rank-sum for diet A is 18, that for B 10. (The total in any case for 7 animals will be $1+2+\ldots+7 = 28$.)

On the hypothesis that the observed values all come from the same population, each possible arrangement of four As and three Bs has equal probability. There are 35 of them. (Although pupils may not be able to calculate the number of arrangements for themselves, there is no conceptual difficulty involved. In simple cases all possible arrangements may be written down.) If the median yield with diet B were very much greater than with A, an arrangement

1	2	3	4	5	6	7
B	B	B	A	A	A	A

would be expected. Low values for the rank-sum of B indicate the greater plausibility of the hypothesis that B is better than A. If it is desired to test whether B is significantly better than A, it must be asked whether a rank-sum for B of 10 (as here) or less is sufficiently improbable on the hypothesis of "no difference between diets" for that hypothesis to be rejected. A rank-sum for B of 10 or less is obtained when Bs occupy the following ranks:

123, 124, 125, 126, 127, 134, 135, 136, 145, 234, 235.

There are 11 such cases, so the probability of obtaining a value of 10 or less (given "no difference") is $\frac{11}{35}$, which is not small enough for significance.

These non-parametric tests may have disadvantages as tests. For example, they discard information in the experimental data and they offer only a limited range of discrete values for significance levels. But they do enable the pupil to appreciate the rationale of a statistical test, and to calculate the boundaries of critical regions and their associated probabilities.

A2.2 Kendall's Coefficient of Rank Correlation

Kendall's coefficient has from a teaching point of view the advantage over Spearman's coefficient in that it is easier to explain why it is a reasonable measure of correlation between rankings. Suppose that it is required to measure the degree of disarrangement between the set 1, 2, 3, 4, 5, 6 and the set 1, 3, 2, 6, 4, 5. The two extreme cases of no disarrangement and complete reversal can be illustrated as in figure A2.1.

In (ii) the arrows have been curved to avoid the crossing of more than two at any one point. The total number of cross-overs in (ii) is 15. The number of cross-overs is a guide to the degree of re-arrangement. For example, in figure A2.2 the transposition of 1 and 2 counts one, whereas that between 4 and 6 counts 2.

If the number of cross-overs is used as a measure of disarrangement, then for the two sets originally proposed as an example, the disarrangement number is 3. The maximum possible number is 15; hence this example

$$\text{index of disarrangement} = \frac{\text{disarrangement number}}{\text{maximum possible disarrangement number}} = \frac{3}{15}.$$

To convert this index to a correlation coefficient it is necessary to arrange that a value of $+1$ should be obtained from an index 0, and -1 from an index 15. This may be done graphically as in figure A2.4, or alternatively we may say that an index of $\frac{3}{15}$ corresponds to a correlation coefficient $\frac{3}{15}$ of the way between $+1$ and -1, i.e. $1 + \frac{3}{15} \times (-2) = \frac{9}{15} = 0 \cdot 6$.

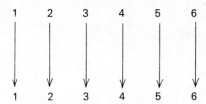

Figure A2.1(i)   Perfect positive correlation.

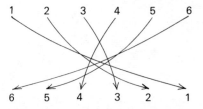

Figure A2.1(ii)   Perfect negative correlation.

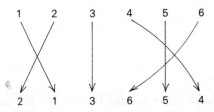

Figure A2.2.

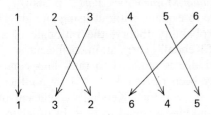

Figure A2.3.

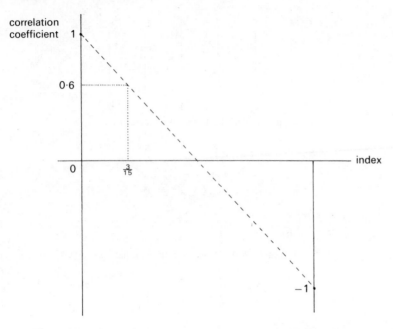

Figure A2.4   Conversion of disarrangement index to correlation coefficient.

of correlation could arise from a purely random allocation of rank orders to the four contestants? There are 24 possible permutations of 1 2 3 4, and for each of them the correlation coefficient can be found. The distribution is as follows:

Correlation coefficient	-1	$-\frac{2}{3}$	$-\frac{1}{3}$	0	$\frac{1}{3}$	$\frac{2}{3}$	1
Number of permutations with this correlation coefficient	1	3	5	6	5	3	1

At this point it is important to note that the question being asked is whether there is significant correlation. The term *correlation* covers both agreement (positive correlation) and disagreement (negative correlation). Although in this example it might appear pointless to bracket together the properties of agreement and disagreement (we are generally interested in how far judges approach complete agreement and not how far they approach total disagreement) in most applications it is correlation (of either kind) which is of interest. If Kendall's coefficient is denoted by τ, then $|\tau|$ is a measure of correlation, and we may derive the following table from that above:

$|\tau|$	0	$\frac{1}{3}$	$\frac{2}{3}$	1
Number of permutations	6	10	6	2

It follows that the probability of obtaining a degree of correlation equal to or better than that indicated by $\tau = \frac{2}{3}$ is $\frac{8}{24}$ or $\frac{1}{3}$, or $33\frac{1}{3}$ per cent. Such a result is far from significant if 5 per cent is taken as the level of significance.

This simple example is worked here in order to show what is involved in the construction of tables giving the ranges of significant values of the correlation coefficient for various numbers of ranked individuals. Short tables can be found in e.g. R. Loveday: *Statistics, A First Course* (2nd edn., CUP 1969), p. 68 and *SMP Additional Mathematics, Part 2*, CUP, p. 366. Fuller tables in graphical form are in: *New Form Statistical Tables*, University of London Press.

When dealing with tied ranks the method hitherto described breaks down and the standard procedure for Kendall's coefficient needs to be used (the standard procedure may be found in *SMP Additional Mathematics, Part 2*, p. 366).

It is possible to explain, without using any ideas beyond very elementary probability theory, the rationale of a test of the significance of Kendall's correlation coefficient.

Suppose a judge is required to rank four contestants, these having already been ranked 1, 2, 3, 4 by another judge. If he ranks them 1, 3, 2, 4, then Kendall's coefficient of correlation between the rankings is found to be $\frac{2}{3}$. In order to test whether this is significant, we need to ask: how likely is it that this degree

Index

algebra, 14, 22–27, 55
  See also under separate entries: equations, formulae.
algebraic structure, 130
approximation, 8, 142
area, 9, 31, 142
  similar figures, 118, 126
  surface area, 73–75
  trapezium, 31
  triangles on same base, 34, 118
    See also circle
arithmetic, 5, 14, 68, 107–108, 124, 125–126, 142
  See also decimal arithmetic
arithmetic mean. See mean
arrow diagram, 10, 24
average, 8
  See also mean

bearings, 84, 132–134

calculators, electronic, 6, 9, 21, 98, 142
circle
  area, 31, 39, 40, 85, 89, 92, 114
  circumference, 31, 40, 114, 119, 128
  geometrical properties, 27–28, 33, 112, 113, 117–118, 126, 129–130
    See also close-packing
close-packing
  circles, 99
  spheres, 60–63
codomain, 23
combinatorial problems, 130–131
compound units, 6–7
  See rate, density
constructions, geometrical
  See geometrical constructions
contours, 85, 134
  See also isopleths
coordinates, 83–84, 134

correlation. See statistical methods
critical path analysis, 126
cylinder, 31

decimal arithmetic, 5, 52–55, 68, 112, 113–4, 142
density, 3, 6–7
  areal density, 90
  population density, 7
development of surface, 85, 113
difference notation (Δ), 57
directed numbers. See negative numbers
displacement. See translation, vector
distribution, 77–78, 89–93
domain, 23

electronic calculator. See calculator, electronic
enlargement, 29, 73–75, 112, 113, 115–116
envelope, 138
equations, 23–27
  single linear equation, 23–26, 38, 142
  simultaneous linear equations, 23, 25–27, 39, 55, 65–67, 142
error, experimental, 8
exponential function, 43–44, 57, 77
flow diagram, 13, 24, 35–37, 68–70
formulae
  setting up, 22, 32–33, 40–41, 73
  substitution in, 22, 55, 97–98
  manipulation of, 22–23, 33–34, 40–41, 92, 98, 142
fractions, 15, 37–8, 68, 70, 83, 112, 142
frequency table, 77
  See also graph, frequency
function, functional relationship, 10, 23, 74, 89–93, 107, 109–110

geometrical construction, 45–47, 112–113, 116, 126, 128
gradient, 56, 73, 85, 90, 134
graph, 9–11
  area under graph, 20, 31, 32, 44–45, 125

change of origin, 2, 18–19
  drawing, 10, 43–44, 68, 76
  functional relationship, 24, 41–42
  interpolation, 43–44, 76
  interpretation, 9, 18, 42–43, 56, 68, 75–76, 107–108, 109, 142
  percentage conversion, 8
  speed-time, 31–32, 43
  statistical, 77–78, 85–86
    See also histogram, pie chart
  straight-line, 18, 44, 56, 142
  transformation of scale, 19–20
  use of in formulating model, 18, 86–88, 100–101, 109–110

helix, 113, 123
histogram, 9–10, 68, 91–92

image, 23
index, 88–89, 95–97, 100–101, 104–105, 108–109
invariant, 85
inverse function, 24
isometric projection, 113, 119–120, 141
isopleth, 85, 89–93, 95–96
isosceles triangle, 27–8

latitude. See spherical geometry
linear law, 20
  See also graph, straight-line
linear programming, 35, 87, 101
locus, 89–93, 101, 113, 118–119, 129–130, 138
logarithm, 20–21, 57–58, 142
  logarithmic scale, 31
longitude. See spherical geometry

mapping, 23
matrices
  presentation of information, 10–13, 95–97, 132
  multiplication, 97, 132
  transformation matrices, 25–27

mean, arithmetic, 8, 77–78
measurement, 5, 112, 125, 127, 134
median, 77–78
mode, 77–78
model, mathematical, 2–3, 31, 35, 73, 83, 86–88, 97–101

negative numbers, 15, 142
network (planar graph), 3, 94–97, 132
numeracy, 5–6, 70–71, 107

oblique projection, 113, 119–120
orthographic projection, 112–3, 121–123

parabola (as conic section), 122
parallel lines, properties of, 27–28, 112, 115–116
parallelepiped, 60
percentage, 6, 8, 38, 52–53, 68, 70–72, 82, 88–89, 107, 108–109, 142
    percentage conversion graph, 8
    percentage pie chart, 10, 85
perspective, 138–141
pie chart, 10, 68, 85
planar graph. See network
polyhedra, 39, 60, 134–136, 138
    See also parallelepiped
probability, 78–79, 79–82, 103–104, 108
problem-solving, 35–37
progressions, arithmetic and geometric, 103
    See also exponential function
projection. See isometric projection, oblique
    projection, orthographic projection
proportion, proportionality, 2, 7–8, 10, 15–18, 39–40, 45, 51, 52–55, 56, 68, 85, 142

inverse proportion, 17–18, 39–40, 44, 72
Pythagoras' Theorem, 30, 89, 100, 118

random numbers, 103–104
random sampling. See sampling
range, of numerical data, 77
rate, 17, 72, 73
    pressure, 3, 6
    rate of change, gradient
    See also density
ratio, 7–8, 51, 52–55, 73–75, 114, 142
ready reckoner, 22
reciprocal, 15, 37–8
reflection, 28–29, 45–47
rounding off, 8, 142

sampling, 78
scale, 83, 112, 113, 115, 126, 134
    scale drawing, 35, 82, 115–116, 126
    scale factor, 17, 73–75, 83, 100
scientific notation. See standard index form
sets, 10–13, 68–70
similar figures, areas of, 118, 126
similar triangles, 29, 33, 34
similarity. See enlargement, similar triangles
simulation, 33, 81, 103–104
slide rule, 17, 18, 20–21, 53, 142
sphere
    volume, 31
    See also close-packing
spherical geometry (of the Earth), 84
square root, 15, 19, 78, 82, 85, 118, 142
standard deviation, 78–79

standard index form, 9, 15, 142
stastical data tables, 85
statistical graphs. See graphs, statistical
statistical methods, 78–79
    correlation, 104, 145–146
    hypothesis testing, 78–79, 105
    nearest neighbour analysis, 104–105
    non-parametric tests, 79, 143–146
structure, algebraic
surface area, See area
symbols
    use of, 14
    translation into, 35
symmetry, 64–65, 112, 117, 126

tables, mathematical, 22, 142
tables, statistical data. See statistical data tables
tessellation
    in two dimensions, 99–100, 137, 138
    in three dimensions, 60, 138
three-dimensional geometry, 57, 112, 134–136
    See also polyhedra
transformation, 85, 93–94
    See also mapping
translation, 60
tree diagram, 10–13, 69
trigonometry, 30, 35, 49–50, 57, 58, 63–64, 82, 142

variation, continuous and discontinuous, 77
vector, 29–30, 33, 34, 41, 65–67
Venn diagram, 10–13
volume, 9, 31, 73–75, 142
    of cylinder, 31
    of sphere, 31